P9-BTO-625

The Ministry of God's Word

The Ministry of God's Word

WATCHMAN NEE

Christian Fellowship Publishers, Inc.
New York

Available from the Publishers at:
Box 58
Hollis, New York 11423

PRINTED IN U.S.A.

CONTENTS

The contents of this volume comprise a series of messages which were delivered in Chinese by the author during a training period for workers held in Kuling, Foochow, China, in 1948.

All quotations from the Old Testament are from the American Standard Version of the Bible (1901), unless otherwise indicated.

All quotations from the New Testament are from the New American Standard Bible: The New Testament (1960), unless otherwise indicated.

PART ONE

THE MINISTER

1. Three Kinds of Ministry
2. The Contents and Delivery of the Word
3. The Course and Ministry of Paul
4. The Peak of the Ministry of the Word

1 | Three Kinds of Ministry

"But we will devote ourselves . . . to the ministry of the word" (Acts 6.4). The *matter* of serving people with God's word is called the ministry of the word; the *person* who so serves is called a minister. "Ministry" points to the matter, while "minister" speaks of the person. The ministry of the word occupies an important place in the work of God. There are definite principles to be learned by those who preach the word of God and serve people with God's word.

From the Old Testament time to the New, God always is found speaking. He spoke in the Old Testament days; He spoke while the Lord Jesus was on earth; and He continues to speak in the New Testament church. We learn from the Bible that God has a prime work to perform on earth, which is, to utter His own word. If the word of God is taken away, then almost nothing is left of God's work. No word, no work. When the word is eliminated, the work is reduced to near zero. We must therefore recognize the place of God's word in His work. Once the word is removed the work of God ceases immediately, for God operates through His word; He treats His word as His work. The work of God is filled with His word.

How does God utter His word? This is a very special and quite remarkable method: God's word is spoken through the mouth of man. Not only is there the word in the Bible; there is also the minister of the word. Were God to speak directly by Himself, He would have no need for the minister of the word. Since His word is delivered by man, the minister of the word becomes a real concern. How very significant is man, therefore, in the work of

God. God employs no way other than man to deliver His word. God is in need of a special class of people to be the ministers of His word.

Briefly stated, one can find throughout the whole Bible three different kinds of people whom God uses to preach the word. In the Old Testament God's word is spread by the prophets; hence we have the ministry of the prophets. Once again, at the time of the earthly pilgrimage of the Lord Jesus, God's word became flesh; and thus we have the ministry of the Lord Jesus. And finally, in the New Testament God's word is propagated by the apostles; with the result that we have the ministry of the apostles.

The Old Testament Ministers of the Word: The Prophets

In the Old Testament God chose the prophets as the men to speak His word. These many prophets spoke according to the visions they received. Even a person such as Balaam could speak for God, for Balaam was a prophet; his prophecies were some of the greater ones in the Old Testament. The way by which the Old Testament prophets could serve as ministers of God's word was through the word of God coming to them. Balaam, for example, prophesied as the Spirit of God came upon him. He spoke in spite of himself. God set aside his feeling and his thought and gave him revelation. The word of God came to him irrespective of his condition. He neither added his own opinion nor mingled his own feeling or thought in with God's word. In other words, God merely employed the man's mouth to utter His word. This is typical of the Old Testament ministers of the word. The Holy Spirit gave the word to a particular individual and so controlled that person that there could be no error in God's word as propagated by him. Though God used the person, there was little, if any, human element involved in this type of revelation. Man merely spoke the word of God without adding anything to it.

Nevertheless, in the Old Testament we do find people such as Moses, David, Isaiah, and Jeremiah whom God employed as mouthpieces in a way which was more advanced than that of Balaam and other prophets. The words which Moses wrote were mainly what

God had commanded him. As the Lord spoke, so spoke Moses. Isaiah recorded vision after vision which the Lord had shown him. In this respect these prophets functioned under the same principle as Balaam. But in another respect Moses and Isaiah were quite different from Balaam. For we know that whenever Balaam himself came forward, his personal feeling was so wrong that he was condemned before God. While under revelation, Balaam spoke the word of God; but as soon as he spoke by himself, he manifested sin, error and darkness. This was not true of Moses. Though he largely spoke according to what God commanded, yet there were times before God when he spoke as he felt. During these occasions he was not looked upon as doing anything wrong; instead, his word was recognized as also being God's word. This shows that Moses was more used by God than was Balaam. The same is true of Isaiah. Most of his prophecies came directly from the visions he received from God, but sometimes he himself began to speak. David and Jeremiah expressed their own feelings before God even more than Moses and Isaiah. All of these prophets approached the way of the later New Testament ministers; even so, they acted mostly under the same principles as the rest of the Old Testament prophets. They spoke when the word of God came to them.

The Minister of the Word in the Gospels: The Lord Jesus

When the Lord Jesus came to the earth, the Word became flesh (John 1.14). The Lord Jesus Himself is the word of God. He clothed Himself with flesh and became a man in the flesh. Whatever He did and said were all God's word. His ministry was the ministry of God's word. The way God's word was spread through the Lord Jesus is totally different from that through the Old Testament prophets. Earlier God merely engaged man's voice to propagate His word. Even John the Baptist, the last of the prophets, was but a voice in the wilderness. The word of God simply used his voice.

Not so with the Lord Jesus. He is the Word become flesh. The very Person is the word of God. In the Old Testament the word came upon man. The word and the man were two separate entities. The former was simply spoken by the latter's voice. Although with Moses and David it was somewhat different, the basic principle of the Old Testament was that God merely engaged the human voice. In incarnation, however, the word of God was clothed with a human body; God's word became man. It was no longer the word coming to man, nor was it God's word using the human voice. The word instead was dressed in man; therefore it had human feeling, thought and opinion, though it remained God's word.

If man's opinion had entered into God's word during the Old Testament period, that word would have ceased to be the word of God. For in the instant that human feeling, thought or opinion is mixed in with God's word, the latter turns imperfect, impure, and unclean. It is the ruination of God's word. To maintain the purity of His word, nothing of man's opinion, thought and feeling may be mingled in. When the word of God was voiced by Balaam it became a prophecy. But if Balaam had attempted to add his own feeling and idea to it, it would have immediately ceased to be God's word, for the nature of the word would have been changed. This fairly well sums up the Old Testament situation.

With the Lord Jesus, however, God's word used not only man's voice but his thought, feeling and opinion as well. His human thought was God's thought; so too were his feeling and opinion God's. This is the ministry of the word which God was able to obtain in the Lord Jesus. How vastly unalike it was from the Old Testament way. God did not want His word to be merely word; He wished it to be like a person. He delighted in having His word become flesh. This is one of the greatest mysteries in the New Testament. It was God's desire that His word should carry human feeling, thought, and idea through a personality. It was this kind of ministry which the Lord Jesus possessed.

In the Lord Jesus God's word was not objective, but rather, subjective. It possessed human feeling, thought, and idea; yet it remained God's word. In this do we find a great principle of the

Bible: that it is possible for the word of God to be unimpaired by man's feeling. The presence of human feeling does not necessarily ruin God's word; it does so only when such feeling is inadequate.

Herein lies a tremendous problem. The great principle is that human elements must not be of such a nature as to hinder God's word. In the life of the Lord Jesus who is the Word become flesh the thought of His flesh is the thought of God. Naturally speaking, the thought of the flesh is only man's thought; but in incarnation the word became flesh in a Man, so that this Man's thought is fully adequate. When it is blended with God's word it fulfills rather than spoils the word of God. The word of God in the Lord Jesus rises higher than the Old Testament word. "You have heard," spoke Jesus one day, "that the ancients were told" thus and so (Matt. 5.21). This tells us that the Lord God spoke to Moses, giving His revelation to His servant. Yet the Lord Jesus proceeded further with, "But I say to you . . . ." (v.22). We find here that Jesus Himself was speaking on earth, using His own thought and His own idea. And in so speaking, far from overturning God's authority, He fulfilled it. He did not overthrow God's word, but raised it to a height beyond that of the Old Testament.

The characteristic of the Lord Jesus as the minister of God's word lies in the fulfilling of God's word. Not only is there a voice, there is likewise feeling and thought emanating from a sinless person. God's word in the Lord Jesus is no longer a revelation; it has become a Person. It not only engages a Man's voice but is the Person of the Lord Jesus Himself. The word of God has taken up personality. It is united with man's word. And when that Man speaks, God speaks. How glorious is this union! When Jesus of Nazareth speaks, God speaks! None has ever spoken like Jesus of Nazareth, nor will any ever afterward speak like Him. He knows absolutely no sin. He is the Holy One of God, and He is wholly of God. The word of God is upon Him because He is the Word become flesh. He is God's word. What He says is said by God. In Him the word of God is absolutely subjective, for He is God's word.

In the Old Testament we can find certain prophets who spoke the word for God, but in the Gospels we can point to the Lord Jesus and say, this Man *is* God's word. In the first instance we are only able to testify that when the prophet opened his mouth the word of God came forth. As to the Lord Jesus, though, we can refer to Him as the word of God. His feeling was the feeling of God's word, and His thought, the thought of God's word. When he opened His mouth there was God's word; even when He shut His mouth, God's word was still there, for as a Person He is the word of God.

Through our Lord Jesus the word was advanced from revelation to personality. Upon the Old Testament prophets the word of God came as revelation, but in the Lord Jesus it was personified. In the Old Testament the word and the person were two separate entities. Although the word was using him, the man remained a man. At the coming of the Lord Jesus, the word of God became flesh. This fleshly Man was God's word. What He spoke was the word of God. To Him revelation was unnecessary, for He Himself was the word. There was no need to have the word of God come to Him from outside before He could speak God's word. For was not *His* word the word of God already? He did not need anything extra, because He Himself was God's word. In Him God's word was unaffected and unrestricted by man. The word He spoke was the pure word of God. Jesus was a man; even so, the word of God never suffered because of Him. Indeed, God's word found its fullest expression through Him. This is the ministry of Jesus of Nazareth.

The Ministers of the Word in the New Testament: The Apostles

The ministry of the word in the Old Testament is entirely objective, whereas that of the Lord Jesus is absolutely subjective. Beginning with the apostles, however, the ministry of the word follows the nature of that of the Lord Jesus together with the addition of Old Testament revelation. The difference between the ministry of the word in the New Testament and the ministry of the Lord Jesus is as follows: in the Lord Jesus it is the Word become flesh, that is, first the word, then the flesh to fit the word. His consciousness, feelings, and thoughts are harmonious with God's word. However, in the New Testament ministry of the word we have the flesh first; in order to make it a minister of the word, this flesh must be transformed according to the requirements of God's word. The feeling, thought, and idea of the flesh must undergo a change that it may be suitable to God's word. Hence, this New Testament ministry is different from both the Old Testament ministry and the ministry of the Lord Jesus. That of the Lord Jesus is wholly subjective, for the word is Himself. The New Testament ministry is that of the Lord Jesus added to that of the Old Testament prophets. The word of God comes to man as revelation along with that man's feeling, thought and idea. It is consequently God's revelation plus human elements.

Those who are chosen in the New Testament are not holy as is the Lord Jesus, who alone is the Holy One of God with no impurity, whose word is the word of God. God must not only put His word in these New Testament ministers but must deal with them as well. He needs to raise them to the level He demands. He will use their thoughts, feelings and characteristics, but these have to be dealt with first. So God deals with these New Testament ministers in respect to their experiences, words, feelings, cleverness, opinion, characteristics and other areas, in order that His word might be communicated through them. The word of God is not just imparted through a human voice but is also manifested in deed through these various areas of the man. God takes pleasure in putting His word in man and then in letting it be exhibited through man. The Lord Jesus is the Word become flesh; the New Testament ministers have their flesh wrought upon for the sake of conveying the word of God.

Human Element in Revelation

It is a mistake to assume that there is no human element in God's revelation or that the first necessarily destroys the second. The revelation of God does indeed contain the human element, for God's word is manifested in it. Even with respect to Old Testament prophetic ministry, however small a place the human element occupies, we cannot say there is absolutely none of it present, since the word of God at least needs to be uttered by man's mouth. In incarnation, the Word has become flesh, and so the entire human element of Christ is now the word of God. Today God desires that His word, delivered through New Testament ministers, should be blended with human elements.

In carefully perusing the New Testament we discover that certain words are constantly employed by Paul which were never employed by Peter or John or Matthew. Likewise, Luke has his favorite words, and so has Mark. In their writings, each maintains his peculiarity. The Gospel of Matthew is different from that of Mark, Mark from Luke, and Luke from John. Paul's writings have their own definite tone; Peter's are in another strain. But the Gospel of John and John's Epistles share the same subject and are continuous in nature. For instance, the Gospel of John commences with "In the beginning. . . .", and his First Epistle opens with "What was from the beginning. . . ." One refers to the very beginning, the other starts from that beginning and proceeds onward. And his Revelation joins these two together, using the same style of writing.

Pursuing this matter further, we find that each writer of the Bible possesses his own idiosyncrasies. As a physician Luke invokes certain medical terms with which to describe various sicknesses, while the other three Evangelists employ common words. Again, because the Book of Acts is also written by Luke, medical words once more appear. Each Gospel possesses its special phraseology and has its particular topics. In Mark, "immediately" is frequently found; in Matthew, "the kingdom of heaven"; in Luke, "the kingdom of God." On each book the writer leaves his indelible mark; yet all are the word of God.

The New Testament is full of human elements; still, it is God's word. Each writer maintains his emphasis, uses his special phrases, and retains his characteristics. Through these, God's word is delivered without suffering any loss. Having man's marks and possessing human characteristics, but nonetheless remaining God's word—such is the New Testament ministry. God's word is entrusted to man and is conveyed through that man's elements. God does not turn man into a tape recorder—first recording every word and subsequently sending them out verbatim. He does not wish it so. Since the Lord Jesus has already come and the Holy Spirit has now entered into the believing man, God will work in man until his human elements do not damage God's word. This is the basis of New Testament ministry. The Holy Spirit so operates in man, so controls and disciplines him, that the latter's own elements can exist without impairing God's word; on the contrary, they fulfill it. Were no human element involved, man would become a tape recorder. Today the human element is in God's word, and the word is fulfilled by man.

Do we know why Paul does not stress that all believers must speak in tongues in the meeting? Yet are not tongues a gift of God? The explanation is because, in the speaking in tongues, man's thought is not involved. In other words, human thought is not included. This makes it more like the Old Testament ministry than that of the New; because this is God putting unknown tongues on the lips of man. God's emphasis in New Testament ministry is in bringing into play the human element in the word. Under the discipline, control and work of the Holy Spirit, all human elements can be properly engaged by God. The word of God is to be released through man. It is God's word, yet it also involves human elements.

Let us use an illustration. Suppose a musician is capable of playing piano, organ, and violin. He may perform the same music on different instruments. Since each musical instrument possesses its unique characteristics, the sounds are distinctly unique. The various characteristics of these musical instruments help to express the feeling of the music. The ministries of the New Testament word somewhat resemble these musical instruments. Some are like pianos, others like organs or violins. The same music played produces a distinct sound according to the different instruments employed. From one minister the word of God comes through with his particular human element; from another there is a different sort of human element. Each and every one of those who are used by God has his own human element implanted in the word. Under the discipline, government and education of the Holy Spirit, this personal element of man no longer hinders the coming forth of God's word but on the contrary renders its manifestation more glorious.

In view of the fact that God's word is to pass through man using human elements, it is obvious that the elements of all those who have not been dealt with by God are unusable. If the personal element is questionable before God, His word cannot come through that person. He is unsuitable; he cannot be a minister of God's word. In the Old Testament God once spoke through an ass, but today the New Testament ministry is quite different. In New Testament times God's word comes through the human element; as a consequence the Lord must be strict in selecting His instrument. We cannot propagate God's word like a tape recorder. God desires to change us. If we are not up to His standard, we are not usable.

To be one who delivers God's word we must be pruned and refined. God has to lay aside those whose human makeup contains many uncleannesses, fleshly things, and matters condemned by God. Others He has to bypass because they have never been broken before God, or their thoughts are not straightforward, or their lives are undisciplined, their necks stiff, their emotions untamed, or they have a controversy with God. Even if these individuals receive God's word, they are not able to deliver it for it is blocked within them. Should they force themselves to preach, the word is ineffective. Hence man's condition before God is a basic problem for New Testament ministers.

Today God wishes His word to be uttered like man's word. It is truly God's word, yet it is also man's word. Which verse in the entire New Testament is not spoken by man? A characteristic maintained from the beginning to the end of the New Testament is that all words spoken by men are *human* to the nth degree, yet also *divine* to the nth degree, being purely the word of God. This is the New Testament ministry of the word.

"For out of much affliction and anguish of heart I wrote to you with many tears," said Paul (2 Cor. 2.4). Paul here is ministering God's word to the Corinthians. He wrote under much affliction. He wrote with many tears. Here was one whose whole being was involved in the word. What he wrote was full of human feeling. The word of God in him made him suffer and caused him to shed many tears. When he wrote, his human element was mingled with God's word and magnified it. He was not void of feeling or thought. His was not like one speaking in tongues with the word coming in and going out without so much as touching the thoughts of the heart. He wrote with his inward being full of thought and feeling. As the word of God came forth, word after word, he was in much affliction and with many tears. This represents the New Testament minister of the word.

Since God's word is to pass through man, his characteristics, idiosyncrasies, tone, and experiences before God may all be manifested in the word. The degree of discipline he has received from the Lord and the measure of trial he has undergone may likewise be disclosed in the word. A minister of the New Testament word may, without any error, add his personal element to the word of God which comes to him. After years of learning before the Lord, he may be brought to a place where he can be freely used by Him as a channel of the word. Should that which man puts into the word be flesh or something of the natural man, the word of God will be adulterated as it passes through man.

God's word contains human elements; only then will it come forth as the perfect word of God. Never misconstrue God's word to be merely one commandment or ten commandments. The Bible demonstrates to us clearly that it possesses a human flavor. God gives His word to man and lets the latter speak. If man's condition is right, God puts him into the word too. The basic law of God's speaking is: "the Word became flesh" (John 1.14). It is God's desire today that there be not only His word but that His word become flesh. This does not suggest that God's word is lowered to be man's word; it simply means that His word has the flavor of humanity without the least sacrificing of its purity. Truly it is God's word, yet it is in addition man's word; man's word indeed, but God's word too. In New Testament ministry men propagate God's word. We find this in Acts, in Corinthians, in Timothy, in Titus, in Philemon, and so forth. God's word is unveiled through man's word and is magnified through the human element. It is man who is speaking; nonetheless, God recognizes it as His own word.

How very great, then, is the responsibility of those who preach God's word! If the man is wrong and mingles his own unclean things in with the word, he defiles the word of God, greatly damaging it. The fundamental problem in preaching rests not on how much one knows of the Bible, for the mere knowledge of doctrine is of little avail. Knowledge may be wholly objective; it can be delivered without being personally involved. As ministers, though, we can never be like the Lord Jesus who is the Word become flesh; still the word of God is deposited in our flesh and is to be released through this flesh. This flesh must therefore be wrought upon by God. We need to be daily disciplined. Any defect in us will defile the word and destroy its power.

Do not think that just anybody can preach the word of God. We know of only one kind of person who may preach it—those who have been dealt with by God. The greatest difficulty we confront in preaching the word is not whether the subject is proper or the phraseology correct, but whether the man is right. If the *man* is wrong, all which emanates from him is likewise wrong. May God show us the true way of the ministry of the word. Preaching is not as simple as we usually regard it. It is to serve God's people with God's word. Only when the word is not adversely affected by us can people hear the pure word of God. We know the stories of Paul, Peter, Matthew, Mark, Luke, John and many other servants of the Lord. They blend their personal elements with God's word, yet we do not touch blood or flesh through them; instead we sense that the word of God is all the more glorified. How marvelous it is—God's word is man's word, and man's word is God's word.

2 The Contents and Delivery of the Word

God's way of proclaiming His word transcends completely the thought of man. According to man's thinking, God might adopt one of two different ways if He desires man to know His word.

First, God might create a giant tape recorder and hang it in the universe to proclaim His word. If it is within man's ability to invent a tape recorder, how far easier for God to create such an instrument to announce word by word what He intends to say. Each time it could deliver verbatim the word of God. And after a few days it could repeat itself. Were this the means of propagation, there would be no possiblity of error and the people could accurately hear the pure word of God. But God has not chosen to do so.

Or second, He might command the angels to proclaim His word. The Bible does record some instances of angels delivering the word of God, but these are very rare and only used as an exceptional or emergency measure. This is not the normal and regular way of God's speaking. Nevertheless, should it please God to propagate His word by the angels, He could simply compile many articles similar to the Ten Commandments and command the angels to deliver them to men to learn. No personal experience would be involved, and no human error would be possible. We might think this would eliminate many theological problems, arguments, and heresies. How simple it would be if God's word were reduced to the form of a law of five or six hundred articles. By hearing or reading these items men would know God's word in toto. Perhaps many believe that the Bible would be easier to comprehend if it were one thousand one hundred and eighty-six articles instead of that many chapters. It would not be unlike a handbook of Christianity. A quick glance would give a general summary of the Christian faith. But God has not so done.

We realize that were God to use a recorder—like mechanism to deliver His word there would be little likelihood of mistake and the word could be proclaimed continuously. God's word would not be so scarce, nor would men be able to say that His vision is infrequent. His word would always be in the earth. At the same time, though, there would also be a basic lack: in such a word as this there would be no human, personal element. God alone would be able to understand His word. Since no relationship would exist between God and men and no place would be provided for the conversation of the two parties, how would man be able to apprehend what God is saying? The word would sound like thunder to us, beyond human power to decipher. But as a matter of fact, God does not adopt this manner of speaking.

Neither does God systematize His word into many doctrines or articles and impart them through His angels. Yes, God's word does include doctrines, quite true; but it is more than something merely for mental understanding. Yet how people today delight to choose the doctrinal part of the word of God, deeming it the best. Many unbelievers are annoyed by the "you" or the "we" or the "they" of the Bible, but how they are attracted to the Ten Commandments. Men always expect God to compile His words into many articles, which include the words of the angels as well as the utterances of God: thunderous and lightning words, but devoid of any human flavor. We ought to recognize, however, that one characteristic of God's word is the fact that there is the human, personal element in it. Which book is any more personal than the Word of God? How many times Paul uses "I" in his letters! In ordinary letters we consider too many instances of "I" to be impolite and unrefined. But we find the Bible to be full of this personal aspect. God chooses men to be His ministers in order that His word may carry a human flavor. This is very basic.

The Contents of the Word

Let us explain what we mean by human element. Looking at the contents of the Bible we discover that it is full of human element. Take that away and very little is left of the Bible, so great in importance is the human element in the word of God. For example: Galatians speaks of the promise of God, but illustrates it with the story of Abraham. Take away Abraham, and the promise of God descends into abstraction. The Lord Jesus is the Lamb of God who redeems the world, but in the Old Testament men offered bullocks and sheep as sacrifices, from the first offering of Abel to the many offerings in Leviticus. These types show us how the Lord Jesus as God's Lamb makes propitiation for our sins.

Or again, we see in the Old Testament a man called David—how he triumphed in battle, how he obeyed God and became a man after God's own heart, and how he prepared materials of gold, silver, and precious stones in abundance for Solomon to build the temple. We see David and we see Solomon. These examples enlighten us as to how the Lord Jesus fights to victory and how He is ascended to heaven to be crowned King. Take the records of David and Solomon away, and we can barely see the Lord Jesus. He is greater than David and greater than Solomon, yet He needs to be preceded by both David and Solomon; otherwise people cannot understand Him. Also, the Scriptures record in detail how Moses led the Israelites out of Egypt and through the wilderness, how Joshua guided them into Canaan, and how they overcame the thirty-one kings of Canaan. Remove these records, and very little will be left of the books of Exodus, Numbers, and Joshua. Without the book of Joshua it would be difficult to understand the Letter to the Ephesians. All these indicate to us the significance of the human element in the word of God.

The distinctive feature of God's word is that it includes many, many human elements. His word is not spoken abstractly, it is instead uttered through man. It is manifested through the many affairs of men. Hence it is simple, easily heard, and easily understood. Whenever God speaks, men are able to hear, for the word of God is not only spoken by God but is also comprehensible to men. It is both supernatural and natural, divine and human. Through the lives of various men we may see the words of God and understand the words He is speaking.

In the book of Acts we find very little preaching. Its narrative is preeminently concerned with the works the apostles performed under the leading of the Holy Spirit. We behold what Peter was like, and that is the word of God. We see also what Paul did, and again it is God's word. We notice the beginning of the church in Jerusalem, in Samaria, and also in Antioch; these are not only histories but the word of God as well. Men work out the word of God in history; they speak God's word in history too. In history the Holy Spirit reveals God's word through the lives of men. The word of God is full of human element. Such is the peculiar feature of the Bible. The Bible is not a collection of devotional articles; it is men performing or living out the word of God.

The governing principle of the Bible is the Word becoming flesh. For those who do not know the meaning of incarnation, it is extremely hard for them to understand what the word of God is. God's word is neither abstract nor spiritual to such an extent that it eliminates all human savor. It is not so elevated that it is beyond human sight or touch. "In the beginning was the Word, and the Word was with God," opens John's Gospel; but he goes on to add that "the Word became flesh and dwelt among us, full of grace and truth" (John 1.1,14). This is the word of God. The Word dwells among men. The basic principle which controls the ministry of the word is the principle of the Word becoming flesh. Consequently although it is most heavenly, nevertheless it is not in heaven but on earth. Though intensely heavenly, the word is definitely manifested through men. Heavenly, yet it can be seen and touched by men. This is the testimony of the apostle in 1 John, where he declares: "What was from the beginning, what we have heard, what we have seen with our eyes, what we beheld and our hands handled concerning the Word of life" (v.1).

To use another example: we at one time did not know what holiness is. But today holiness is no longer an abstraction, for in the life of the Lord Jesus we have seen holiness, how it lives and walks among men. By seeing the Lord Jesus we know what holiness is. Holiness, as it were, has become flesh. Similarly, we did not know patience, but in the Lord Jesus we have seen patience. God is love, yet we were ignorant of how He loves. Now we have beheld this love in Jesus of Nazareth. We misunderstood spirituality, thinking a spiritual person should neither smile nor cry and should be totally devoid of any feeling; now, in the person of Jesus of Nazareth we comprehend what spirituality in actual fact is.

We do not know the holiness of God, but we can comprehend the holiness of the Lord Jesus. So it is with God's love, patience, glory, or spiritual nature. All need to be understood in the Lord Jesus. This is the meaning of the Word becoming flesh. Holiness, love, patience, glory, or spirituality must all become flesh. As we touch *this* flesh, we touch God. The love of Jesus is God's love, the glory of Jesus is God's glory, and so forth. If something is merely in God, we are unable to apprehend it; but we shall know it when we see the Lord Jesus.

Hence the Word becoming flesh is the basic principle. It governs all the dealings of God with men, and it regulates the communion between the two. Though the word had not yet become flesh in the Old Testament, God was pushing in that direction. Today the incarnated Word has already ascended to heaven, nonetheless God is still working according to this principle. God at this present moment is not an abstract God, One who is intangible and who hides Himself. Not so; He has become flesh, He has come. How gladly do we proclaim to the world that God has already come. In the Old Testament it seems as if God were yet to come, for "He made darkness his hiding place, his pavilion round about him" (Ps. 18.11). In our day, however, God is in the light; He reveals Himself in that light for us to see. When He hid Himself in darkness, none could see Him; but in these latter days He is seen in the light. God has come forth. He has come in the Person of His Son, Jesus Christ.

The Delivery of the Word

Since the word of God is full of the human element, its delivery must be by human beings. God does not enlist a tape recorder, thunder and lightning, or angels to proclaim His word; rather, He uses man to propagate it, and not as a machine but as an integral part of the word. He does not ask men to merely send out the voice He gives, for His word needs to pass through man's spirit, thought, feeling and understanding until it becomes that man's word. Only then may it be delivered. This is called the ministry of the word. Receiving with one hand and handing out with the other hand is not considered to be the ministry of the word. If so, it would be similar to a sound machine. No, God does not want us to announce His word mechanically. He puts His word in us that we may meditate on it, feel after it, be afflicted by it, or rejoice in it, before the word is released by us.

"On the last day, the great day of the feast, Jesus stood and cried out, saying, 'If any man is thirsty, let him come to me and drink'" (John 7.37). If I am thirsty I can come to the Lord Jesus and drink. But His proclamation continues with, "He who believes in me, as the Scripture said, 'From his innermost being shall flow rivers of living water'" (v.38). When I am thirsty I may go to the Lord Jesus and drink of Him. But if I meet others in need, do I simply pour out a cupful to them? No, the Lord indicates that whoever drinks of Him shall find the water in the deepest part of his being, and that out of his *depths* the living water shall flow. This constitutes the ministry of the word. The word of God first enters a person, then out of his depths it flows to others. Such a turning becomes the ministry of the word. It does not depend on how many Scripture verses we can recite to others, nor on how many sermons we can give; rather is it the turning of the living water deep down within us. Such a process demands a costly price. Sometimes the living water fails to flow out after it has flowed in; at other moments it ceases to be living after it has entered in; and at still other times it may issue forth with many of the impure things of the heart. Under all these circumstances the ministry of the word is arrested.

Thus the ministry of the word is not the mere delivery of sermons we memorize. We must allow the word to come to us, to drill and to grind us, until it flows out with—yes, our personal elements in it—and yet not spoiled or corrupted in the least. The Lord wishes to use us as a channel of living water. The very depth of our being is the channel. For the living water to flow freely from us we must be right before God; otherwise we will hinder His word. True preaching never brings in cleverness or eloquence. It depends on whether we perfect or corrupt the word of God as it passes through us and mingles with our personal makeup. The great problem is that many living waters cease to be living after they flow through men! How extremely necessary, therefore, is the discipline of the Holy Spirit in our lives. Should anyone fail to see the necessity of having himself dealt with by God, fail to see how his habits, temperament and life need to be pruned and refined, he is of no use to the word of God.

How very far from the truth it would be if you should accept eloquence and cleverness as the prerequisites of a minister of the word! The word of God comes to you. You are satisfied as it passes through you, yet you are at the same time being tried, drilled, ground, and dealt with by the word. You undergo much affliction, pay some costly price, till gradually you begin to be clear in regard to that word. In this manner God's word is being increased in you. Word after word and line upon line is knit and woven into you. The time arrives for its delivery. It issues forth not only with words but also with the spirit. The water remains pure, being wholly of God. Your words do not lessen but rather increase the perfectness of the word. You do not diminish, but instead add to, its holiness. You, as a person, have come forth; so also has the living water. You are speaking, but God is speaking too. This, then, is the ministry of the word.

In the ministry of the word two streams instead of one seem to flow, and they flow together. It is the consequence of the working of the Holy Spirit within us as well as His disciplining us through the arrangement of our environment. We become channels of living water only after the Holy Spirit has succeeded in breaking and grinding us down. Our outward man needs this breaking by God. It needs drastic and thorough dealings. Whereupon our spirit may begin to breathe freely—the Holy Spirit being freed within us—and the word of God may commence to flow from us. The word of God and ourselves are consequently like two streams merging and flowing together.

Never forget what the ministry of the word is. It is the outflowing of the Spirit of God in man as well as in the word. One part of it consists of God's word and the other part of man's ministry. The word of God comes to man, who adds in his ministry, and then the two flow out together. God's word is not delivered if it is just the word without the human ministry.

Some might think they could preach the word if they managed to learn how to speak well. We would reply, It is not that simple. The ministry of the word is a convergent, not a single, flow. It is not God's way to flow singly, because this would be contradictory to the basic principle of the ministry of the word. Without man, God's word cannot be released. God needs man. Yet because of our peculiar temperament, hardness of heart, uncleanness of mind, or rebellious state, might we not be correct in saying that it would be more convenient for God to use an ass than to use us? Nevertheless, God still wants to use man. He has decided to have the human element in both the content and the delivery of His word.

He chooses man to proclaim His word. It therefore follows that today if there is a minister, there can be a word; otherwise there can be no word. If God can find a minister, He will speak; otherwise, He will not speak. We cannot expect God to speak without supplying Him with usable ministers. The appointed way of the Lord is to entrust His word to the minister, to one who has been dealt with by the Holy Spirit.

We all know that the Spirit of God abides in God's word, but He also dwells in us. In other words, God's Spirit is in the minister as well as in the word. He begins to work when His abiding in the word and dwelling in the minister are joined in one. The seven sons of Sceva tried to cast out a demon in the name of Jesus whom Paul preached. Not only could they not cast out the demon, but two of them were even overwhelmed by the evil spirit. The word was there, yet the Spirit did not work. Word alone is futile; there must also be the minister. When God's Spirit joins the minister and the word together, living water flows.

All the problems today rest on the shoulders of the minister. Neither is vision infrequent nor the word rare, but the minister of the word is hard to be found on this earth. How often God's light disappears when it is discharged from *our* mouth. Some ministers may speak of the Holy Spirit, yet people touch the flesh and not the Holy Spirit. Some may speak of God's holiness, but what the audience touches is not holiness but a lightness of spirit. Still more may talk about the cross, yet where are the marks of the cross on them? They are undisciplined persons. And others may preach on the love of the Lord, yet the impression conveyed to their hearers is not of their love but of their temper.

These all suggest problems which are with the ministers. Were all the messages on earth today truly the ministry of the word, how rich the church would be! But alas, there is much preaching yet so little word! This is the difficulty in the church of today. Since there is no minister, there can be no revelation. Many messages are far from revelation. God does not want to speak alone, yet man is unusable—this is the crux of the problem.

Brethren, if God wills not to speak alone, and if the ministers are incompetent to speak, what must be the condition of the church? All the barrenness, poverty, and corruption found in her are due to the inadequacy of the human element in the word of God. Would that God could find those who are broken and stricken to the ground so as to allow His word to flow out from them. We are always trying to find God's word, but God is continually looking for those whom He can use. We are seeking for the word of God, but God is seeking for His ministers.

If we have not been chastened we cannot do the work of the Lord. Let us not think that whether we are dealt with or not does not matter. Let us not imagine that we may deliver as many messages as we have heard. If we are not right, the word of God is blocked. The Holy Spirit does not side with the word alone; He also sides with the man who is broken and bears the marks of the cross. A broken, stricken human spirit is a usable spirit. Should the Holy Spirit fail to be released, it is because of the hindrance of our outward man. Our emotions, temper, and will can each one hinder the word. We may speak well, yet it actually can be merely word, doctrine or teaching–not the word of God. God's word needs to enter into your being, into your feeling, understanding, heart, and spirit. It needs to make a turn in you and flow out again. Then the word is intimately knit with you, it is pressed and pushed forth in you. But if there should be any defect in your emotion, thought, understanding, heart, or spirit, the word of God will be damaged by you. Not only will your word be defective but the whole church will be adversely affected. You will have ruined God's word as well as despoiled God's church. We must learn to let His word pass through us without hindrance. If God is merciful to us, we shall see light.

3 | The Course and Ministry of Paul

We have already seen the nature of the word of God, that it includes the human touch of many people yet is not thereby in the least spoiled. The word still remains eternal, transcendent, divine, holy, and pure. We have seen the ministry of the word as being the delivery of this word containing human elements through men, that is, through men's memory, understanding, thought, heart, and spirit. We earlier stressed the fact that the minister of the word must be in a right state before God if the word is to be proclaimed, because any improper condition in the minister will automatically corrupt the word of God.

Now let us focus our attention on Paul—who was most used by the Lord according to the record of the New Testament—that we may learn how he was used to be a minister of God's word.

First

"I have finished the course," said Paul (2 Tim. 4.7). The course which Paul had finished had been well planned and laid out. God gives to each of those whom He wants to use a definite course to run, a course which is carefully calculated and specifically appointed both as to the road and the distance. Paul received such mercy from God that he was able to finish this course just before his departure. He could say, "I have finished the course."

We believe God put this course before Paul on the first day Paul trusted the Lord. We know, of course, God worked in his life long before he was saved. Paul himself told the Galatians, "But when He who had set me apart, even from my mother's womb, and called me through his grace, was pleased to reveal His Son in me, that I might preach Him among the Gentiles, I did not immediately consult with flesh and blood" (1.15,16). He first mentioned, "He who had set me apart before I was born, and had called me through his grace," to show that he was actually set apart from his mother's womb; then he continued to tell how he became a minister of God's word. Even when he was in his mother's womb God had set him apart and prepared a course for him. And the moment he was saved he began to run. We thus realize that the preparation and beginning of a minister are determined by God even while he is still in his mother's womb.

Hence all which happens to us before we are saved has a definite meaning. Whatever may be your characteristics, temperament, inclination, and strength are prearranged and prepared by God. There can be no accident, for everything is within God's providence. Nothing comes by chance. Even a man's natural ability and experience are prearranged for future service. God had set Paul apart before he was born and had ordered his course beforehand; even the profession he learned before regeneration was prearranged.

Peter was fishing when he was called. Accordingly, his life work was to bring men to the Lord. The "keys of the kingdom of the heavens" were given to him that he might open the door to the kingdom. He opened the door of the kingdom at Pentecost, and he did it again in the house of Cornelius. A fisherman is therefore for the purpose of bringing people in.

John too was a fisherman, but when he was called by the Lord he was not fishing but mending nets. The Gospel of John is the last one written of the four Gospels; it tells people what eternal life is. Should there be only three Gospels, with John's "mending" one left out, people probably would never know what eternal life is. John wrote his epistles several decades after Peter and Paul wrote theirs. During that period the Gnostics tried to mix in human philosophy with the pure gospel of Jesus Christ. This is why John led people back to review eternal life. He wrote of the conditions and the manifestations for one to be born of

God. In the beginning of apostasy he was called to mend the nets by re-emphasizing eternal life. John also wrote the book of Revelation as the last of the sixty-six books of the Bible. Were this volume missing, how incomplete the Bible would be, for many things would remain without endings. So, again John mended, this time with the book of Revelation. God shows us that John's ministry is one of mending.

Let us now return to Paul. His course was determined by God; even his earthly profession was divinely prearranged. He was a tentmaker, not a weaver. He made use of available materials, cut and sewed them together to make a habitable home, a mobile house. Here we see a ministry which follows the work of the Lord Jesus and that of Peter. It stands between the work of Peter and the work of the coming kingdom. The days of the kingdom are yet to come, but people have already been saved, so they should be built up as the church. Paul's ministry is like tent-making, putting the materials together to build a habitable home. His was not to weave a large piece of cloth but to make something habitable. This profession was also prearranged by God.

Having been set apart as a minister of God's word from our mother's womb, none of us can afford to be foolish before God. Each must know what the Lord has arranged for him. A person's environment, family, profession: each of these human matters has God's arrangement in it. God never intends to destroy these human aspects. He does not want us to be spoiled—to be pretentious and unnatural. He desires us to be innocent people, though at the same time He will work to break down our outward man. That about you which is the human element is something established by the Spirit of God; but you as a person, that is, your natural skill, your natural life with its thought, will and emotion, must assuredly be broken down by God. The breaking of the outward man does not at all imply that God also rejects our human elements.

The great problem is: we do not know where to start and where to end; that is, we know not how much in our life is to be retained and how much is to be broken by God. But those who have been taught before Him can quickly discern if a ministry is clean or unclean. This way is not as simplistic as we usually think. We all need to submit ourselves under the discipline of God, under the cross. The cross has already set aside all which He condemns and hates; it has broken everything which He wishes to break. We must learn to submit, praying: "Oh Lord, I have many problems in me which I do not know how to solve. I ask for your light to enlighten, to slay, and to deal, so that I may be brought to the place where my personal makeup does not hinder your work but can be used to release your work." Paul's life from beginning to end was arranged by the Lord. His salvation was exemplary: God's light cast him to the ground. This is a tremendous salvation. After he arose from the ground God's word came out continuously from him. He wrote so many of the books of the New Testament. God's word kept coming from him. He indeed was a minister greatly used by the Lord.

Second

Let us read especially the first letter to the Corinthians to discover what kind of a ministry of the word Paul had. For some observers contend that in the Corinthian letters, particularly in Chapter 7 of 1 Corinthians, the Bible reaches its peak so far as human experience is concerned. This is quite true. Paul's experience bears out this judgment. Note the following passages.

"This I say by way of concession, not of command" (v.6). Plainly, Paul himself was speaking.

"I wish that all men were even as I myself am" (v.7). This wish was Paul's own. Verse 6 showed Paul's own word; verse 7 revealed his own wish. He did not say God had commanded or God had so decided. He even mentioned later on, "But each has his own special gift from God, one of one kind and one of another." God worked differently in different people, but according to my personal opinion, Paul mused, I wish that all were as myself.

"I say to the unmarried and to widows that it is good for them if they remain even as I" (v.8). Again, Paul spoke the word.

"To the married I give instructions; not I, but the Lord, that the wife should not leave her husband" (v.10). He first said, "I give instructions"; immediately afterwards he caught himself by saying, "not I, but the Lord." Of the entire Bible only 1 Corinthians 7 contains this way of speaking. Paul was here giving a charge, and yet he insisted that it was not he but the Lord who gave the charge.

"To the rest I say, not the Lord" (v.12)–Paul was once again speaking. From verse 12 through 24 it was Paul who spoke, not the Lord. How did he dare say these things? How bold he was! On what authority did he give such a charge? Paul tells his readers in the succeeding verses.

"Now concerning virgins I have no command of the Lord" (v.25). He did not lie, but honestly confessed that he had no command of the Lord. "But I give an opinion as one who by the mercy of the Lord is trustworthy." This was the opinion of one who had received the mercy of the Lord and who was given power by God to be faithful. The Lord had done a deep work in his life that he might be trustworthy. Paul was saying: since God through his mercy has made me a trustworthy person, I can today give my opinion. There is no command of the Lord, it is solely my opinion–it is only the way I look at these problems.

"I think . . . that this is good in view of the present distress" (v.26). Paul was telling his opinion here.

"And I am trying to spare you" (v.28). Again, Paul's own opinion.

"And this I say, brethren. . . ." (v.29). It was Paul who said this.

"I want you to be free from concern" (v.32). Paul's word again.

"And this I say. . . ." (v.35). And still Paul speaking.

"But in my opinion. . . ." (v.40). Paul's personal judgment here.

Finally, let us return to verse 17. "And thus I direct in all the churches." Paul had not only the Corinthians but all the churches in view when he gave charge.

All of this may seem strange to us. Is it not contrary to what we usually understand? "I do nothing on My own initiative," said Jesus, "but I speak these things as the Father taught Me"; "the things I speak, I speak just as the Father has told Me." (John 8.28, 12.50). If this was the guiding principle in the life of the Lord Jesus then how was it that Paul dared to say, "I wish," "In my opinion," even, "I direct in all the churches"? Here we touch either the highest or the lowest of spiritual experience. Thank God we are touching the height, for 1 Corinthians 7 is unique in the Bible. After Paul had said these words, he ended on this note: "And I think that I also have the Spirit of God" (v.40). He knew very clearly he did not have the command of the Lord. He knew the Lord had not spoken, because he spoke according to the mercy which God had shown him. His sole basis for speaking rested on the mercy and grace which God gave him. He therefore concluded his words by saying, "I think that I have the Spirit of God."

This of which we have been discussing is a distinctive illustration of how that which we call the human element is used in the word of God. Here was a man who had been so disciplined, controlled, and dealt with by the Lord that he could speak, though knowing the Lord had not spoken, and that what he spoke was after all the words of the Holy Spirit. Paul said, "I wish," "In my judgment," yet the result was that the Spirit of God likewise so wished and so judged. Because he was completely yielded to the Spirit of the Lord and allowed God's Spirit to work in him so thoroughly, the words he spoke became the words of the Holy Spirit.

How vastly opposite is this to the speaking of Balaam's ass! The latter only spoke when God's word was put in its mouth. When God took His word away there was nothing left but an ass. But Paul had followed the Lord for many years and had received mercy to be trustworthy. When he spoke, the Holy Spirit spoke. Paul confessed that it was his opinion, but the Holy Spirit acknowledged it as God's opinion. God had so worked in Paul's life that it was possible for him to speak His word even though the word had not been given to him. What is this? This is the ministry of the word.

Most servants of the Lord can speak only when the word is put in their mouth, but Paul reached the point where he had the word of the Lord whether or not it was put in his mouth. He was so edified that he could be trusted by the Lord. For this we seek the mercy of God today. Brethren, we must not speak as an ass, able to say something only after the word has been put in our mouth. How are we ever to establish a more intimate relationship with the word? Here was one who was so closely related to God's word that his thought became God's thought. How perfectly one was he with the Spirit of God! When he spoke, he spoke for God. Indisputably Paul had arrived at the highest spiritual plateau. Consequently, we can only conclude that a minister of the word is not one who simply proclaims the word of God, but that he is additionally one who himself is rightly related to His word. He has God's thought; he has God's idea. What he wishes represents the wish of God. So that this is not the same as our doing the will of God after we have come to know it. Rather, this means God has disciplined a person to such an extent that He can own the person's thought and idea as his.

This that we have just said is what we have stressed throughout these years as "the incorporating work of the Holy Spirit." God is incorporated in us. As the golden lampstand is of beaten work, so is God beaten into us. Let us remember that God gives to us on the one hand and beats into us on the other. After we are repeatedly hammered, we cease to be a formless lump of gold but take on the shape of a lampstand. The work of the Holy Spirit includes beating God's desired form into us as well as putting God's word in our mouth. The problem which confronts us here is deeper than that of having God's word put in our mouth, because it involves our being beaten to the degree of being entrusted with His word. Paul had God so wonderfully incorporated into him that his opinion and thought became trustworthy in expressing God's word. When the word of God was put in this man, it would not suffer loss.

Thus, a minister of the word is one whom God can trust. Such ministry requires not only the word, but also a suitable minister in whom God's word will neither be corrupted nor misunderstood. He has received such dealings that his opinion, thought, and demand are trusted by God. His human elements can be blended with God's word without producing any adverse effect. Are we contradicting ourselves when we state this? Earlier we said we should not mix in any human thing with the work of God. Now we maintain that the word of God contains human elements. We are not suggesting that we can blend *any and every* human element into God's word. The truth is, only the human element of those persons who have been dealt with by God can be combined with the word of God.

Let us return to Paul's words. He claimed that by the Lord's mercy he had become trustworthy. Mercy came from God; trustworthiness was the result of mercy, being the incorporation of God in him. God had so worked in his life that he became almost like God's word; and he was able to utter His word in many places afterwards. How could he say, "I wish," "I say" "I direct in all the churches"? Because he as a man had met God and knew God; therefore, when he spoke, God spoke. Let us be reminded that God's word does not come forth supernaturally; it emerges from man and carries with it human elements. If the person is wrong he cannot be successful in being a minister of the word, for the word of God will not be released through him. Never for a moment imagine that one can deliver a message simply because he remembers it. God's word must "churn about" within the man. In case the man is unfit, God's word is damaged as it turns about within him. It is corrupted when man's frivolity and flesh are added to it. Hence man must be brought to a place where there is the incorporation of God in him; then the word of the Lord will not be damaged when it passes through him.

In 1 Corinthians 7 the word of God suffered no loss in Paul, because he was a mature person. We know he was right when he said, "In my judgment," "I say," "My rule in all the churches," because the word of the Lord came through him when he gave charges. It was not he alone who came forth. He was trusted by God. A minister of the word needs to rise very high before God; only then will His word come through. The pureness of the word released depends on the amount of discipline received before God. The more the man is broken, the purer the word; the less that has been learned, the more corrupt its release. The ministry of the word is based on the condition of the man before the Lord.

Third

"Let two or three prophets speak, and let the others pass judgment. But if a revelation is made to another who is seated, let the first keep silent. For you can all prophesy one by one, so that all may learn and all may be exhorted; and the spirits of prophets are subject to prophets" (1 Cor. 14.29-32). Prophesying is the highest among all ministries of God's word. The Holy Spirit gives this word to the prophet. The Holy Spirit is upon him, and the spirit of the prophet is also with him that he may speak God's word. Certain observations are made, however. The one who speaks first should notice if another is given revelation. If so, he has to make room for the next. Moreover, should four or five persons have been given revelation, only two or at the most three may speak. The rest should remain silent, for the spirits of the prophets are subject to the prophets.

Herein lies a fundamental rule concerning the word of God: the Holy Spirit determines what to say, but the prophet decides how and when to say it. If, in a meeting, two or three persons have already spoken according to revelation, the fourth or the fifth person who has equally received revelation should remain silent. Although he is given the word by the Holy Spirit, he himself must decide when to speak. He should not be careless. Even if he is speaking, he must be ready to stop and let another—who has just received revelation—speak. All of this indicates that the word is given by the Holy Spirit but that the time and the manner of speaking is left to the prophet to decide. The spirit of the prophet is subject to that prophet.

How extremely serious, then, is the responsibility of a minister of God's word. Many responsibilities rest on his shoulder, not on God's. The word will be damaged if he is incompetent, if his attitude is not right, or if his speaking is untimely. The word will fail to be released if he is untrustworthy. It would be easy for him if he could just speak whenever the word of the Lord comes to him and keep quiet if the word does not come. But the Lord leaves it to the prophet to decide how and when to speak. Unless one has been dealt with by God and has the work of the Holy Spirit incorporated in him, he will surely corrupt God's word. Let us never overlook such a serious responsibility.

The word of God was never meant to be broadcast by a tape recorder. It is entrusted to man for him to consider how and when to say it. The spirit of the prophet is subject to that prophet. The Lord wills that the prophet's spirit should obey that prophet himself. How to speak and when to speak are the responsibilities of the prophet, not of his spirit. Except the prophet has been disciplined, the spirit of the prophet will cause trouble during its operation. The question today is more than whether or not a man is a prophet; it preeminently comes to this, what kind of a man is the prophet? The differentiation is not between prophets and ordinary people, but between prophets and prophets, such as between a Jeremiah and a Balaam. This fundamental principle we must learn clearly before God. Today there is need not only for the word, but also for the ministers of the word. If there is no word, there can be no ministry of the word; if there is no suitable person, there will not be such ministry either.

The main trouble in the church is the lack of ministers of the word. It is not the rarity of God's word nor the infrequency of vision and light, but the scarcity of those who can be used by the Lord. God wants the spirits of the prophets to be subject to the prophets. What kind of a prophet can command the subjection of his own spirit? Can the spirit of the prophet be subject to him who is licentious, self-willed, heady, or excessively emotional? He who has no mark of the cross in his spirit and who remains wild and proud after many strokes by the Lord is disqualified. Is vision infrequent? Is light scanty? Or is the word rare? Not at all! The sad fact is, usable prophets are what are scarce.

The distinctive feature of Paul is that he was suitable and faithful. How can God trust His word to those who are unfit? How would you deliver the word if it were given to you? Would you speak by yourself? What if your thought were not right, your emotion not fitting, your intention not pure, or your opinion not correct? You know that if your spirit is not right, what is released will similarly not be right, even though you do say the right word. How much the word of God has suffered in the hands of men!

The more dealings we receive the nearer we approach revelation. When the Holy Spirit finds it possible to put the word in a person's mouth because the emotion, thought, will, and spirit of that man are under His control, then there is revelation. The revelation mentioned in the Bible points to that ministry of the word in which all the human elements of man are under the control of the Holy Spirit. Every area of our life must therefore be dealt with by God. Always remember that to be a minister of the word is not a cheap matter. Never think for a moment that it can be cheap. Can a clever person be a minister of the word? No such thing. Do not imagine that man's wisdom, knowledge, and eloquence can help in God's word. We need to be beaten, pressed, and broken by God. All who know the Lord can see that His hand is heavy on those whom He wants to use. This is because He must bring them to the place of utility.

We know some who have been dealt with by God for many years, perhaps twenty or thirty years. The Lord's hand has always been heavy on them. He has dealt and dealt and dealt with them. Are we so unusable? Are we like those who slumber? We really need to prostrate ourselves before God, saying, "I am an unfit person. I need to be beaten and broken by Thee that I might be usable. Otherwise, how can I ever serve Thy purpose?"

In conclusion. What the Holy Spirit does is to put the word of God in you that you may know what to say, but He entrusts you with the decision of how and when to say it. God trusts you and commands that your spirit be subject to you as a prophet. How great is the prophet's responsibility! The way of the ministry of the word lies in the release of the word through the mind and word of man. But what if we mix in things which are improper? These matters will change the nature of God's word. It would be very simple if God just spoke from heaven; it would be equally plain if He merely spoke by the angels; but God has chosen men such as we. How sad that the word meets obstacles in us at each and every turn. We often are unsuitable. Let us look to God for mercy that He may obtain His ministers. Without mercy we are simply undone, and the word of God is blocked in us.

Today's entire responsibility rests on us. We may claim we have preached for ten or twenty years, but how many times have we really proclaimed the word? The basic principle of the ministry of the word is found in the word becoming flesh. The word cannot bypass the flesh. There is word when there is a minister; there is no word when no minister can be found. Hence the responsibility of the minister is serious before God. If you are a minister, you know the responsibility is yours.

Today God does not speak directly, nor does heaven open its mouth, neither do the angels raise their voices. Should men refrain from speaking, the world will not be able to hear God's word. During these two thousand years, the Lord speaks whenever He finds a usable person. If He can get a minister today, His word will come out copiously. We need to be brought to where Paul was: we are speaking, yet the Lord also is speaking. Then shall we see the abundance of God's word. May the Lord be merciful to us in giving us word. May He also raise up many ministers of the word.

4 | The Peak of the Ministry of the Word

First

Besides the Lord Jesus who Himself is the Word become flesh, there are two other kinds of ministers of the word: the Old Testament ministers and the New Testament ministers. In principle, Old Testament ministry is entirely objective, that is, the ministers do not have any subjective experience. Though prophets like Jeremiah and Isaiah did have many subjective experiences, these were only their personal experiences and are not to be considered as touching the principle of Old Testament ministry. So far as this principle goes, God puts His word into the mouth of man for him to utter, thus constituting him as one who proclaims the word of God. Man receives word on the one hand and sends the same out on the other. Even Saul and Balaam ranked among the prophets. So in the principle of Old Testament ministry, we do not find much relationship between the word of God and the one who delivers the word. Man in this case is like a water pipe through which water flows in and out. So long as the word is accurately passed on, God's revelation is preserved without any other complication.

The New Testament ministry, however, is quite another story. Should it succeed in attaining God's purpose it excels the Old Testament ministry in glory; but should it fail to arrive at God's aim, it exceeds the Old Testament ministry in danger. In the New Testament God commits the word to man for him to exercise his own thought, feeling, understanding, memory, and words in the delivery. If he is able to deliver God's word in pureness, his glory far surpasses that of the Old Testament ministers. For though man has been blended in, the outcome is still God's word. The word has not been changed or damaged. This is manifestly most glorious. But contrariwise, should there be any defect in the messenger—even the slightest defect—the word of God immediately incurs loss.

Perhaps some will wonder why God employs such a troublesome way to proclaim His word. A question of this kind belongs to the same category of questions often asked by unbelievers, such as: Why does God not take away the tree of knowledge of good and evil? Why does He not create a species of man who cannot sin? For would not man then avoid the plight of sinning and God escape the dilemma of atonement? The same answer can be given to the question concerning the ministers of the word as to these similar inquiries. God does not will that the man He creates be like a machine, having no freedom of choice but having to obey perfectly. It would be easy for Him to make such a perfect machine. There would be no trouble with man, but neither would there be glory for God. Such obedience and goodness have no spiritual value. There may not be any fault or sin, yet neither can there be holiness, for the obedience is passive. God rejects such a thing.

What God desires to have is the kind of man who knows his right hand from his left. He accordingly creates a mankind that is capable of choosing the evil as well as the good, the wrong as well as the right. If the man God created were capable of choosing obedience to Him only, the glory he would render to God would not exceed that which a machine can present. God gave man a free will, capable of choosing good or evil. In such a circumstance, if man should choose good, a glorious thing is done by him. Although the possibility of doing evil is a great danger, that of doing good is of exceeding glory. This explains why God does not create a machine-like man who can only do good and obey God, but why instead He makes a man free to choose good or evil. God decrees it to be a matter of glory for man to choose good and to choose to obey under his own initiative.

Now God applies this same principle to ministry of the New

Testament order. In terms of difficulties, it surely gives God much trouble to speak through man. He would have no trouble, though, if He were to speak directly, nor would He incur any trouble if He used angels to communicate His word. Even speaking by an ass is less troublesome than speaking through man, since an ass is far less complicated and, therefore, poses less obstacles in the areas of the mind, understanding, memory, intention, and so on. Nonetheless, speaking by an ass is an exceptional case. God used the ass to speak only after the prophet failed. He never intended to make an ass a prophet, because He always calls man to be the prophet.

God's wish is to use man. Man was created for God's specific purpose. As He did not make an obedient machine at the time of creation, so He now rejects the use of a preaching machine. He does not want an automaton; He wants a man with free will. It is a calculated risk with God to choose man as a minister of His word. Yet in spite of the complexity of man and his many problems such as sin, defilement, weakness, the outward man, and natural resistance, God still entrusts His word to man. Through the greatest rigor God obtains His highest glory.

Second

1 Corinthians 7 shows us how perfect it was that Paul was chosen to be a minister of God's word. His ministry is ministry which is apocalyptic and accurate to a letter. Not only his words *contain* God's word, but every word of his *is* God's word. How does he attain to such a ministry? It is through his being personally dealt with by God. He has been brought by the Lord to the place where all his thought, decision and opinion are correct and accurate in His sight. This is not the precision of a machine, but the precision of a man. God does not put His word in man for him to repeat verbatim. He puts His word in man for the latter to search out with his mind. He gives light to man that man may grasp it and think on it. He places a burden in man for him to find appropriate words to express that burden. It is man who thinks, searches, and speaks; even so, God is able to acknowledge

that it is in truth His very own word.

New Testament ministry does not come through God reading His word to you for you to recite word by word to others. God's word in the New Testament comes forth through the following process: first, God sheds light in your spirit, causing a burden in the spirit. The light flashes as a fleeting ray; it requires your thought to fix this light firmly or else it will simply fade away. After the thought succeeds in fixing the light, you need to seek God for words—perhaps just a few words—which can interpret that light. While thinking, you may think of some words which you later write down. Or you may sense something which you utter afterwards. Then you voice the decision or opinion you have in a particular matter. As you express your inward feeling, decision or opinion, the burden in your spirit begins to diminish. The more you talk, the more the light in your spirit which has been fixed by your thought is released. You keep on speaking till your burden is completely discharged. You are talking in your own words, expressing feeling, decision or opinion of your own, yet after you have finished speaking God acknowledges it all as His word.

Do you see the difference between this and the human concept of reciting articles of faith? You are speaking, writing, or thinking, but God accepts it as His word because you have been so thoroughly wrought upon by Him. This is the ministry of the word. You only receive light and burden in you; the opinion, decision and feeling are your own. As you think, feel and decide, God gives you a few words to enable you to express your thought. But as you speak, He is able to acknowledge it as His word. How imperative, then, for man to rise up high so as to be a minister of the word. Any defect in thinking, feeling, or emotion will disqualify you from being a minister of the word. If you as a person have not been pruned and refined by God, your opinion will not be dependable. Any bit of its projection will spoil the word of God.

How God has trusted you as His minister! He gives you light and burden, and then allows you to think out and feel His word, even permitting you to form your own opinion. He trusts you. He so works in you that all your opinion, thought and feeling will be like His. This is New Testament prophesying, New Testament ministry of the word.

Third

Let us review Paul's condition in 1 Corinthians 7: "This I say by way of concession, not of command" (v.6). He knew the operation within him. He merely permitted; he did not command. How very delicate and distinctive was his inner operation. Paul was clear not only of the rightness of this matter but also of his permitting, not commanding, what had been proposed to him. "And I think that I also have the Spirit of God" (v.40). Here the Holy Spirit agreed to that to which Paul had consented. Paul felt this thing could be done, and the Holy Spirit acknowledged this feeling as His own. God here was using Paul's delicate feeling. This is similar to all of us, when in referring to the authority of God we say the Lord Jesus has given His name to us. It is a weighty thing.

It is likewise a weighty thing for God to commit His word to us. For instance, if people have some difficulty and seek your help, you can send a young brother to them by telling him, "You go and speak to them." When the young one remonstrates with "I do not know what to say," you can simply reply, "Whatever you say is reckoned as mine; it represents my opinion." How serious is such a commitment! What a disaster it can create if the man in question is unusable. This is the way God trusts His ministers today. God does not predetermine every word, asking you to repeat them. Should this be the way, there would not be much difficulty, for you would discharge your responsibility by simply repeating every word. No, God does not wish to proclaim His word in this fashion. He puts His word, like living water, in us to be taken in first before it flows out. He gives us light, burden and a few distinctive words, that we may stand before men and proclaim them. It is as if in sending you from heaven to earth to speak to men, God allows you to say whatever you feel like saying. Those who know God dare not be careless.

The responsibility of a minister of the word is great, since he is to speak for God according to his inward feeling, thought, opinion and judgment. What if his feeling, thought, opinion, judgment or spirit is wrong or doubtful? All that he says will be wrong or doubtful. How, then, can he be a minister of God's word? Therefore, the basic problem is to bring a person to the place where his most delicate feeling can fully represent God's feeling–it is independent and personal, yet dependent and of God. The way which Paul spoke in 1 Corinthians 7 is unquestionably not a small matter.

In verse 7 of that chapter, Paul said "I wish," and this was repeated in verse 32, "I want." This indicates to us that Paul had a definite feeling–he wished all were as he himself was. This feeling was endorsed in verse 40 as that which the Holy Spirit wished. So, what Paul wished was what God wished. How careful must this "wish" operate in Paul. Should there be any blemish, the word of God would be totally confused. This "wish" is a most delicate spiritual sense. It allows for no deviation. God Himself regulated the delicate feeling of this man so that he would sense what the Holy Spirit desired to have. His feeling was usable, and the Lord had confidence in his feeling.

Brethren, is our feeling usable? Can the Lord trust us? We need to be broken indeed, or else the Lord cannot trust our feeling. How usable and trustworthy was Paul's feeling. "To the rest I say, not the Lord. . . ." (v.12). He did not have the distinct sense that the Lord was speaking, hence here he said, "I say, not the Lord." But wait till the end; He concluded with, "and I think that I have the Spirit of God." How marvelous that a man like Paul had arrived at such a position!

In verse 25 Paul revealed his own situation before the Lord. He declares: "Now concerning virgins I have no command of the Lord, but I give an opinion as one who by the mercy of the Lord is trustworthy." Here was one who had followed the Lord for many years and had received mercy to be trustworthy. In what respect was he trustworthy? His ministry was trustworthy. He was a servant of Christ and steward of the mysteries of God. He was entrusted by God with His mysteries and word.

What is important to a minister of the word is trustworthiness. Paul meant here that since the Lord had been merciful to him and made him a faithful servant, he would like to communicate his opinion to the Corinthians. The Lord had not given command, so this was simply how he, Paul, wished. Though he dare not say anything, for God had not commanded him, yet he would share his own opinion concerning certain matters on the basis of his having proclaimed the mysteries of God many times in the past. It was as if he were saying that having been in touch constantly with spiritual things through the mercy of God and having somewhat learned before God, he would now like to communicate what he had seen and learned through the years in spite of the fact that he had not received any fresh command from the Lord. He dare not presume this to be the Lord's command; he only presumed to tell his own opinion. Nonetheless, God endorsed his opinion. How glorious is this endorsement! We praise God for such a man who by the mercy of God became trustworthy and whose opinion was endorsed by the Lord.

Fourth

At this point we must take note of one matter, which is, what is the inward fashioning work of the Holy Spirit in us? We know the Spirit of God not only dwells in man but also does the work of fashioning and incorporating Christ in him. What the Holy Spirit incorporates in man cannot be taken away. The Holy Spirit dwells in man and is joined in one with him; He never ceases to fashion man according to the image of Christ. How could anyone treat the Spirit of the Lord as a guest when He has been living in his house for ten or twenty years? He is in the man—fashioning, building, and organizing till the character of the Lord is gradually stabilized in him.

After a house has been occupied by a person for a long while it begins to reveal the character of that person. Though the gift of the Holy Spirit may not transform a man, the indwelling Spirit will enable him to bear the fruit of the Spirit, thus manifesting a heavenly character. The Holy Spirit's fruit in man is the transformation of his character, for God builds up man's character through His Spirit. The Spirit of God works in his thought and effects a change there; in just the same way are his feeling, opinion, and judgment transformed. The Spirit's work of fashioning and incorporating is for the transformation of man's character.

The Holy Spirit was not only able to speak through Paul as a minister of His word, He in addition could use this man's character. He succeeded in building something out of the man's character. This is the fruit of the triune God. He works day after day, fashioning and forming in man until a new character is developed. The character is the man's; yet it is built in the man by the Holy Spirit. It is completely personal though it is produced by the Holy Spirit. As the Holy Spirit works and builds, the man is changed from glory to glory.

We need to see that transformation is a basic doctrine and experience of the Bible. Both the third chapter of Philippians and the third chapter of 2 Corinthians refer to basic experiences. On the one hand we acknowledge the unchangeableness of the flesh, yet on the other hand we believe the Lord's transforming work and His building work in our character. The Spirit of God not only dwells in us, He is also our life. It would be most strange indeed if a person had been indwelt by the Lord as his life for ten or twenty years without having undergone any change. Due to this fact that the Spirit of the Lord dwells in you as life, your thought, your feeling, your judgment, your opinion, your heart, and your spirit are each and all transformed. Formerly, you were inwardly full of the flesh; now, there is a new incorporation, there is new fruit in your feeling, thought, judgment, heart, and spirit. It came through the cross having dealt with, and having overcome, your flesh. What then is the incorporating task of the Holy Spirit? It is what God has worked and built and inwrought in man; it is that which can never be lost.

Paul became a trustworthy person through the merciful workings of the Lord. This trustworthiness points to his ministry. He confessed that he had no command of the Lord but that he would tell his own opinion. This opinion of his came from the incorporating work of the Holy Spirit in him. What Paul said was not ordinary revelation but was God's incorporation in him, which, as we see, was equal to revelation. This is a wonderful feat. When one is under the revelation of the Holy Spirit, he knows this is God's word; but when he is under the incorporating work of the Holy Spirit, he does not sense that it is God who is speaking. Rather, he seems himself to be giving opinion, nevertheless, what he says is reckoned as being of the Holy Spirit because of the Holy Spirit's incorporating action in him. Hence Paul summed up by saying, "I think that I have the Spirit of God." What we need is the incorporating work of the Holy Spirit. We need Him to work in us and to so fashion us that all our opinions, words, thoughts and feelings do not contradict God's word. Thus shall we be ministers of His word.

The character incorporated by the Holy Spirit in man varies with different persons. Thus Paul's preaching had its own charateristics, and Peter's preaching had its distinctiveness. Peter's letters differed from Paul's in style; so were John's different from all the rest. Each had his own style; style was something wholly personal. Upon experiencing the incorporating action of the Holy Spirit, a person's style can also be used by God. Had the sixty-six books of the Bible been written only in one style, how dead it would be. Today the glory of God is manifested in permitting each man to have his own style so that, no matter how it is said, it is the result of the Holy Spirit's incorporating work in him.

Each man's special characteristic is brought out only when he is subject to the Holy Spirit. Consider the grass God has created; no two blades are alike. Of the many trees, no two of them are the same; of the countless stars, each has its own glory; and of the endless faces, every one is unique. Similarly, the incorporation of Christ in you is distinct from that in me. Paul was full of the love of the Holy Spirit, so was John full of the Spirit's love;

yet all who have learned of the Lord know that each of them exhibited a different aspect of the love of the Holy Spirit. God has no need for uniformity. Each one who has the incorporating work of the Spirit in him maintains his own peculiar features.

Brethren, do not misconstrue what has been said to mean that we can all imitate Paul's way of speaking in 1 Corinthians 7. It is unique in the entire Bible; it represents the greatest height to which one can reach. If we speak without God's sanction, we commit a serious mistake. 1 Corinthians 7 shows us what kind of person Paul was, that we may better understand such writings as Ephesians, Colossians, Romans, and Galatians. It opens up Paul as a man to us, that we may know the person behind the writings. This is the preciousness of that chapter. We find here a man whose feeling, thought, opinion and word were trusted by God. When the word of God was put in him it became the highest revelation and suffered no loss. Without that chapter we would only see what the Holy Spirit does *through* Paul, not what the Holy Spirit does *in* him. His personal feeling, thought and word were so trustworthy that the word of God encountered no difficulty in Paul.

God is unable to entrust His revelation to some, for they are not dependable. He cannot appoint them to be ministers of His word because their thought, feeling, opinion and word are not trustworthy. In Paul's letters such as Romans, Galatians, Colossians, and Ephesians, we behold great revelations, but in 1 Corinthians we see what is the kind of man to whom God can entrust such revelations. The kind of person governs the degree of revelation. If we had all the other letters except 1 Corinthians with its Chapter 7, we would never know what kind of man Paul is. He is so trustworthy that not only has God's revelation not suffered loss in him but the word of God has even been more glorified—in the style, personality, and peculiarities of this man. How glorious that man can be used by God, that his personal elements may be blended with the word of God without causing any trouble but instead glorifying, enriching and perfecting it.

May God be merciful to us that we may be used in releasing

His word. There is hardly any greater need today than the word of God. Let brethren recognize the way of God's ministers of the word. We should ask God to give us inward light and word, and the kind of dealing that is deep and drastic, chiseling and grinding us so as to make the most delicate of our feelings trustworthy. Then when we express our feeling, it will be the Lord's feeling; when we show any inclination, it will be the result of the Holy Spirit's working in us; and when we exhibit love or patience, it will be the fruit of the Holy Spirit. Due to the many deep and thorough undertakings of the Spirit in us we will be able to exhibit these fruits. Because of what He incorporates in us, we can become such people. Bearing fruit is a natural process: the consequence of an inner working.

Brethren, after God by the Holy Spirit has done His work in you, you will naturally feel as the Holy Spirit feels, think as the Holy Spirit thinks, and desire as He desires. When God puts His word in you and sends you out, you will be able to give great glory to God by causing people to hear His word.

The root question today then is this: Can the Lord trust us? We shall see that the difficulty is not in God's word, rather does it reside in the minister. Without ministers there can be no word. God speaks in our day as He always has. He has no intention to take the ministry of the prophets away from the church, even as He never intends to remove the ministries of the teachers and the evangelists from the church. But there is a scarcity of the ministers of the word today. Whether there can be ministry and more ministry in the church depends upon us. The poverty and darkness of the church is due to our condition. May we solemnly pray: Oh Lord, break us that Thy word may flow through us.

May God be gracious to us.

PART TWO

THE WORD OF GOD

5. The Basis of the Word
6. The Need for the Holy Spirit's Interpretation
7. The Need for the Holy Spirit's Revelation
8. God's Word in Christ
9. Knowing God's Word through Christ

5 The Basis of the Word

To be a minister of God's word, as we have seen already, is not as simple as is usually understood. The word of God cannot be communicated by just anyone. A fundamental issue in being a minister of God's word is the man himself. Let us now turn to another matter, the word of God itself.

(1)

When we spoke earlier about the ministry of God's word, we did not assert that there could be God's word outside of the Bible. As we categorically deny that beyond the sixty-six books of the Bible someone could write a sixty-seventh book, we equally reject the notion that men today can receive revelation not found in the Bible or can possess ministry additional to what the Bible permits. We firmly believe God's word is in the Old Testament and His word is in the New Testament; we do not intend to add anything to the Bible. Even so, we additionally understand that not all who are familiar with the Bible can preach God's word. It is therefore necessary for every minister of God's word to know what the word of God is. The lack of such knowledge precludes him from being God's minister.

The whole Bible contains sixty-six books, written by approximately forty persons. Each of the writers has his own peculiarities, style, and phraseology; each possesses his personal feeling, thought, and individual traits. When the word of God came to these writers, God used their personal human elements. Some were used more while some were used less. But all have been used by God, and all have received revelation. The word of God is like a symphony and the writers are like the musical instruments. There are many and various musical instruments in an orchestra, each emitting its own sound; but when they play together they render harmonious music. We can still distinguish the sound of the piano, violin, trumpet, clarinet, or flute. Yet what we hear is not a jarring discord but a symphonic blending. Each of the instruments has its individual characteristics, yet all play the same musical score. If they each were playing independent musical numbers there then would be the jarring notes and the unbearable sounds. The same is true of the ministers of the word. Each has his personal characteristics; nonetheless, all speak the word of God.

From beginning to end the Bible maintains an organic unity. It is not a chaotic compilation. Though each minister says a little, they all nevertheless come together into an organic oneness. Many are those who speak—almost forty in number—but the Word is one. There is absolutely no confusion, nor are they unreconcilable bits and pieces. Many instruments, but one music. Something extra added in would hurt our ear and make us sense that something is wrong. God's word is one. There can be different voices but no jolting notes. Not because one knows how to make some sound can he justifiably stand up and deliver God's word. The word of God is an organic unit. The ministry of the word in the present is one with that of the past. Nothing foreign can be added. God's word is the Lord Jesus Himself; it is livingly and organically one. No one can mix anything else into it; any addition would be confusion and disturbance and impairment to the word of God.

There are thirty-nine books in the Old Testament. Chronologically the book of Job may have been the first one written, but the five books of Moses stand at the very beginning of the compilation. Let us grasp a very significant point here—that all who wrote after Moses did not write independently, but wrote according to what had been written before. Moses wrote his Pentateuch independently, yet Joshua set down his book on the foundation of the Pentateuch. In other words, Joshua's ministry of the word of God was not an independent one; he became a minister according to what he knew of the Pentateuch. So was it with the one who wrote the Books of Samuel; he too based his ministry on the five books of Moses. This is to say, therefore, that aside from Moses—who was called of God to write independently—all those who followed became ministers of God's word according to the word already given. Every book in the Old Testament was composed in this fashion. The writers are various, yet they all write on the basis of the previous writings. Every minister of the word after Moses speaks in accordance with the words already uttered. The word of God is one; no one can speak what he wants to; those who follow must speak according to the words given by their predecessors.

We now come to the New Testament. Except for the mystery of the Gentiles and the Jews forming one body, as unfolded in the Letter to the Ephesians, nothing is new; all else can be found in the Old Testament. Any revelation of truth can be located in the Old Testament, even that of the new heavens and the new earth. There is a certain edition of the Bible which capitalizes all of the many Old Testament quotations in the New Testament. It becomes quite evident that many words used in the New Testament were already seen in the Old. Many are direct quotations, and many more repeat what the Old Testament had already expressed. There are more than a thousand five hundred places in the New Testament which are quotations of Old Testament words. Let us remember that the ministry of the New Testament word is based upon God's word in the Old Testament; they were not independently spoken. Hence if anyone should stand up today and claim to have received an independent revelation, we would know for sure that it was undependable.

No one today can have God's word extraneous to the Bible; even the New Testament cannot exist alone, nor can the words of Paul. You cannot cut the Old Testament away and retain much of the New Testament; neither can you excise the four Gospels and keep the letters of Paul. We must see that all the later words follow those previously uttered. The words spoken later arose from light in the former words; they were not isolatedly spoken. Should another word ever come forth independently, it is heresy and not God's word. All the ministries in the Bible are interdependent; none possesses an unconnected revelation totally unrelated to the others and entirely disconnected. Even the twenty-seven books of the New Testament are based on those of the Old Testament. The subsequent ministers received what was handed down to them by their predecessors.

(2)

We should understand that any independent revelation and ministry is basically wrong. "No prophecy of scripture is of private interpretation" (2 Peter 1.20 ASV). The word "private" points not to man but to prophecy. It means no prophecy of Scripture is explained by its own meaning. For example: Matthew 24 cannot be explained by itself but must be interpreted by combining with it the other places in Scripture which have bearing on it. No prophecy is self-interpreting. Daniel 2 cannot be explained by Daniel 2 alone, nor can Daniel 9 be interpreted exclusively by Daniel 9. To do so would cause us to fall into private interpretation. We must always remember that God's word is one. It cannot be privately interpreted, that is, based upon itself; it must be explained by joining it together with many other passages. Today God has already put His word in the Bible; hence we are not allowed to speak independently nor give any word which is unable to be joined to the word already spoken by God. To do so would be heresy, a deception of the evil one.

The first group of ministers was used by God to speak in an independent fashion, for there was no one preceding them. The second group, though, spoke according to what the first group had previously said. They repeated and enlarged upon the words spoken earlier. The third group of ministers spoke on the basis of the first and second groups. They do not speak independently;

they only expand on the light received from the first and second groups. No doubt God had given them new understanding and new revelation; nonetheless these are all founded on what He has already before spoken. The nobility of the Jews in Berea was shown in their eagerness to examine the Scriptures daily to see if these things were so (Acts 17.10-11). God does not say one thing yesterday and say another thing today. His word is one; there is no change from the beginning to the end. He adds one word after another, because He aims at establishing His own work. Those who were used by God to enlarge on the light, both of the Old and the New Testaments, did not have independent revelations; they all based their enlargement on the revelation given first. Light continued to flow out from the initial revelation. It shone brighter and fuller until we have before us the entire Old and New Testaments.

Therefore, all who wish to speak for God today must receive His word from the Old and New Testaments; they are not to obtain anything from outside the Bible. This is a most important axiom: just as the ministers of old were not independent, neither are today's ministers of the word to be independent. Each one must depend on what God has already said. None are able to secure any revelation outside of the scope of the Bible.

Some of God's children harbor a great misunderstanding with regard to the Old and New Testaments. They think these Testaments are contradictory; they look upon law and grace as opposites. Are they really so? The mere reading of Romans and Galatians reveals to us especially that the Old and the New are one. How many misjudge that God's ways of dealing with people vary from the Old to the New Testaments, that He acts differently under law and grace. What they do not realize is that the New Testament is a progression from, not an opposition to, the Old Testament; so too is grace in relation to law. The New Testament is the continuation as well as the expansion of the Old Testament. These two are not in the least contradictory.

Paul reminds us that grace does not begin with the New Testament. By reading Galatians we know that at the time when God called Abraham the "promise" was already there. In other words, God preached to Abraham the gospel that through the coming of Christ the whole earth would be blessed. There was not any trace of the law. Galatians plainly indicates that what God gave to Abraham was not the law but the promise which is the gospel (3.8). According to Galatians, today's gospel is based upon the gospel spoken to Abraham; our blessing is founded on the blessing of Abraham; the promise we have today is traced back to God's promise to Abraham; and even the Christ we receive is the seed of Abraham. Paul demonstrates to us that the Old Testament and the New form a straight line.

Why, then, we may ask, was the law ever given? "It was added because of transgressions" (Gal 3.19). God first gave man grace and the gospel. But after man fell, he could not tell what sin was, hence he was unable to receive grace and the gospel. The law was then added to condemn sin in order that man might be made partakers of God's gospel and promise. This is the gist of Galatians. To put it differently: God has not at one time given us grace and at another time law; neither has He bestowed His promise and then demanded work for awhile. God's work from start to finish has never changed. The Letter to the Galatians consequently shows us that the grace we today receive is not something new but is the same grace which Abraham received. We have become children of Abraham, so we today inherit the grace and promise which God gave to Abraham. Thus the promise at first, the law in between, and the finished work of Christ afterwards all fall into one straight line. The word of God is one, not two, and is progressive in nature.

God first promised Abraham and later gave the law to the Israelites. Are these contradictory? Not at all. They are actually progressive. Today God has given grace to us. Is there any discrepancy? No, it is progress. God's way with men becomes clearer and clearer. The promise God gave Abraham cannot be annulled by the law given four hundred and thirty years later.

The later law does not annul the promise but on the contrary fulfills it, for men can accept promise only after they have known their sins. But now God has kept us all in custody under the law that we may accept the grace which comes from the Son sent by God. As the Old Testament is progressive, so the New Testament continues on from it and is also progressive. The New Testament is not in opposition to the Old. God's word is one. The later ministry is but to enlarge on the past revelation of God.

Today's ministers of the word must know what God has said in the Old Testament as well as in the New. It is evident that those ministers of the word who wrote the New Testament were familiar with the Old Testament. Today's ministers must be well acquainted with both. By knowing the words of our predecessors we are able to utter what harmonizes with these two Testaments. We will not speak independently. God does not put an additional word in our mouths; He only gives us new light on what He has already spoken in the Old and New Testaments that we may stand before men and deliver His word.

Whenever we begin to speak, we should already be in possession of many Old and New Testament words. When the first group of Old Testament ministers rose to speak they did not have God's previous word. When the second group came along, though, they could quote what the first group had said—but nothing more. Generation after generation, group upon group keep arising to minister the word of God. What they can quote to support their words increases in quantity, because many utterances have proceeded from God. We may say that in our day we have the richest deposit of God's word. But to be a minister of His word one must at least be acquainted with the Bible that he may put it to living use. If one is not familiar with the Scriptures and has not seen new light in it, the word he speaks has no basis. And if he speaks wrongly he will not be conscious of it. Hence we must know the Bible well, else it becomes difficult to be a minister of God's word.

We stress that a minister of the word needs to be familiar with the Bible. If we do not hear what God has spoken in the past we have no way to obtain revelation. Revelation is born out of previous revelation, never isolatedly given. First God puts His revelation in the word said before, then God's Spirit enlightens that word and enlarges the revelation. Thus the process continues. This is the way of revelation. It is not a light given in isolation, but is a light which comes from within the word and increases in brightness as time goes on. This is God's revelation. Without past revelation God's light has no ground in which to operate. God's revelation today cannot be given in the same way as at the very first. When He revealed to the first man He spoke without there being any previous background on man's part. In the advanced word of today, however, He speaks only on the basis of what He has already said. All His subsequent revelations are derived from the first one.

(3)

Psalm 68.18 is the Old Testament passage on the gifts which would be poured out upon men at the ascension of the Lord Jesus. When Paul wrote the first and fourth chapters of Ephesians he derived his message from that portion. In Ephesians 1 he speaks of Christ being ascended to heaven and made to sit at the right hand of God the Father (vv.20-21). In Ephesians 4 he describes how at His ascension Christ led forth a host of captives and gave gifts to men (v.8). In looking back further, we find that Peter on the Day of Pentecost said the same word: "Therefore having been exalted to the right hand of God, and having received from the Father the promise of the Holy Spirit, He has poured forth this which you both see and hear" (Acts 2.33). So both the outpouring of which Peter spoke on Pentecost and the gifts to build the church resulting from the ascension of which Paul spoke, come from an understanding of the light in Psalm 68. God did not give the light directly to Paul; on the contrary, He gave to the apostle the light which He had stored in Psalm 68. In order to get that light one must be familiar with Psalm 68.

The Book of Hebrews ably explains many offerings to us and shows us that the Lord Jesus is *the* offering. If one is unfamiliar with the Old Testament sacrifices, how can he understand Christ as *the* sacrifice? God's light is hidden in the Old Testament offerings. The writer of Hebrews knew the revelation in the Old Testament; otherwise he would have been unable to write Hebrews. The light of God is deposited in the Old Testament; this means it is deposited in Abraham, in Isaac, in Jacob, in Joseph, in Moses, in Joshua, in Samuel, in David, and in Solomon. If we fail to see these men, we fail to see all that light. For example, light is contained in the candle. Without the candle how can there be light? Light is shown through the lamp and lampstand, and without these there can be no light. We need to see that the Old and New Testaments are where God deposits His light. We shall not be able to meet today's need if we do not know the word in these Testaments. To repeat, the word of God is one; in it God puts His light that shines forth unceasingly.

Abraham "believed (God), and he reckoned it to him for righteousness." This is found in Genesis 15.6. This word is used three times in the New Testament—in Romans 4, Galatians 3, and James 2. The word once spoken in the Old Testament is repeated thrice in the New Testament. There are three key words in this statement: believe, reckon, and righteousness. First God gives His word in the Old Testament; in this word is hidden God's light. When Paul wrote Romans he stressed the term "reckon"; whoever believes is reckoned as righteous by God. In writing Galatians, he again quoted the same statement but his emphasis this time was different, for he underscored the term "believe"—believe unto righteousness. But when James was speaking, he neither took up the word reckon nor the word believe; he took up instead the term "righteousness": a person is undone without righteousness. Hence God's light shines forth in three different directions. It emits from three distinct points. If Paul had never read Genesis 15, if he had forgotten what he had read or if he had read without receiving any revelation, then the word would surely have been lost. Should one be careless with God's word in the Scriptures he will not be qualified to be a minister of His word.

A minister must be able to discover many facts in the Bible, and the more the better. He must search into the delicate parts of the word of God. One obtains God's light by first entering into God's facts—without the facts of the Bible there is no way to obtain the light. Without the lamp how can there be light? If the lamp is not lit, how can the light be manifested? We need God's previously spoken word in the Bible to help us in speaking the word of God.

Another instance is in Habakkuk 2.4, "the righteous shall live by his faith." This too is quoted three times in the New Testament: in Romans 1, Galatians 3, and in Hebrews 10. It also has three key words: the righteous, faith, and live. Romans 1 lays stress on "the righteous"—the righteous shall live by faith. Galatians 3 emphasizes "faith"—only by faith can man live. Hebrews 10 takes up "live"—by faith the righteous shall live. God again deposits His light in the Old Testament but releases it in the New. The light is released once, twice, and three times by the word in the Bible. It is therefore established beyond question that revelation is light emitted from the word which God has earlier spoken. It is never independent but always has its foundation.

(4)

As we have mentioned before, the New Testament includes nothing new except that which pertains to the mystery of the body—composed of the Gentiles and the Jews—as described in Ephesians. What the New Testament has is but the enlargement of the Old. The operating rule here is: God deposits His light in His word. We must therefore learn to know more of the word of God already given and recorded in the Scriptures. If those who are quite familiar with the Bible are not necessarily God's ministers of the word, how much less qualified are we if we are not thoroughly acquainted with the Bible! We cannot be lazy in this matter of knowing the Scriptures. We need to seek for spiritual understanding; knowing the letter alone is insufficient. We must read the previously given word of God before the Lord, asking for light that the Book may be an enlightened one. Oh that the word already spoken may speak again in us. This alone is effective. Where can we meet God's light if it is not in His already spoken word which is to be found in the Bible? Today's word is hidden in the New Testament word, even as the New Testament word is hidden in the Old Testament word. Just as the word of the apostles is derived from Moses and the prophets, so our word comes from the apostles. We need to learn to get a word from the apostles' word.

All the revelation today is but the light regained from the word of the past. At the beginning God gave His word; thereafter it is word begetting word. The governing rule for our day is for us to obtain a word from that which was once spoken and for us to attempt to speak something else. If we are unable to gain a word from the word already given, then we cannot be ministers of the word. We need to approach God's word as the apostles did, not as the scribes and Pharisees. We must see light in the word of the past, and word must beget more word. The first grain of wheat was created by God; from this initial grain all other grains were produced. The first grain produced many grains—from singular to plural. And the process continues on. The first one came from God; it was created, for it never existed before.

The same principle can be applied to God's word. The first word was created by God, for it had no precedent. This word then begat many subsequent words as it continued forth. Generations have passed with the word becoming clearer and clearer. It has increased enormously. Just as we cannot expect God today to create a new grain to sow, neither can we wait for Him to create a new word. We get our words from God's previously spoken word; we obtain light in the light already given; we receive revelation from the revelation once shown. This is the way for today's minister of God's word. Anyone who trespasses this principle falls into heresy.

Beloved, do not accept indiscriminately those who claim themselves to be apostles or prophets. We know that anyone who surpasses the Scriptural word of God is heretical and devilish. Serious error can be produced by careless speaking. Today's light is included in the light already given, today's word is hidden in the word previously spoken, and today's revelation is implied in the revelation once shown. What issues from the Bible is right; what does not come from the Bible but from another source is wrong. Today's word must come from the previous word. This is not the day of creation. The principle for today is one of begetting. Revelation begets revelation, light begets light, and word begets word. We are learning step by step, hoping that we may begin to have the ministry of the word.

6 The Need for the Holy Spirit's Interpretation

We have observed that ministers of God's word today must not speak independent words, words outside the scope of the Bible. All God's latter day utterances are based upon His earlier statements. The New Testament words are derived from those of the Old Testament, while today's words are grounded in the New and Old Testaments. The word of God is living and organically one. If anyone, being unfamiliar with the Old and New Testament words and failing to form an organic unity with these past words of God, attempts to speak independently, he is undoubtedly propounding heresy, the doctrine of the devil. Even so, God still has ministers of His word today; none of them speaks carelessly without a proper foundation.

Now we wish to proceed further to see that the words these ministers speak are not only rooted in God's former words but are also interpreted by Him. The ministry of the word requires God's interpretation as well as God's written word. His former words alone are not sufficient. One who has laid hold of God's speaking in the past is not necessarily thereby qualified to deliver God's word. He who is familiar with the Old Testament is not automatically enabled to write the New Testament; neither is one who is well versed in the New Testament necessarily competent as a minister of today's word. Upon the basis of God's recorded word there needs to be God's interpretation. God must explain His own past word to His minister; otherwise there can be no ministry.

Just as we must set aside all words which have no foundation, so we cannot accept anything that does not come from God's interpretation. God alone is able to explain what He has said before. We should not depend upon our good memory, lucid thought, and diligent study of the Bible. It is not the one who can recite by memory the 150 psalms who is able to speak on Psalms, nor is it he who knows the Song of Songs by heart who is competent to lecture on it. A person may remember all the prophecies of Isaiah, or recollect vividly the book of Daniel after having spent five to ten years on it; yet such a one does not automatically become a qualified expounder of either of these writings. We should not only know that no one can preach God's word if such preaching is not based on the past speaking of God, but also realize that not all who have a Scriptural foundation are necessarily ministers of God's word either. He who does not speak according to God's former word is unquestionably rejected; but he who does so speak may likewise not be accepted. In the early days many were the scribes and Pharisees who were well versed in the Old Testament, but none of them became a minister of the word. It is possible today for us to be well acquainted with the Bible and yet fail to be ministers of the word. A minister is one who has God's interpretation as well as God's word. He must have a foundation to his speaking and likewise an interpretation.

How does God intepret the Bible? How does He explain the words of the Old Testament to the New Testament minister? There are at least three distinct ways of interpretation in the New Testament: (1) prophetic interpretation, (2) historical interpretation, and (3) comprehensive interpretation. When the New Testament ministers study the Old Testament words, they will approach the Scriptures from these different angles: they look to the Holy Spirit for interpretation of prophetic words, historical records, or comprehensive messages.

Pertaining to Prophetic Interpretation

Let us illustrate this method by seeing how Matthew wrote his Gospel.

The Holy Spirit controlled Matthew in his narration of the story of the Lord Jesus. In the first chapter he quoted from

Isaiah 7: "Behold, the virgin shall be with child, and shall bear a son, and they shall call his name Immanuel." At the moment of writing his Gospel, Matthew was enlightened by the Holy Spirit with these words from the Old Testament. He did not spend time in attempting to arrive at some interpretation of the Old Testament. As a tax-collector Matthew might not have read much of the sacred scrolls, but afterwards he must have read a lot. It was the Holy Spirit who brought to his memory the words in Isaiah. But what did this word mean? It required the Holy Spirit to interpret this word as pointing to the birth of the Lord Jesus. Hereafter God is to be with us. In the past, God was not with us; but now, through the coming of the Lord Jesus, God is with us. This is the Holy Spirit's interpretation. The Spirit alone determines the meaning of God's word.

In 2.15, Matthew referred back to Hosea 11.1. A cursory reading of Hosea might not give us the impression that it points to the Lord Jesus, but the Holy Spirit explained to Matthew that it was so.

Again, in 2.18 the words of Jeremiah 31.15 are quoted: "A voice was heard in Ramah, weeping and great mourning, Rachael weeping for her children; and she refused to be comforted, because they were no more." We would not have known—unless the Holy Spirit had given His interpretation—that these words in Jeremiah prophesied about Herod setting his heart on killing Jesus.

Chapter 3 cites Isaiah 40.3—"The voice of one crying in the wilderness, make ready the way of the Lord, make his paths straight!" How would we have known that this referred to John the Baptist if the Holy Spirit had not expounded it as such to Matthew?

In recording the journey of the Lord Jesus to Capernaum by the sea in the territory of Zebulun and Naphtali (4.13-16), Matthew used the word in Isaiah 9.1: "This was to fulfill what was spoken through Isaiah the prophet, saying 'The land of Zebulun and the land of Naphtali, by way of the sea, beyond the Jordan, Galilee of the Gentiles. The people who were sitting in darkness saw a great light, and to those who were sitting in the land and shadow of death upon them a light dawned.'" Who would have thought of Isaiah 9 as referring to the Lord Jesus? But the Holy Spirit so interpreted it, and by His interpretation we realize it does speak of the Lord Jesus. Thus are we shown that the minister of God's word needs the Holy Spirit's interpretation as well as God's past word. Without His interpretation the Bible is sealed; it can serve no ground for further speaking.

In Chapter 8 we observe that the Lord Jesus healed many who were sick and cast out demons from the possessed. Matthew took up the words in Isaiah 53.4 by stating: "in order that what was spoken through Isaiah the prophet might be fulfilled, saying, 'He Himself took our infirmities and carried away our diseases'" (v.17). The words of Isaiah were opened to Matthew and became the ground for speaking. Only the Scriptures opened gives one the ministry of the word.

In Matthew 12.10-16 the Lord Jesus is recorded as again healing the sick. He saw a man with a withered hand on the Sabbath and commanded him to stretch it forth. The man did so, and it was restored whole like the other. The Lord withdrew from them. Many followed Him and He healed them all. However, He ordered them not to make Him known. Whereupon the Gospel writer immediately quotes the words from Isaiah 42.1-4 as follows:

> Behold, my servant whom I have chosen, my beloved with whom my soul is well pleased. I will put my Spirit upon him, and he shall proclaim justice to the Gentiles. He will not quarrel, nor cry out; nor will anyone hear his voice in the streets. A battered reed he will not break off, and a smoldering wick he will not put out, until he leads justice to victory. And in his name the Gentiles will hope. (vv.18-21)

It is the Holy Spirit's interpretation which joins the two passages of Isaiah 42 and Matthew 12 together. The Holy Spirit gave the explanation and Matthew became a minister of the word.

Consequently, in the ministry of the word it is imperative to have the Holy Spirit's interpretation—an interpretation which ordinary people do not see and which neither the Pharisees nor the scribes so understood. God Himself gives the interpretation and makes one a minister of His word. As a minister of God's word Matthew did not speak arbitrarily. He based his words on the Old Testament. But how? Before he could take the Old Testament words as his ground for speaking, he first had to be thoroughly acquainted with them and then be given the Holy Spirit's interpretation or unveiling. The ministry of the word is therefore based upon the Biblical word of God as interpreted by the Holy Spirit. In the Gospel of Matthew there are many quotations from the Old Testament, some of them cited by the Lord Jesus Himself. But the passages referred to above were all spoken exclusively by Matthew. He often said that such-and-such was to fulfill the prophecy of Isaiah or that something else fulfilled the words of some other prophet. It is very precious to find that one who by training was a tax-collector is quoting so many Old Testament words. Though not reared a scribe, nor educated a Pharisee as was Paul, he nonetheless had the ministry of the word.

Matthew spoke once more in Chapter 27. The Lord Jesus was soon to depart from the world; Judas had hanged himself; and the chief priests were taking counsel to buy the potter's field with the betrayal money. Wrote Matthew, "For this reason that field has been called the Field of Blood to this day" (v.8). Let us note especially that this was Matthew's own judgment. But immediately afterwards, however, he said this: "Then that which was spoken through Jeremiah the prophet was fulfilled, saying, 'And they took the thirty pieces of silver, the price of the one whose price had been set by the children of Israel; and they gave them for the Potter's Field, as the Lord directed me'" (vv.9-10) He declared this incident to be the fulfillment of what Jeremiah had said. *We* would hardly draw such a conclusion, yet the Spirit of God gave Matthew such an interpretation, and thus he was able to make the judgment. Matthew had the ministry of the word.

Pertaining to Historical Interpretation

1 Timothy 2.13-14 mentions the story of Adam and Eve. "For it was Adam who was first (formed), and then Eve. And it was not Adam who was deceived, but the woman being quite deceived, fell into transgression." Satan had not tempted Adam directly; this he did to Eve. Satan tempted Eve, and Eve, Adam. As Eve fell when tempted by Satan, so Adam fell when tempted by Eve. The Old Testament merely records this fact, but in the New Testament the Holy Spirit explains it by showing us that no woman should be the head or have authority over man. In the incident set before us a basic principle is involved. Sin was brought into the world by a woman turning to become head. This indeed is a part of history. But the unveiling of such an historical fact forms the basis of the ministry of the word.

In narrating the story of Abraham, Paul in Romans 9 cited the words of Genesis 21: " Through Isaac your descendants will be named"; "At this time I will come and Sarah shall have a son" (v.7,9). These are historical events as recorded in the Old Testament. But the Holy Spirit expounded them to Paul so that the apostle now realized that not all who were descended from Israel necessarily belonged to Israel since not all the seed of Abraham were children of Abraham just because they were his descendants. Only those who were born of Sarah were considered as Abraham's descendants. Isaac was born of promise and he alone was Abraham's seed. In like manner are those who believe in the Lord Jesus. Since they are born of God's promise they alone become children of God. The Holy Spirit had thus opened up the history of how Abraham had begotten Isaac, and so Paul was given the ministry of God's word. Had Paul merely read the story of Abraham and Sarah, without the Holy Spirit's interpretation, those words would have remained a mere story and Paul would not have had the ministry of the word through them.

The narrative of Isaac was explained even more clearly in the Letter to the Galatians. "If you belong to Christ, then you are Abraham's offspring, heirs according to promise" (3.29); "And you brethren, like Isaac, are children of promise" (4.28). These were Paul's words as one who had the the ministry of the word. His words were derived from the episode in the Old Testament. The Holy Spirit interpreted that particular section of history to him, unfolding to Paul the secret of "the promise." Wherein was this secret? It was in Genesis 18.10: The Lord said, "I will certainly return unto thee (in the spring); and, lo, Sarah thy wife shall have a son." This was God's promise–not today, but next year. Hence Isaac was born of promise. We all, like Isaac, are born of promise. This matter is crystal clear. The reason Paul could supply us with God's word was because the Holy Spirit had explained this Old Testament word to him. It is not only prophecy that needs the Spirit's interpretation; history too requires explanation. All Old Testament history needs such comments.

Another matter is made quite plain in Galatians 3. "Brethren, I speak in terms of human relations: even though it is only a man's covenant, yet when it has been ratified, no one sets it aside or adds conditions to it" (v.15). Paul meant by this to say that not only in divine, but even in human, affairs a will once ratified cannot be annulled or addition made to it. "Now the promises were spoken to Abraham and to his seed. He does not say, 'and to seeds,' as referring to many; but rather to one, 'and to your seed,' that is, Christ" (v.16). Notice how careful a man Paul was. In Genesis God told Abraham that He would bless the nations of the earth through his offspring. In Galatians the Spirit of God has explained it even more precisely to Paul. The word "offspring" or "seed" in Hebrew is singular in number. The opening up of this one word gave understanding to Paul. God was not going to bless the nations by the many seeds of Abraham. For if this be the meaning, then the grace of God is solely for the Jews, and only the Jews can spread the blessings to the whole world. What is said here is seed or offspring in the singular, that is, Christ, because through Him alone shall blessings come upon all the earth. The fact is rather simple: merely in the singular or plural number lies the difference; yet in this simple fact is hidden a most important truth. It was the Holy Spirit who expounded such a simple fact to Paul, and it made him a minister of the word.

Let us mention one further matter. Abraham believed God and it was accordingly reckoned to him as righteousness. This was recorded in Genesis 15. Paul now shows us through this record that God does not reckon *man's righteousness* as his righteousness but accounts *man's faith* as his righteousness. This is Paul's ministry. He shows us today that the way Abraham was justified is the way all his descendants shall be justified. As Abraham was justified by faith, so all who are likewise justified are children of Abraham. The record in Genesis 15 is mory than a fact of history; it in addition embodies the principle of justification by faith.

Let it be understood that the Old Testament with its history is as valuable as Old Testament prophecy. Some may think of the biblical prophecies, laws, and teachings as highly valuable, while considering the histories included therein to be mere stories. But we should remember that the histories narrated in the Scriptures are equally the word of God. If the Bible is entrusted to an unbeliever, he may choose Proverbs and discard Genesis. But we know the prophecies, teaching, laws, and histories recorded in the Old Testament are all God's word. His word is one, and the inner principle is also one. What is spoken through history is the word of God as much as what is spoken through prophecy. Both require the Holy Spirit's interpretation. Many New Testament truths and revelations are derived from the opening up of the Old Testament history. In Paul's ministry we discover that sometimes the Holy Spirit unveils Old Testament prophecies to him while at other times, Old Testament histories.

Pertaining to Comprehensive Interpretation

Comprehensive interpretation is especially used by God in the ministry of His word. Let us see how Peter ministered God's word on Pentecost. A most wonderful thing happened on that day—the Holy Spirit was poured out and gifts were distributed. Man spoke in tongues and many tongues were spoken. The one hundred and twenty persons received what the Israelites had never received before. Formerly the Holy Spirit might come upon one or two prophets or even upon a group of prophets. Yet on that Pentecost day all one hundred and twenty were filled with the Spirit as though drunk with new wine. At that time God distinctly placed the key of heaven into Peter's hands. Of the eleven, he unmistakably walked at the front. He seized this opportunity to testify. Peter stood up and told the Jews what had taken place. He explained the day's happenings and exhorted his listeners to receive the same thing themselves. Peter was on that day a minister of the word. He received words from God—and not words from just one part of Scripture but words from three parts combined. In grouping these three parts together light began to shine. It was not an analysis but a synthesis. God did not explain simply one thing to him; He instead brought three parts of the Scriptures together and so revealed His thought.

On that day of Pentecost, Peter based his message on Joel 2, Psalm 16, and Psalm 110. The Holy Spirit combined these three passages and expounded them to Peter, thus giving light to men. It accordingly indicates that when one is ministering he does not need to limit himself to just one passage. Oftentimes He explains several passages together. In today's ministry this comprehensive interpretation plays a major role.

For instance. In the Old Testament there were four objects which the people had vicariously worshiped: the golden calf, the brazen serpent, Gideon's ephod, and Micah's graven image. If you are going to give a message on unlawful worship, you could gather together these four cases in the Old Testament and comment on them. Many matters are solved in this way.

Peter took this comprehensive line at Pentecost. He used Joel 2 to speak on the outpouring of the Holy Spirit, Psalm 16 on the resurrection of the Lord Jesus, and Psalm 110 on His ascension. He joined these three passages together, saying that the Lord

Jesus had been resurrected, had ascended to heaven after the resurrection, and that the outpouring of the Holy Spirit which his hearers now witnessed was the result of His ascension. Upon being raised from the dead the Lord must ascend to heaven. Death having no power to bind Him, He went up to the Father, awaiting His enemies to become His footstool. The heavenly Father presently glorified Him and the outpouring of the Holy Spirit is this day the evidence of this glorification. By these three passages having been expounded to him by the Spirit, Peter could speak with authority.

We can find quite a few messages in the Book of Acts whose words are of this comprehensive nature. Although but few words of the message are recorded in Chapter 3, it nevertheless puts Deuteronomy and Genesis together. In Chapter 7 Stephen had a very special ministry of the word. He spoke with great power, yet he rarely explained. He merely related some history of the Old Testament, beginning from the call of Abraham in Genesis 12, then touching upon the period of Moses in Egypt, and ending with the rebellion of the Israelites in the Wilderness. He spoke from Genesis to Exodus and from Exodus to Deuteronomy, quoting the words of Amos and Isaiah as he narrated. He gave little interpretation, and yet his message so roused the anger of his listeners that they stoned him to death. This shows us that a special ministry of the word does not require much explanation; all which is needed is to marshal the facts one after another. Stephen's message was pressed out of his spirit, hence it was irresistible. As recorded in Chapter 13, while preaching in Antioch of Pisidia Paul cited words of 1 Samuel 13, Psalm 89, Psalm 2, Isaiah 55, Psalm 16, and concluded with a word from Habakkuk. On the basis of these comprehensive words, he drew a conclusion for his listeners: they must receive Jesus of Nazareth as their Savior.

Now of the three different modes of interpretation which we have mentioned, we would place special emphasis on the comprehensive way. The book of Hebrews is written in this fashion, and so are Romans and Galatians. When the Holy Spirit directed an apostle to a certain subject, He selected numerous Scripture verses and expounded them to him. This principle still governs today's ministry of God's word. Just as Peter, Paul, Matthew and many other apostles ministered with the words which the Holy Spirit taught them out of the Old Testament, so today we have our ministry of the word by following what the Holy Spirit instructs us from both the New and the Old Testaments. The apostles never spoke carelessly, because they always spoke according to the interpretation which the Holy Spirit gave concerning God's former words. Today's ministers of the word should observe the same rule. We speak what God would have us to say today by our having both the words of the New and Old Testaments and with them the Holy Spirit's interpretation. This constitutes the ministry of the word.

However, not all who at that time read the Old Testament could speak like Peter, Paul, or Matthew. The ministry of the word came only after the Holy Spirit's interpretation. The Spirit would enlighten one of them, expound the meaning of a particular word to him, show him the fact in the Old Testament word, and point out to him its characteristic.

As those in the New Testament had the ministry of the word, we today must have such ministry. Should we desire to be ministers of God's word we must diligently read the recorded word of God, and not merely with our head but looking to the Spirit of the Lord to reveal to us what characterizes His word that we may take of the facts and receive the interpretation. When a minister of the word speaks, he must speak from background. Never speak without foundation, nor consider familiarity with God's past words as sufficient. Always seek for the Holy Spirit's interpretation.

Let us remember that ministry of the word in our day ought to be richer than that of those who wrote the New Testament. This does not mean that today we see deeper than they did. The Bible was completed when the Book of Revelation was written. All God's truths have been released, the highest as well as the deepest. How, then, do we say that today's ministry of the word should be richer? Because Paul had in his hand only the Old Testament as the basis of his speaking, but we have in our hand the writings of Paul and Peter and others in addition to the Old Testament. Paul had only thirty-nine books in his hand, but we have sixty-six books. Hence our ministry should be richer in word. We have more materials at the disposal of the Spirit of God, more opportunities for God's Spirit to explain. Our ministry therefore ought not be poorer but richer.

We need to study the Bible carefully; we also need the Holy Spirit to interpret the Bible to us. In the past many have spent time studying the Bible, and the Holy Spirit has given them much light. Some have noticed differences in words, such as the difference between "Christ" and "the Christ," "law" and "the law," "faith" and "the faith." Others have discovered that before His resurrection the Lord Jesus is "Jesus Christ," but that afterwards He is "Christ Jesus." Nowhere in the whole Bible is there the phrase "in Jesus"; it is always "in Christ."

We should allow the Spirit of the Lord to speak to us and show us how accurate the Bible is. No one can carelessly change the word of the Bible, not even the pronouns. Each time the blood is mentioned it relates to redemption; but every time the cross is used it has reference to the dealing of man's self. "Crucified on the cross" speaks of the dealing of the old creation; "bearing the cross" speaks of the dealing of the natural self. Never is there any confusion. Confusion comes from us, it is not in God's word. As to the works of the Holy Spirit, His constituting and His forming are inward, whereas the gift is outward. All these prove to us the accuracy of the Bible. Just as the writers of the New Testament saw the accuracy of the Old Testament when the words were explained to them, so we shall see the accuracy of the New and Old Testaments when the Spirit of the Lord interprets His recorded word to us.

To be a minister of the word is not to receive independently a great revelation never before given, rather is it seeing increased light in the word already spoken by God. Some ministers came before Paul, and Paul and other apostles have come before us.

The sixty-six books are the word of God already written down. Today's revelation must coincide with the revelation those preceding us have received. Today's light must be one with the earlier light given. Today's word must be united with the word spoken by our predecessors. If Paul became a minister of the word through the Holy Spirit's interpretation, we too must have His interpretation in order to be ministers of the word. God's word passes on from generation to generation; His word begets further word. No one speaks independently. Those who come later see more than the earlier ones. God did something independently in the first man, but the second man follows the first and so walks farther, while the third follows the second and moves on still more. God's word comes forth endlessly; His word begets word till there are many words. Today we have more words.

If God is gracious and merciful to us we shall see His former word and be the minister of His word on this basis. The ministers are many, but the word is one. Ministers are raised up from generation to generation, yet all ministry comes from the same word. Hence those who come later should ask God to interpret the word spoken by their predecessors so that their word may be united with God's greatest word—the Bible—and that they themselves may join the ranks of the many, many ministers. The fundamental truth is: one word but many ministers.

7 | The Need for the Holy Spirit's Revelation

We have already seen how a minister of the word must speak according to God's former word and with the interpretation of the Holy Spirit. We will now venture a step further: the minister of the word must fulfill another basic requirement: he must have revelation. Without the spirit of revelation, no one can be a minister of the word. He should have both revelation and the Holy Spirit's anointing in order to minister God's word.

One

The Bible is a wonderful book. Its special characteristic rests in the fact that it speaks with human words, yet is truly God's word. Though written by human hands, it is nevertheless recognized as having been written by God's hand too. Its many terms, phrases and statements are all God-breathed. The original for "inspired by God" (2 Tim. 3.16) is "God-breathed." The Bible is God-breathed, as "men moved by the Holy Spirit spoke from God" (2 Peter 1.21). When God was creating heaven and earth, He formed man of dust of the ground; but man was not a living soul until God breathed the breath of life into him. Though the Bible was written by human hands and spoken from human mouths, even so, God breathed on it and made it a living book. It became a living word spoken by the living God. This is the meaning of inspiration in the Bible.

There are human elements and men's words in the Bible. Many, in reading it, touch these elements and words, but they so often miss what God intends to say through them. The distinctiveness of this Book is its dual feature: on the one hand the

Bible has its outer shell—the physical part of the Bible—similar to that part of man which is made of dust; on the other hand it has its spiritual part, that which is in the Holy Spirit, what is God-breathed and God-spoken. The outer shell is something which comes from man's memory (hence it can be memorized by man), from the human mouth (hence can be heard by man's ears), which is written in human language (it may be apprehended by man's understanding), and was also spoken by man as doctrine or teaching (it can thus be remembered, understood and propagated by more people). This, however, is the outer shell of the Bible, that which is merely physical. Even doctrine and teaching are included in this realm, because they are the physical part of the Book, able to be memorized and understood by the wise. But the Bible has still another part. "The words that I have spoken to you are spirit and are life," declared the Lord Jesus (John 6.63). This is the spirit and life side. It is God who speaks in man. Neither the wise nor the understanding know it. It requires an organ other than the eyes, ears, or brain for its apprehension.

A minister of the word is not to serve the church with the physical part of the Bible. He is to minister the spiritual portion. He who serves only with the physical is not a minister of God's word. Were there no physical side to the Scriptures, the matter of whether or not one is a minister of God's word could easily be settled. But since the Bible has a physical part comprised of human elements, and since it can thus be understood and accepted by man, there arises a great danger and difficulty. Man may use his human elements to propagate whatever in the Bible corresponds to him, regarding this as being a ministry of the word. He merely selects the human elements of the Bible and places these before the church. Since what he preaches is undeniably Scriptural, orthodox and fundamental, he regards himself as serving the church with the word of God. We ought to know, however, that such human aspects do not belong to the spiritual part of the Bible and therefore constitute things which are in a far different realm.

Some young people think they will unquestionably understand God's word if only they study Greek, not realizing that many Greek scholars comprehend little or nothing of the true word of God. Not all who are acquainted with Hebrew understand the Old Testament, nor are those who are familiar with Hebrew and Chaldean necessarily those who know the Book of Daniel. There is a word in the Bible which is beyond Greek or Hebrew or Chaldean. It is the word which all ministers seek to know. It is the word of God. To know the language is one thing, but to know God's word is a totally opposite matter. One should never deceive himself by thinking he can be a minister of God's word if he simply reads the Bible. The question is not whether he has read the Bible: it is instead, *how* has he read it? God's word needs to be heard before Him, His voice needs to be recognized. Only such as have experienced this can be ministers of His word.

We are called to preach the gospel, not to present the background of the gospel. We serve people with the gospel, not with arguments about the gospel. The Bible does furnish the background of the gospel; it is the ground of God's speaking. God has indeed spoken once in the Bible. But today He must breathe on the written word once again to make it alive. The Spirit of God must breathe upon and quicken it. Only through revelation will the Bible become living. The words in the Bible and the word of the Bible quickened today are quite distinct. What is the word of God? It is what God is speaking today, not what He has once spoken. Once He spoke; and so we have the past word of God. Now, though, we need Him to breathe anew on His former word. God's word is more than what He once uttered; it is in addition the word which He speaks today.

Let us remember that the word of God covers two disparate realms. One includes the letters and the words, with the doctrine, knowledge, teaching, types and various truths of the Bible. Things in this realm can be heard by man's ears, can be memorized with his mind, and delivered through his mouth. This is the physical realm. For example, you may have heard that Abraham's faith was reckoned to him as righteousness. God reckons faith as righteousness. It is possible for you to endorse this doctrine, and if your power of memory and understanding is strong you may even propagate this statement to others. You are merely speaking the physical external part of the word, but this cannot be considered the ministry of God's word.

Let us note that the Bible is what God has once spoken, that which the Holy Spirit breathed upon once before. When the word of the Bible is released, some people will meet the word of God while others may miss it completely. In Paul's letter to the Roman believers we find two things. One is the physical side of his letter, what we can read externally, written perhaps with ink made from sap and recorded on lamb skin. When the Roman believers receive the letter, they might read the mere letters of the epistle. What they would then have would be just an epistle from Paul, not the word of God. But if the breath of God were to blow once more on the epistle at the time of their reading—breathing upon word after word—then they would see how they were sinners and how they could be justified by faith. They would believe in God's word and accept it as such. *This* constitutes the ministry of the word. As they read they meet the other word, that which Paul was trying to convey in the epistle. It is possible for those who are clever and strong in memory to be so familiar with the epistle that they can recite it verbatim, yet they can be totally ignorant of what justification by faith in reality is. They may even know the teaching concerning justification by faith without in any wise touching its reality. Yes, men can touch the physical part of the Bible without touching its spiritual counterpart. They merely touch the doctrine of the Bible without touching its contents. They know only the appearance of God's word without knowing its life.

Two

What is inspiration? And what is revelation? Inspiration means God has once breathed upon this book the Bible. Without inspiration something cannot be written so as to become a part of the Bible. Consequently, inspiration is the foundation of the

Bible. God inspired Paul to write Romans; that is, God breathed on him that he might write the Letter to the Romans.

What, then, is revelation? Revelation means God again breathes on His word when I read Romans two thousand years later in order that I may know it as the word of God. Inspiration is given only once; revelation is given repeatedly. By revelation we mean that today God again breathes on His word, the Holy Spirit imparts light to me; the anointing of the Holy Spirit is upon this word so that once again I see what Paul saw in his day. God does something today to make alive the inspiration of yesterday. This is a tremendous event! It is a most glorious act!!

What again is revelation? Revelation occurs when God reactivates His word by His Spirit that it may be living and full of life as at the time when it was first written. As in the beginning when Paul, full of life, was used by God to write and thus the word became so living, so today the Holy Spirit once more anoints and fills His word that it may have the same power, light and life as it had formerly. This is revelation. It is futile to simply read, for a person can read through the Book without ever hearing God speak once to him. The Bible is the word of God: God has indeed once spoken these words. But to make it living a person must ask God to speak afresh. When God speaks again, things will happen—God's word, light and life come forth. Unless there is this speaking afresh, the Bible will remain a sealed book.

Suppose a hundred brothers and sisters are gathered in a meeting. God is speaking there. Not all, however, hear His word. All hear the sound and the sentences, yet some hear God's word whereas others do not. Some meet things in both realms; some meet things in one realm only. Some have heard the doctrine, the truth, or the argument expressed by voice; they understand and, if their memory is good, can repeat these to others; yet they may not have heard the word of God. To hear the word of God is something quite different. God's word is not simply doctrine or teaching. We need to hear something beyond what we hear physically. This extra hearing comes from God's speaking to us. We have heard and accepted it; we can thank God for letting us hear His voice. Thus do we know that we have unquestionably met something.

Here is another illustration. A hundred people may be listening to the gospel. Ninety-nine of them may understand the meaning, doctrine, teaching, and truth of what is said and may even nod their heads and show their approval; but perhaps only one person apprehends that doctrine and word which is beyond what is presented. That person, having heard the voice of God, will bow his head and pray: I am a sinner; oh God, save me! This man alone has heard God's word; the ninety and nine touched only the human and physical side of the word. How basically unalike these two realms are.

The same is true of the Bible. It is indeed the word of God. God has once spoken through Paul, through Peter, and through John. But when one reads them today he may gain all the words, phrases, doctrines, truths and teachings, yet God has not spoken to him. He may read the Bible for ten years without ever hearing God speak one single word to him. Have you not heard people confess, "I have read the Bible for twenty years, but I have to admit today that I know absolutely nothing about it." Or you have heard someone say, "I have read the Bible for five (or ten) years. I thought I knew it all. But one day I received God's mercy; He spoke to me; then I knew I had known nothing before." All who are experienced know the difference therein described.

In the ministry of the word there must be God's word beyond man's word; in addition to man opening his mouth, God must open His mouth. Should God keep His mouth shut, nothing spiritual can be done. These are two diametrical worlds. The one is the world of doctrine, truth, teaching, letters, language, phraseology; those who are diligent, clever and wise, and possessing a good memory, may be able to comprehend the one world. But the other is wholly at variance, for God speaks again what He had once spoken before. Do we now see the difference? The Bible records without any error what God once promised, but the word of God today is His speaking to us again what He has said before. In God's word there is the need for Him to again speak to us; in God's light there needs to be another enlightenment from Him; in God's revelation, there awaits a fresh revealing of what has already been revealed. This is the foundation of the ministry of God's word.

To help some who may still not be clear as to the relationship between the word of the Bible and the word of revelation today, let us use the following illustration. Suppose you have had the experience of feeling that the Lord had spoken through you. Though the delivery might not have been strong, yet at least you had the sense that the Lord gave you some special words during that time. You had the anointing of the Holy Spirit. Two months later you meet the same type of situation, facing the same kind of people with the same kind of need. You are confident you can help them now, for is it not true that you "successfully" spoke to such a group just two months ago? Yet today, upon finishing speaking to them, you feel defeated and powerless. Wherein lies the trouble? The trouble is you surmised that if you delivered the same word as before, the Holy Spirit would permanently anoint that which He had once anointed. But this, to your surprise, was not true. There is no assurance that the word previously anointed by the Holy Spirit will again be anointed each time it is spoken. Let us remember that the word of revelation we earlier receive is not guaranteed to always be such a word whenever it is uttered. The word remains, but revelation does not linger. You may repeat the word, yet you cannot repeat the revelation or the anointing. Revelation and anointing are in God's hand. You can only repeat words, you cannot recall revelation. Today you preach to a sinner the Gospel of John Chapter three and verse sixteen, and he may be saved. Subsequently you meet another person—perhaps in the same room—and to him you preach on the same Scripture a second time. This time, though, the Holy Spirit is silent, and thus the man remains unsaved. The Scripture has not changed. The issue is whether or not there is an anointing or a revelation.

Three

Every minister of God's word must learn one lesson. Not because I understand something of the letters of the Bible, not because I see somewhat concerning the truth in the Bible, nor because I am able to quote Scripture verses am I a minister of the word. I need to understand, see, and be able to quote, but besides these there is a still more basic requirement. The possession or lack of possession of this basic requirement determines whether or not I have the ministry of the word. This determining factor is the revelation of the Holy Spirit. The ministry of the word requires the revelation of the Holy Spirit. There must not only be similar words; there must also be corresponding revelation. The absence of corresponding revelation terminates the presence of ministry. This we must know deep in our heart.

To secure results today similar to what He did once before, God has to speak again. The word which may be repeated is effective only when it is anointed afresh by God. In this can we see the balance of truth. On the one side, God uses again what He once spoke before. The one preaching the word of God today does not seek independently for new words but bases his ministry upon the old word given by God previously. On the other side, though, what he preaches is not the old word. It is the same word and yet not exactly the same. It is the same word inasmuch as God will not speak if the fundamental foundation is lacking, for the word of God is one. Nevertheless, it is not the same word because there is now a fresh anointing and a fresh revelation of the Holy Spirit. Without the Holy Spirit's fresh anointing and revelation the same old word will not produce the same result. This balance—of the old plus the new—must be carefully maintained before God.

A great temptation looms before man, which is, that man merely seeks to speak the same word. He thinks by so speaking he will have the same power, light, and revelation. Let it be recognized, however, that these are worlds apart. One may use the same word with the same truth, testimony, example, and presentation—for these can be repeated—they are within human ability to reproduce; yet God may not return its effectiveness. One may be able to repeat the outward things but he is totally unable to reproduce the inward. God's world remains God's, while man's world belongs to man.

Perhaps an example will clarify the point. The principle of God's speaking is the same as that of resurrection. What is resurrection? It is not giving life but is life out of death. When a child is born he is not resurrected; only when a dead man comes out of the grave is there resurrection. The daughter of Jairus, the only son of a widow in Nain, and the man Lazarus, were all of them resurrected because they had first died and had then been raised from the dead.

It is on the principle of resurrection that one ministers the word of God. Once upon a time God put life in His word. Today this word needs new life from God. This is the resurrection principle, quite separate from the creation principle. The first speaking is according to the principle of creation, but today's ministry of the word is different. God's word is already here, but God must speak again. When God again puts life into the word so as to make it alive in man, this is resurrection. Take for instance Aaron's rod which represents resurrection. All the rods in the story were at one time living, for they were made of wood. In the story, however, life has left them, so they become dead rods. When placed before the ark, Aaron's rod alone sprouted, blossomed and bore fruit. This is resurrection.

God's word stands on the ground of resurrection. It is not the cutting of another rod, but the budding of the original one. Since God's word is one and only one, no person can preach His word if he casts aside the Bible. It is still the same rod, but resurrection life has entered into it. The rod must be the same one, nonetheless life must enter into it the second time. The word is the same, yet life passes through it time and again. Only as the word each time receives life, light, and revelation is it living. Whoever casts aside the Bible is himself rejected by God, for he has rejected the written word of God. All Scripture is inspired by God and must therefore be respected. Without the Bible as the foundation there can be no pure faith nor any revelation of God. Yet even *with* the word of the Bible, man has to seek still further revelation and enlightenment from God.

The principle is: one inspiration but many revelations; one word but spoken repeatedly by God; one Bible but frequent anointings of the Holy Spirit. Thus is the ministry of God's word established. Whenever anointing, enlightenment and revelation are lacking and hence what is left is but the outward expounding of the Scriptures, the ministry of the word has ceased. We must take note of this before God. Useful indeed are man's diligence, memory, understanding, and cleverness, yet these by themselves are inadequate. To be effective, there must be God's further mercy and renewed speaking. As a matter of fact, unless God is willing to speak, men will never hear the word of God. It is something beyond human ability. If the Lord is silent, the speakings of all the ministers are in vain. It is therefore of the greatest importance that the Lord should speak. Anyone who has learned to speak in the spirit has seen the utter uselessness of human competency alone. The words may be the same, even the tone or feeling seems to correspond, yet what is spoken can be vastly different in effect.

Always remember that God's word needs to be spoken by God. The Bible is the word of God and it requires of Him to speak again. The work of a minister is to allow God to speak through him. He is to serve God in this spiritual realm. Ministering the word of God and ministering theology are separated by an unbridgeable gulf. Whenever listening to a sermon, do not pay attention only to the correctness of the doctrine, teaching, or truth. We do not think lightly of these things, but all who have learned before God and have had their eyes opened search for something more. Perhaps the one who is speaking has very good thoughts, but he just does not have the word of God. Another speaker may not be as gifted in thinking; he nonetheless has the word of God in his delivery. Whether God is speaking or not marks the great divide.

If brethren today learn this lesson, there will not be such an over-emphasis in the church on gifts; people will think more of ministry instead. In our day the trouble is that many young brothers and sisters do not know how to discern; and as a result, gifts are especially welcomed in the church while ministry is overlooked. The words may be exactly alike, even so, the realms are diametrically opposite. Those with discernment can tell. A brother once said, "I have preached what brother so-and-so preached!" He had a big brain; he thought he had succeeded in preaching as the other one had; actually he knew not in what realm he had been speaking. Some speak with their mind, others in the spirit. These belong to two separate worlds.

Four

From church history we can see that God began the work of recovery at the time of Martin Luther. He commenced it by raising up Luther and his contemporaries to recover the truth of justification by faith. Much later, especially after 1828, many more truths were recovered. Today, in the hearts of all throughout the world who love the Lord, there is one question: How far has the Lord advanced on this road of recovery?

To speak what the apostles spoke and to proclaim the truths the Bible presents is not to be viewed as recovery. Proclaiming New Testament truth may not bring in New Testament revelation, nor does the preaching of apostolic messages necessarily mean the carrying on of their word. Nowadays many may preach on baptism without knowing what baptism really is, may expound on laying on of hands without comprehending its meaning, may speak on the church without actually seeing what the church is, and may touch upon obedience without recognizing God's authority. Do not conclude that the same topic means the same content or the same word gives the same substance. Much preaching is done in the realm of the letter of the word. This is not the ministry of the word.

To be a New Testament minister one must have New Testament revelation of the word. Only at the time when we receive the same anointing as the apostles did do we have the ministry of the word. Each fresh revelation in common with that of the apostles supplies us with one time of ministry. Repeating the words of the apostles alone does not give us the same word of God that they had, for God's word is something far beyond that. Suppose there is currently a church which is being enticed waywardly in the same way as the Galatians were. How would you help? Could you just copy the Letter to the Galatians and send it off to them? The Letter to the Galatians was written by Paul, but from it the Galatians received the word of God. If you were to send a copy of this letter to that church today, they might touch your copied words—but not the word of God. It is possible for people to meet the Bible without in the least meeting life. This, in fact, is quite a common occurrence. People touch the letter God uses but not the word of God. They touch the God-inspired Bible, but not the revelation of the Holy Spirit.

Why is it, brethren, that many read the Bible today but get little from it, that many preach the Bible but rarely have God's word? This is because men only meet the outer shell of God's word. They encounter what God has once spoken, yet they lack the speaking again of God through His recorded word.

We ought to see that getting God to speak through the Bible is the responsibility of a minister of the word. He must be a person through whom God can speak. When he opens the Bible and speaks, people must hear more than what the Book says; they must hear the current voice of God. Should the hearers close their own spirits, hearts, and minds intentionally, they turn deaf to God's voice; yet if they are willing to be open, they cannot but hear His voice. Should people fail to hear the word of God when we expound the doctrines of the Bible, it indicates our complete failure as ministers of the word. When a true minister of the word preaches from the Bible, God is willing to speak to men. Then people will feel that God has spoken to them today and they will be completely subdued.

The destitution of the church in these days is caused by the poverty of the ministers. You may blame others for not possessing more revelations, but why do *you* not give them revelation?

Giving them revelation is your job. You may accuse the church of poverty; why however, do you not give her the needed abundance? To make the church rich is your responsibility. The effectiveness of a minister of the word is demonstrated by his enabling the people to hear the word of God, not the word of the Bible alone. In his mouth the word of the Bible becomes the word of God. It is life and light, not mere letters. How can anyone be so mistaken as to view the ability to preach Bible doctrines and expound Bible types as being the qualification for a minister of the word? One who preaches in that way gives only the outer shell of the Bible to others. He is not recognized as a minister of the word.

Some suggest that the church needs revelation; we acknowledge the validity of this suggestion; but let us inquire who is going to impart revelation to the church. We cannot place all responsibility upon the brothers and sisters. This poverty of God's ministers is what makes the church poor. The lack of prophets and of vision deprive God's people of light. Since God gives light to the church through His ministers, their task is tremendous.

Never assume that because you speak on the same Bible word as the apostle of old that therefore you are a successor to the apostles. Not so. You are a true successor to the apostles only when you receive the same revelation and anointing as the apostles had. The deciding factor is not in preaching the same doctrine but in receiving the same anointing. What can be more serious in the church than that there is no one to supply the peoply with God's word, revelation, and light? The ministers of the word must be responsible for supplying the church with God's word. A minister is one in whom there is light, revelation, and the anointing of the Holy Spirit. When he arises and speaks on the Bible, God is willing to speak through the Bible. This is how a minister supplies the church with God's word.

The current trouble lies just here: many can preach on the Bible but God does not speak. Knowing the word in the Bible is quite different from obtaining the word of God. You may read the Bible for days without God's speaking. Then one morning the Lord speaks to you. Everything is changed and turns to good. You exclaim, "Ah, for years I have read the Bible with such vagueness that I literally knew nothing—but now I know." Hence the determining factor is whether or not the Lord is speaking.

Some people never have spiritual insight other than the one time when they are saved. Since God has not spoken much to them, they are naturally strangers to spiritual things. Or, a certain person may hear a message as much as ten times in the meetings with absolutely no impression; then one day he hears a brother speak on that same message again and, strangely enough, he cannot bear it. This proves that for ten times he heard only the word of the Bible, whereas this time he heard the word of God. What a contrast! What is God's word? It is God Himself coming forth. God must speak to you, and He must also speak through you. If God is silent, you will have no way to deliver His word. A minister therefore needs to be one who has revelation from God.

All the problems concerning the building up of the church so that the body of Christ may attain to the full stature of Christ and be one in faith are focused on the ministers of the word. God desires to establish His ministers that they may perform the work of the ministry. Does not Ephesians 4 reveal to us that the full growth and unity of the church are realized through the work of the ministry? Today's difficulty is the lack of ministers. It is possible that there is no lack of preaching, yet how little the word of God is released. The fact that God's people currently lack light and revelation is a responsibility which we cannot push onto the shoulders of other brothers and sisters. The failure of the ministers to give out the word is the reason for sinners unsaved and believers not edified. If the ministers are incompetent, how can we expect the church to be competent?

The crux of the matter is in our being closed to God's revelation. Because we are unenlightened we cannot help others towards enlightenment. The difficulty is in us, not in them. How very serious this is. One reason for the prevailing impotency of the church is that our Lord does not find a way through us. The

Lord is now looking for ministers of His word. God's word is not scarce, nor has His light lessened; the difficulty lies in the lack in men. God is unable to manifest Himself through us, and His light is blocked in us.

How absurd that many so-called spokesmen of God do not even expect to speak God's word nor anticipate His revealing Himself while they preach on the Bible. Their whole interest is to display the doctrine they formulate. They are primarily if not entirely interested in their own doctrine, in their own good thoughts. As long as their doctrine or thoughts are released, they feel content. But let us not forget that the word of God is the coming forth of God. If He does not come out, people hear only *your* words. When *He* comes forth, men begin to obtain revelation. Without God, whatever is said merely passes from one person to another, from one mouth to another, and from one brain to another.

Brethren, have you seen the difference between preaching the word of the Bible and letting God reveal Himself to men? Do you see that, though to you many words are most logical, clever and precious, yet God does not speak in them? If and when you realize this, you cannot but fall before God, saying, "Oh Lord, I do not want to do the work which is void of revelation, that which cannot impart revelation to others I hate to do." Do not be a professional preacher. Once you turn professional you speak not because you have something to say from God but because you are obliged to utter something. Unless you live before God you cannot be a minister of the word. God must obtain His ministers in our midst. May we receive mercy from Him that we may get revelation in His word and that we may impart it to others. What else can we look for except for God's mercy? If all we have is a book—even the Bible—it is dead. A minister of the word must minister according to the Bible—yet he needs more; he requires the revelation of the Holy Spirit.

Brethren, may we learn to expect the anointing of the Holy Spirit. We need to pray frequently, "Oh Lord, anoint Your word once again, and give it to me." When we stand up to speak, let us tell the Lord, "Oh Lord, do anoint the word that I am going to speak." Today is the time to ask for mercy. How the ministers have failed to bring God's word to men! The poverty of the ministers causes the poverty of the church. Many are they who set their minds on truth and knowledge; few are they who look for revelation. No wonder men are not saved after they have heard the gospel. The life of God has not been released through the words. The words are empty, possessing no value. We fail in that we allow people to praise us and to praise the doctrine we preach rather than in our striking them to the ground because of the tremendous light and revelation in the word. What is urgently needed today is not to get people to admire God's word, but to have them stricken by God's light. If the ministers of the word fail to produce this result, something is wrong with them. May God be merciful to us all.

8 | God's Word in Christ

One

"In the beginning was the Word, and the Word was with God, and the Word was God. He was in the beginning with God" (John 1.1,2). This definitely indicates that the Son of God is this word; Christ is the word. Hence the ministry of the word is the ministration of God's Son. Serving the church with God's word is ministering the Son of God. If the seven deacons in Acts 6 were those who served tables, the ministers of God's word are those who serve people with God's word. But this word is more than simply a word; it is a Person, even Christ Himself.

Some can only serve with the doctrines of the Bible. They have no way to minister the Lord Jesus because they live in the realm of the letter. Their service ends with truths, doctrines and teachings. It is beyond their ability to minister the Christ behind the doctrine. This is a difficulty to many—they cannot impart Christ to others. Yet the written word of God is Christ. The Bible is more than simply a book in whose pages certain doctrines and teachings can be found. If the Bible is divorced from the Person of Christ it becomes a dead book. In one realm it is just a book, but in another realm it is Christ Himself. He who lives in the first realm, seeing the Bible merely as a book, is not qualified to be a minister of God's word. He can only serve with doctrines, truths and teachings; he is unable to serve with Christ.

Two

Paul's words are clear: "Therefore from now on we (know) no man according to the flesh; even though we have known Christ according to the flesh, yet now we know Him thus no longer" (2 Cor. 5.16). We no longer know Christ after the flesh but know Him after the Holy Spirit. In other words, we know Him not merely as Jesus of Nazareth—the historical Jesus—but more so, we know Him as Christ in the Holy Spirit. We should remember that those who knew Jesus historically may not have known Him as Christ. In His earthly days many Jews professed to have known Him. "Is not this the carpenter's son?" they said. "Is not his mother called Mary, and his brothers, James and Joseph and Simon and Judas? And his sisters, are they not all with us?" (Matt. 13.55,56) They assumed that in knowing these things they knew Him. But we realize they did not truly know Him.

John the Baptist was sent by God. He testified by saying, "After me comes One who is mightier than I, and I am not even fit to stoop down and untie the thong of His sandals. I baptized you with water; but He will baptize you with the Holy Spirit" (Mark 1.7-8). To stoop down and untie sandal thongs was a most menial job. During the days of the Romans it was done by a slave; when the master came to the door, the slave would kneel and untie the thong. John knew that he was far inferior to the One who came after him. But though John was clear about this he did not realize who it was who came after him. He did not know that the Lord Jesus was the One. According to the flesh John was a cousin of the Lord's. They must have known each other from childhood. Yet John had no idea that the Lord Jesus was the One to come. "I did not recognize Him," he confessed; "but He who sent me to baptize in water said to me, 'He upon whom you see the Spirit descending and remaining upon Him, this is the one who baptizes in the Holy Spirit.' And I have seen and have borne witness that this is the Son of God" (John 1.33-34). At the time the Lord Jesus was baptized, the Holy Spirit descended and remained on Him; and by this sign John realized that Jesus, his cousin of thirty years, was the Son of God. Though having lived so near and been so close, John had not known Him. Only after the Holy Spirit opened his eyes did he recognize this Jesus as the One to come. Hence it is possible for men to live with the Lord Jesus for thirty years without really knowing Him. For thirty years John was in constant touch with the Lord Jesus, yet all he knew was his cousin, the historical Jesus, He who was of Nazareth. He never before knew that this Jesus of Nazareth was God.

The Lord Jesus *is* God, but when He traveled incognito on earth men did not recognize Him as such. It takes the unveiling of the Holy Spirit to see Jesus as the Son of God, as Christ. In the same vein, we can say that the Bible is just a book, though perhaps more special than other books in the estimate of men; but when the Spirit of God opens men's eyes they see the Bible as the revelation of God—the Book which reveals God's Son. Since Jesus of Nazareth is the living Son of God, the Scriptures reveal Him as such. If the Bible is but an ordinary book to you, you do not know the Divine Oracle. Whoever does not know the Son of God knows not Jesus; and whoever knows not the Son of God does not know the Bible. Contrariwise, everyone who knows Jesus knows Him as the Son of God; and all who know the Bible also know the Son of God revealed by that Bible.

This book, the Bible, reveals God's Son, the Christ. It is not an ordinary book. While the Lord Jesus was living on earth his contemporaries assumed varying views and criticisms toward Him. Some said He was Jeremiah; others said He was one of the prophets. Some insisted He was this while others maintained He was that. So the Lord Jesus asked His disciples, "But who do *you* say that I am?" Simon Peter replied, "Thou art the Christ, the Son of the living God." What did the Lord Jesus say afterwards? "Blessed are you, Simon Barjonas, because flesh and blood did not reveal this to you, but My Father who is in heaven. And I also say to you that you are Peter, and upon this rock I will build My church" (Matt. 16.15-18). It takes heavenly revelation, not human inspiration, to know the Lord Jesus: without such revelation there can be no church, for the church is built on that foundation. Having seen the historical Jesus as the Christ, the Son of God then becomes the foundation on which the church is built.

Some may regretfully say, "Alas! I was born two thousand years too late. Had it been twenty centuries earlier I would have gone to Jerusalem to see the Lord Jesus with my own eyes. I would have believed in Him, even though the Jews did not believe Him as the Son of God." We must answer in this way: even if you had lived daily with Him, walking with Him and working with Him, you still might not have known Him. You certainly would have known the man Jesus, but you would not have recognized who He was. When the Lord Jesus was on earth men held many ideas concerning Him. They realized He was different from ordinary people, yet they did not understand Him. Here is One who needs to be known, not to be theorized about. But how can anyone know Him? First and foremost, God must enlighten us for us ever to see that Jesus of Nazareth is Christ, the Son of God.

Without the revelation of God not even following the Lord Jesus is of any use. Men may follow Him to Caesarea but they still may know Him not. People may stay with Him day after day, yet fail to really recognize Him. To recognize who He is requires revelation, because He cannot be known through outward familiarity. Revelation, not familiarity, is the way to know Him. You need God's revelation, His speaking to you, His making you see, before you are able to know this Man to be Christ, the Son of God. External acquaintance does not give you a true knowledge of Him.

The same is true of the Bible, for the word of God is not only a person but is also a book. God's word is the Bible as well as Jesus of Nazareth. If our eyes need to be opened by God to see Jesus of Nazareth as God's word, the Son of God, so they must be opened to know the Bible as the word of God, as that which reveals God's Son. Even as one who has had a long acquaintance with the Lord Jesus may not know Him, so he who has been familiar with the Bible through many years of study and research may not necessarily know this book. God's revelation is a must; only what is opened up by God is living.

In the story recorded in Mark 5 of the healing of the woman

who had a flow of blood for twelve years, we find that many thronged about the Lord Jesus but only one touched Him. This woman came up behind Him in the crowd and touched His garment. For, said she, "if I just touch his garments, I shall (be made whole)." This woman had faith, and she had feeling too, because she felt in her body that she was healed of her disease. Our Lord immediately inquired: "Who touched my garments?" And His disciples said to Him, "You see the multitude pressing in on you, and you say, 'Who touched me?'" But our Lord knew and felt the touch. There was no change in the many who thronged around Him. It was solely the one who touched Him who was instantly changed. It is therefore of no use if the Lord stands by you today and you press in about His body. Jesus of Nazareth is not known by pressing around Him. He who touches His garments with conscious faith knows who He is. He is the Son of God as well as Jesus of Nazareth. Alas, many press in on the externalities of Jesus without touching the Son of God within.

By the same token, many throng the Bible but few touch the Son of God. While the Lord Jesus was on earth He could be known in two different realms: in the one sphere men heard Him speak, saw Him walk, yet did not know Him one bit. In the other sphere a simple individual touched His garments and was healed of her disease. Many saw Him, yet only one knew that God was in Jesus of Nazareth. Today we fear lest we only bring to men Jesus of Nazareth according to the flesh; we equally fear to merely present the Bible as a book. Just as crowding Jesus of Nazareth brings no relief, so thronging the Bible produces no effect. Some, though, are enlightened, and thus touch the Son of God in this book. The words which the Lord utters are spirit and life. If you touch this you touch the ministry of the word. The task is not simply presenting a book to men, rather is it presenting the Son of God in the Book. When a minister of the word serves people with God's word, he simultaneously serves with the Son of God. We minister with Christ.

The Lord Jesus drew near to the two disciples on their way to

Emmaus and walked with them. They conversed with one another for quite some time. The Lord also opened to them the Scriptures. As they drew near to the village, they constrained the Lord Jesus to remain, saying, "Stay with us, for it is getting toward evening, and the day is now nearly over" (Luke 24.29). The Lord went in to stay with them, and they invited Him to an evening meal. During this entire lengthy period they failed to recognize that this was the Lord Jesus. When He took the bread and blessed it, however, and broke it and gave it to them, their eyes were at last opened and they recognized Him.

This proves that men may walk and talk with Him and yet not know Him. The Lord whom we desire to know must be known deeper than what we can know of Him when we walk and talk with Him. Only when He opens our eyes are we able to recognize Him. Perhaps you regret that when the Lord was on earth you were not there. Let it be understood, however, that even had you been present you might not have known Him any better. Today the least and the weakest of the saints can know the Lord Jesus as much as Peter knew the Lord while they were together on earth. Remember, the Lord Jesus whom the apostles knew in their spirit is exactly the same whom you know today in your spirit.

The underlying question is this: how can we really know the Lord Jesus? He cannot be recognized outwardly. It takes the revelation of God to open our eyes that we may see Him and therefore really know Him. This is where the responsibility of a minister of the word lies. For one can spend time in searching the Scriptures, memorizing its words, and clarifying its doctrines so that he is capable of answering any question, and yet he may not, even in the smallest measure, know the Son of God. It awaits the day when God opens his eyes for him to see the Son of God. What we stress is that it is God who opens our eyes to see the Son of God in the Bible and in Jesus of Nazareth.

This does not at all imply that the earthly work of the Lord Jesus is unimportant. Everyone who believes that Jesus is the Christ is a child of God. Whoever confesses that Jesus is the Son of God is born of God. We must not only see Jesus as the Christ, the Son of God; we must also see Him in the Bible. None can divorce the Christ the Son of God from Jesus of Nazareth; nor can anyone profess to know Christ the Son of God by casting the Old and New Testaments aside. For it is through the Bible that God enables us to know His Son. Nevertheless, without revelation, even the studying of the Bible will make us understand only the doctrines included, not the Christ within.

The dilemma of Christianity lies in these two entirely contrasting worlds. Were the outside world to be taken away and the inside world alone to be left, things would then be very simple. But here is the outside world of thronging as well as the inside world of touching. Some throng, but some touch. Do you see the difference? Thronging belongs to one sphere, whereas touching belongs to another. Nothing is of any avail in the world of thronging; only in the world of touching are diseases healed and problems solved. In the first sphere there may exist persons with great learning who profess to understand the Bible, its doctrines and teachings; but in the other sphere we meet light, revelation, and the anointing of the Holy Spirit.

Brethren, are you aware of these two worlds? In the first are the scribes of the letter; in the second are the ministers of God's word. What you preach must be what you truly know. You need to be brought by God to a place where you can touch the inside world. In the other world of thronging no one can know the Lord Jesus nor the Bible. Only the world of touch is effective, for only there is the effectual word of God. It is rather interesting to note that the Lord Jesus was not at all conscious of being thronged but He *was* conscious of when He was touched.

Compare two brothers. One is a simple believer. Fully aware of his ignorance and nothingness, he approaches the Bible with fear and trembling; and the presence of the Lord is with him, shedding light upon the pages. The other brother lives in a quite opposite world. He knows Greek and Hebrew as well as English. He reads the Bible many times over and perhaps memorizes numerous passages, yet he does not experience any light from

God. He is not qualified to be a minister of God's word. The most he can do is impart Bible knowledge to others; he is unable to serve the church with Christ. The Bible is living; it is a Person, even the Son of God. If you have not touched this living word, then all you know avails nothing.

Three

While the Lord was on earth He taught frequently and many heard Him. For instance, after He had taught the Jews the lesson of forgiveness He told them this: "You shall know the truth, and the truth shall make you free" (John 8.32). They answered that they were descendants of Abraham and had never been in bondage to anyone. The Lord therefore answered them with: "Truly, truly, I say to you, every one who commits sin is the slave of sin" (v.34). The Jews may or may not have understood these words, but they certainly could not deny that they had heard them. Their ears were not deaf, yet the Lord Jesus said a peculiar thing about them, "He who is of God hears the words of God; for this reason you do not hear them, because you are not of God" (v.47). Thus hearing is more than a matter of hearing the sound. Some hear the word of God as well as the sound, while some hear only the sound but not God's word. These two are poles apart. If you had asked these Jews whether they had heard what the Lord Jesus had just said, they doubtlessly would have answered in the affirmative. Nevertheless, the Lord Jesus commented that they had not heard anything because they were not of God.

How serious is this entire matter. The word of God is not something people hear by just being present. Physical presence does not insure the hearing of the word. The Jews were present and they problably heard every syllable of what the Lord Jesus had said, yet He categorically denied they had heard anything. The hearing He speaks of is of a different sort. We have two kinds of hearing belonging to two different worlds. One may hear the words of this world but fail to hear those of the other world. This constitutes a basic problem.

Many may hear the words of the Bible but do not hear the

word of God. Those to whom the Lord addressed Himself were not fools or idiots or deaf; they were quite ready and able to argue with Him about His words. This they could not have done if they had not heard nor understood. Yet the Lord Jesus insisted that whoever "is of God hears the words of God; the reason you do not hear them is that you are not of God." Many can hear the voice of the one domain but do not hear the voice from the other domain. They understand every word of this realm but completely fail to apprehend that of the other. Why do they neither hear nor understand? Because they are not of God. Something very foundational was wrong with these people, therefore they could not hear. The Lord explained: "Why do you not understand what I am saying? It is because you cannot hear my word" (v.43). Physical ears can hear only physical words, that which belongs to this world. It requires another kind of ear to hear the words of the other realm. Only those who are of God may hear.

Many, in perusing the Bible, can only hear the outer letters of the word of the Lord Jesus, but a minister of the word must hear the inner word of God. We flatly deny that any who merely contact the outside shell of the Bible can be God's ministers of the word. The word of God comes today by adding revelation to revelation. Revelation alone is not enough, for the Bible is itself a revelation to begin with. There needs to be revelation upon the revelation of God.

Let us understand what the word of God means. It means that there is a word behind words, a voice behind voices, and a communication behind the letters. Its peculiar feature lies in the fact that no natural ear can grasp it. Do you think a man hears the word of the Lord Jesus because he is naturally endowed with cleverness and capability? Please realize that that only enables him to contact the outer shell of the word, the physical side of the Bible. The word of God belongs to another world. It is heard by one who is of God. Hence the question narrows down to the person himself. If my physical ears are deaf I cannot hear the Lord's words in the physical sense; but if my spiritual ears are defective I am unable to hear His word in the spiritual sense. Just as I belong to two worlds, so His word spans two worlds—one physical and the other spiritual. The words I hear in the physical domain touch only the physical side of His words. I may have heard and understood, but the Lord insists that I have not heard anything. He does not want me to hear the words only, He wishes that I may hear the other word also. Tens of thousands may have heard the former, but those who hear the latter may only be numbered in terms of eight or ten persons. This is the difficulty in approaching the Bible; men may touch the outside of the Bible without touching the Christ within, in the same way that some thronged around Jesus physically without actually touching the Son of God. Little use is it if we merely touch the Bible as a book.

"We are (of) God; he who knows God listens to us; he who is not (of) God does not listen to us. By this we know the spirit of truth and the spirit of error" (1 John 4.6). The word "listen" in this passage is the same Greek word which is translated "hear" in John 8.47. John candidly declared that he and those with him were sure they were of God, and hence of the truth. Whoever knew God would listen to them, but He who was not of God would not listen. The meaning of the apostle is unmistakable. It was not by hearing the physical voice of a man that one heard. At that time John was quite old. Perhaps people were used to his voice. It was rather surprising for him to say that only those who knew God heard him. This indicates that whether one hears or not does not depend on the physical ears. The word of God belongs to another realm. Not all who are familiar with the Bible know the word of God; neither do all who can preach on the Bible proclaim God's word; nor do all who accept the Bible receive the word of God. One must have a special relationship with the Lord before he is able to hear His word.

In this connection, there are three Scripture verses from John's Gospel which can be read together. "God is spirit, and those who worship him must worship in spirit and truth" (4.24). "That which is born of the Spirit is spirit" (3.6). "The words that I have spoken to you are spirit and life" (6.63). The three instances of "spirit" being mentioned here are very meaningful. God is Spirit, the words of the Lord are spirit, and that which is born of the Spirit is spirit. Because the Lord's words are spirit, it requires a person with spirit to apprehend them, for only those of like nature can understand each other. The outward word is merely a sound, something which one can read or listen to and understand. But the inward word is spirit, that which cannot be heard with the ears nor understood with the mind. The words of the Lord are spirit; they are therefore beyond the reach of one's mind or cleverness to understand or to propagate. Only he who is born of the Spirit may hear them. A man with spirit must learn anew how to listen to the word of God.

Brethren, do you now realize the absolute necessity of having the outward man broken? Unless the outer man is broken, no one can serve as a minister of God's word. This outer man lacks that basic relationship with God. None of one's cleverness, emotion, feeling, thought or understanding is of any avail. (Later we shall see how all these can be useful, though in this basic matter of receiving God's word they are useless.) God's word is spirit; thus His word is effective only when the spirit of man is exercised. Let us recognize this principle: that God is Spirit and therefore He must be worshiped in spirit; similarly God's word is spirit, hence it must be received with spirit.

> The disciples came and said to him, "Why do you speak to them in parables?" And he answered and said to them, "To you it has been granted to know the mysteries of the kingdom of heaven, but to them it has not been granted. For whoever has, to him shall more be given, and he shall have an abundance; but whoever does not have, even what he has shall be taken away from him. Therefore I speak to them in parables; because while seeing they do not see, and while hearing they do not hear, nor do they understand. And in their case

> the prophecy of Isaiah is being fulfilled, which says: 'You will keep on hearing, but will not understand; and you will keep on seeing, but will not perceive. For the heart of this people has become dull, and with their ears they scarcely hear, and they have closed their eyes; lest they should see with their eyes, and hear with their ears, and understand with their heart and turn again, and I should heal them.'"
> (Matt. 13.10-15)

The disciples asked the Lord why He spoke to the multitude in parables. The Lord's answer was: "To you it has been granted to know the mysteries of the kingdom of heaven, but to them it has not been granted." Why was this so? Because something had happened in the preceding chapter; they had blasphemed the Holy Spirit. The Lord had cast out demons in the power of the Holy Spirit, but those among the multitudes insisted that He had cast out demons by Beelzebub. They called the Holy Spirit Beelzebub, which meant "king of flies." Consequently the Lord Jesus turned to the use of parables in Chapter 13. In other words, hereafter they should hear but never understand. They heard of sowing, but they did not know what was sown. They heard of the weeds planted by the enemy, yet they could not figure out what these weeds were. They heard of a net thrown into the sea, but they were at a loss as to what the casting of the net meant. Though they heard of a woman mixing leaven in the measures of meal, they were plainly puzzled as to what the Lord was after. All these things did they hear, yet they understood nothing. After the Jews had blasphemed the Holy Spirit they began to hear many parables.

Today we use parables to make people understand, but the Lord Jesus at the first employed parables to deny to them an understanding. The Lord used parables purposely to allow them to hear the outward words without admitting them into the secrets of the inward meaning. Nowadays many read the Bible in the same way as the Jews at that time had heard the parables. All they know are the sowing, the good soil, the thorns, the rocky ground, the thirty, sixty and hundredfold. They have undoubtedly heard the words, though they apprehend almost nothing. They see the external elements without ever seeing the inward reality.

Four

What is the ministry of the word? It touches what is hidden behind the parables or words and what can only be seen when the person is right before God. If the people's hearts have grown dull they naturally cannot hear. A dull heart brings in closed eyes and heavy ears. Today's difficulty does not stem from a scarcity of God's word; rather does it arise from a lack of understanding among God's children. How people incorrectly take parables and external words as the word of God! Brethren, the man who touches the Bible does not necessarily touch the word of God. It is a fact that to touch God's word one needs to touch the Bible. But touching the Bible alone is not enough. You should ask the Lord, "Oh Lord, let me see Your word behind the words; let me see Your light in the light; and let me receive revelation in Your revelation." If you fail to touch what lies behind, then your words have little to offer to people, for you cannot communicate Christ to them.

The Lord is not to be known by merely understanding the truth of the doctrine of the Bible; He is known when you see the light of His countenance. Because you know the Lord, so you know the Bible as the word of God. This is the only way to supply the church with Christ. After you have seen Christ you can easily find a given aspect of Him in the Bible. Hence it is said, and said truly, that there is no page in the Bible which does not speak of Christ. Yes, when you know Him, everything in the Bible becomes living.

So the issue here is whether or not you have the revelation of Christ. If you have the revelation of Christ, Bible knowledge will strengthen your apprehension of Him. Without that revelation, the Bible and the Lord remain two distinct and separate entities. You may supply the church with the Bible, but you are not able to supply Christ to the church. How do you supply the church with Christ? By presenting something of Him that corresponds to each portion of Scripture which you use. You not only use Bible terms and words, you actually supply Christ to the church. Oh, the futility of just the bare studying and expounding of the Scriptures! Always remember that helping others to know the Bible and helping others to know Christ are two opposite matters.

The ministry of God's word must be exceedingly subjective, something of man's experience. The objective way of expounding the Bible as written cannot be viewed as the ministry of the word. Each and every minister must be a person with revelation, that is, he must see something subjectively. After receiving revelation and seeing something inwardly, he may, basing his word on the Bible, preach Christ to others. To speak according to the Bible and to speak according to Christ are two totally different things. Many currently are preaching on the Bible: some expound it according to its letter while some expound it according to Christ. Those who are able to supply others with the Christ who has been revealed to them are they who have received revelation from God and have found the counterpart in the Scripture.

We acknowledge the usefulness of many expository messages—especially for those who have had little experience—because such messages can deliver us from error and difficulties. But strength of ministry and excellence of service are not to be found in the exposition as such. They are to be seen in the person who, knowing the Lord and selecting the appropriate word in the Bible, supplies the church with Christ.

Accordingly, a basic knowledge of Christ is required of a minister of God's word. Oftentimes you may know something inwardly before the Lord before you know it in the Bible. It takes time for you to find it in the Bible; but when you do, you know the word will be released, because Christ has become the word. It may take a few days or even a year or two before you see it in the Book. You will then say, "Oh, this is what I learned before the Lord on such and such a day." One passage after another begins to come to you—the Christ whom you know in revelation gradually becomes the word. You are sure that the Lord wants you to minister this word and He will providentially arrange the time and opportunity for you to deliver it. And thus the word you preach shall become Christ in others. This is the ministry of the word in us.

The Christ we know in revelation gradually becomes the word in us. We have found Him in the Bible, perhaps in one, two, or nine or ten different passages. We progressively see the reality of Christ in the word, and so we are able to supply Him along with the word. By the mercy of God, those people who receive such a word will find the Holy Spirit working in them to transform the word into Christ in them. This is called the supply of Christ, that is, Christ is supplied through the word of the Bible; and men receive Him when they receive the word. This forms the basis for all ministry of the word.

Brethren, you ought to recognize the disparity which so greatly exists between the inner way and the external way of ministry. Word is important to a minister, but this word must be something which you see before God, something which you meet in Christ. Only then will this Book be quickened into the living word. If all you see is the Book, the best you can do is give some expository preaching—you have no word from God. Though this may help some to understand a little, it is not adequate to bring men to the Lord. You can render help on truth, but you cannot lead others to a living knowledge of the Lord.

We consequently need to know what the word of God is, how to touch it, and how to minister it. We must pay the price of not letting out hearts be dull, our ears heavy, or our eyes closed. We have to really see God so that we may hear and hearken, see and perceive. We must touch both the outside and the inside worlds of the word, for only so do we gradually become useful instruments in God's hand. May God be merciful to us, enabling us to see that just as Jesus of Nazareth is Christ, so the written word of

God is Christ; that just as the Man in the flesh is Christ, so the Bible is likewise Christ. Both the incarnate Son of God and the printed Scriptures are the word of God.

Ministry opens up to those who touch the inside as well as the outside of the word. Though they may receive into themselves the Bible by memory, any who know not Christ are disqualified from being ministers of the word. Hence we must fall before God and look for His revelation. Only in this way shall the words which we speak cause other people similarly to fall before Him. This is not a question of degree but a matter of kind. Many ministers do not possess the right kind of ministry. Should God be gracious to us, we shall begin afresh in ministry. We will touch the Bible through knowing the Lord, and thus be ministers of His word.

9 Knowing God's Word through Christ

One

A minister of the word is one who has the revelation of Christ, one in whom God has been pleased to reveal His Son (see Gal. 1.16). It is more than that he just says this is so, but he inwardly knows that Jesus is the Christ, the Son of the living God. To say so takes only two or three minutes to recite, but the Lord says: "Flesh and blood has not revealed this to you, but my Father who is in the heavens." To know Christ is better than to know words; it is a seeing. As one sees this vision of the Son of God everything but Christ recedes, be it sanctification, righteousness, or life. Out of this entire universe nothing can be compared with Christ; no spiritual thing can vie with Him, for Christ is all and in all.

Outside of Christ there is neither life nor light, sanctification nor righteousness. Once a man is brought by God into this revelation of Christ, he begins to realize there is nothing apart from Christ. Christ is everything: He is the Son of God as well as the word of God; He is love, sanctification, righteousness, salvation, redemption, deliverance, grace, light and work. He fills everything. All which we have seen in the past, however much it may be, fades away before Him. Nothing can stand its ground before this grand revelation. Moses and Elijah disappear, so do Peter, James, and John. The Lord Jesus alone remains. He fills all and is all. Christ is the center as well as the circumference. God's center and periphery are found in Christ.

After a person passes through this basic experience of being brought by God to Christ for a true knowledge of His Son, he begins to know the word of God. Thus shall he be able to supply Christ. Without this revelation of Christ, no one is able to minister Him to others. One cannot minister the Christ one does not know, nor can one serve with only a fragmentary knowledge of Christ. Ministry cannot be based on fragmentary knowledge. From the days of Peter and Paul up to this present hour, all who before God possess the ministry of the word have had a basic vision of the Lord Jesus. To minister Christ one needs to be brought into a face-to-face knowledge of God's Son. He must know the Son of God in the depth of his being, know Him as preeminent over all things, as the All and in all. Then and only then can he supply people with Christ. The Bible thereafter becomes a living book to him.

Have you seen this fact that it is God's revelation which gives us a real understanding of Christ? Searching the Scriptures may convince people that Jesus of Nazareth is the Christ, the Son of God, but it does not guarantee they will have touched Christ. By reading the Bible they may comprehend Him, but they do not necessarily have revelation. Many are crowding Christ along this road; yet few really touch Him. Today we are still in need of God's mercy that we may be enlightened and so receive grace. For God to reveal His Son in us is not the result of research or searching; it is entirely a matter of mercy and revelation. It is an inward seeing, an inner knowing. And thereafter the Bible becomes a new and living book. Many puzzles and discrepancies which you formerly found in the Bible are solved once you have seen Christ. Indeed, the Scriptures become quite clear and refined to you. By knowing Christ inwardly you can commence to understand the Bible. Such basic revelation shows you who the Lord actually is.

Two

What is meant by God revealing His Son in us? We cannot explain it; nobody can, not even Paul. How do we know that some have received this revelation of God while others have not? Some can testify that they have seen, but others cannot so assert. Some are clear, some are blurred in vision. You may often spend time and energy in thinking and seeking, yet nothing happens. Then one day God is merciful to you and you begin to see without any effort. We may have prayed, "May You be my all, may You fill all and be all." We were seeking, though we knew not what we were saying.

But one day God showed mercy to us and revealed His Son in us. Now we can say quite simply and naturally, "Thank God, Christ is all. Today all my past experience and searching are gone. Gone are my love, my faith, my righteousness, my holiness, and even my victory, for Christ has become all to me." Thenceforward we are able to declare that Christ is preeminent and all-inclusive. This is a basic revelation resulting in our learning to understand God's written word. If we learn God's Bible through God's Son we shall understand and appreciate so well that we may exclaim, "Oh, now I begin to know what was hidden from me before!"

Let us be those who learn as little children. How, for example, does a child learn to know an ox? There are two different ways: one is to draw an ox on paper and write the word "ox" beside it; the other is to show the child a real ox. Which of these ways enables the child to really know an ox—the drawing of an ox or the living ox? Since the drawing is only a few inches high, the child may easily misconstrue the ox to be a small cow. But to see a living ox gives the child an entirely different understanding. (It is true, of course, that for the child who has seen an ox and so has an impression of it but knows not its name, the drawing and its caption serve as a help.) Even so, in like manner must we ask God to reveal Christ to us. After we have once met Him we will find the Bible most clear and profitable to us for it unfolds to us many things concerning Christ. If the basis is correct, the rest is all right. With the foundation laid, all else falls into its proper place and can be rightly related.

It is rather difficult to show people things in the Bible. It is like a brother who read a great deal about plants. He found described in one book a certain plant with particular leaves and flowers, and off he went to the hills to find this plant. But his search was without success. Perhaps it is easier to learn words through pictures than to find objects through pictures. The same thing can be said of recognizing people. We would rather see the person first before we see his photo, for it is the simplest way of knowing him. So it is in the lives of all God's children, including Paul and Peter: they all came to know Christ through the mercy of God. The Lord Himself declares that "flesh and blood has not revealed this to you, but my Father who is in heaven." It is through God's mercy and grace that we know Christ by His revealing His Son in us. After that happens we can know the Bible, because the true knowledge of the word comes through Christ.

Three

The salient question therefore is this: Are you merely supplying people with the Bible or are you one who has met Christ and so possesses that basic knowledge of Christ? If you are one who has that basic seeing, you will naturally thank God for making many words of the Bible clear to you. Daily you discover the accuracy of the word as you pore over the Bible. You first know the Lord inwardly, next you know Him in the Bible. Once you have had that subjective knowledge of the Lord, you find all the words of God in the Bible to be correct—fitting in, one with the other. What you considered in the past as difficulties now turns to be profitable; what was unimportant before today becomes significant. Every point falls into perfect place; none can be rejected. Henceforward your days are days of knowing the Bible. You do not see everything all at once, but gradually there is an increasing harmony between what you have been shown and the word of the Bible. We know the things of the Bible through inner light and revelation, not through the Bible itself.

The folly of human thought manifests itself in following the way of the mind, that is, in man considering himself competent to study the Bible. If only he can spend time studying it, he feels he can comprehend it—with or without prayer. This is the wrong way. At the time the Lord Jesus was born many Jews were so thoroughly conversant with the Scriptures that they could reply immediately—without need of further research at home—to Herod's inquiry as to where Christ should be born. They referred to the Old Testament by quoting the prophet, "And you, Bethlehem, Land of Judah, are by no means least among the leaders of Judah; for out of you shall come forth a ruler who will shepherd my people Israel"(Matt.2.6). They could recite Scripture by memory, yet did they know Christ? Their familiarity with the Scriptures did not help them to seek Christ, it instead helped to "kill" Christ by giving assistance to Herod in his attempt to slay God's Anointed. How absurd is such familiarity with the Bible! And how distorted is the use to which such Bible knowledge may be put!

When the Lord Jesus came to the earth He fulfilled the words of the Bible one after another. All who know the Scriptures know for certain, from all these fulfillments of prophecy, that Jesus of Nazareth is the Son of God. But did the Pharisees know Him? They neither recognized Him nor accepted Him. They inscribed Scripture verses on their phylacteries and the fringes of their garments. They possessed Bible knowledge and the ability to explain prophecies, to expound and to teach doctrines, yet they shut out Christ. They touched the Bible without touching Christ. They handled the Old Testament as a book to be read, as something upon which to do research work, yet they rejected the Giver of salvation!

During this same period there was another group of people, including those such as the tax-collector Matthew and the fisherman Peter. Even in the time of the Book of Acts these same people were despised as "uneducated and untrained men" (4.13). Yet they truly knew the Lord, because they had met Christ and because God had revealed His Son in them. God revealed His Son to Peter in the district of Caesarea Philippi, enabling him to know from within that Jesus was the Son of God, God's Anointed. Now according to the Lord's ministry, Jesus is the Christ of God; according to His person, He is the Son of God. So far as His work is concerned, Jesus is God's Christ; but as to His own self, He is God's Son. These two revelations are one, and are the greatest revelation of all; the entire church is built upon them. The uneducated, common people knew God's Son; they all became experts on the Bible. Being a tax-collector, Matthew had little knowledge of the Scriptures. Yet after he knew the Lord, great was his understanding of the Old Testament. This is not learning words through pictures; this is learning pictures through fact. First know the Lord, next find Him in the Book, even as you would immediately recognize who was in a picture if you had previously known the person. Know Christ first, then know His Book.

Man's problem is that he reverses the order of Christ and the Bible. Men insist on knowing the Bible first and knowing the Lord afterwards. Consequently they may know the Bible without knowing Christ. We may not fully appreciate this difference since we are not Jews. Suppose we were Jews born in the land of Judea under the old covenant. As we read the Old Testament according to its letter we would find the whole book a giant puzzle. Even today the Old Testament is still perplexing to many so-called "theologians" and unbelievers. Not so with Peter, Matthew, John and James. They understood the Old Testament clearly because they had met Jesus of Nazareth, divinely revealed to them as the Son of God. As they read their Old Testament they could say that this was that. From the first chapter of Genesis through the fourth chapter of Malachi they continually found Jesus of Nazareth as the Christ, the Son of God. They knew the Bible, not directly from its pages, but through Christ. All who know Christ just naturally know the Bible. Nowadays many nominal Christians cannot make sense out of the Scriptures after even perhaps years of reading; but one day they see Jesus the Savior and immediately the Bible becomes a new book to them.

Knowing the Lord is therefore knowing the Bible, for revelation comes from Christ. He who has the revelation of Christ has revelation on the Bible, while he who professes to know the word through the Book may not have any revelation at all. The experience of many who know the Lord proves to us that studying the Bible alone is inadequate. We need to remember that we must first know Christ before we can know the Bible.

The experience of Paul supports this axiom. Though he was a good and pious Pharisee, thoroughly acquainted with the Scriptures, he nonetheless persecuted those of the Way everywhere. It is possible for man to be so conversant with the sacred writings and still persecute the Lord Jesus. Paul was not suddenly awakened to the fact that Jesus of Nazareth was God's Son only after he had diligently studied the Scriptures. No, he knew the Lord when one day God's light shone on him. He was previously one who hated and persecuted the Lord by searching out men or women who belonged to the Way, bringing them bound to Jerusalem. In those days he may have been looked upon as being the worst enemy of the church. How he must have been in total darkness! Yet, as he was enlightened by God's light, he instantly fell to the ground. He heard a voice saying to him, "Saul, Saul, why do you persecute me?" And he replied, "Who are you, Lord?", followed by "What shall I do, Lord?" His prostration was a genuine one. His entire being fell with his body. The Paul of flesh and blood was weakened, the Paul within was also weakened. What kind of Paul do you find in Acts and in his Epistles after he had received this revelation? He persistently explained the Old Testament by telling us Jesus of Nazareth is the Christ, the Son of God. To him the Old Testament was an open and living book.

The Bible will become a sealed volume if the knowledge of Christ is shut out. Many with good brains and great learning cannot make any sense out of reading the Bible. They shake their heads when told how precious is this Book. *You* are clear but they are puzzled, because they do not know Christ. The person who knows Christ is the one who knows the word of God. This, however, does not preclude the possibility of men finding God through the Bible. Some have indeed found God this way. This is because God has mercifully enlightened them. As they were reading the Scriptures it pleased God to reveal His Son in them that they might be saved. Even so, the way to know the Bible is through knowing Christ. As you read Romans, Galatians, and

Ephesians you will find a man who had great understanding of the Old Testament. How did Paul come to such knowledge? By his knowing Christ inwardly first.

Four

Once Paul had been enlightened to know Christ, he at once began to proclaim in the synagogues that Jesus is Christ. "For several days he was with the disciples who were at Damascus, and immediately he began to proclaim Jesus in the synagogues, saying, 'He is the Son of God.'"But when the Jews refused to believe what he proclaimed, Paul "kept increasing in strength and confounding the Jews who lived at Damascus by proving that this Jesus is the Christ" (Acts 9.19-20,22). Since the Jews believed in the Old Testament, Paul proved to them from its words that Jesus was the Christ. How strange to find a man, who only a few days before had made havoc in Jerusalem of those who called on this Name and had come to Damascus to take them bound before the chief priests, now proving with such strength that Jesus was the Christ by the words of the Old Testament. This indicates to us that the ministry of the word is based on knowing Christ.

Again and again we pledge our respect for the Bible. The foundation of all the words of God is in that Book. But we also stress that the use of the Bible alone does not make anyone a minister of the word. There is no word of God for those who do not read the Bible; but familiarity with the Bible does not automatically constitute a ministry of the word. Knowing Christ is the key to ministry. If you are to proclaim the word of the Lord you need to have a strong and thorough enlightenment which causes you to know that Jesus of Nazareth is the Christ, the Son of God. Such knowledge makes you fall to the ground and turn a hundred and eighty degrees. And so shall the Bible become a new and open book to you.

After Peter had received this basic revelation of Christ, the Lord Jesus told him: "Upon this rock I will build My church" (Matt. 16.18). This rock points not only to Christ but to the revelation of Christ as well. Peter's confession was not the outcome of what flesh and blood had revealed, but was the result of what was revealed by the Father who is in heaven. Through revelation we come to know that the rock is the Christ, the Son of God. The church is built upon this Rock. The foundation of the church is laid on Jesus as Christ, the Son of God. The gates of hades shall not prevail against the church because its foundation is Christ, the Son of God. But how is this Christ recognized? How is this Son of God known? He is known as such through revelation, not through Bible instruction given by flesh and blood. Supposing someone is speaking on the Bible today, that is to say, flesh and blood is teaching the Book; do you therefore know Christ? No. You know Christ when the heavenly Father reveals Him to you apart from the instruction of flesh and blood. As God speaks, you come to know who Jesus of Nazareth is. Thus is the church built upon this revelation of Christ.

Whether or not there is the revelation of Christ is a matter which concerns not only Peter, Paul, John, and Matthew; it also concerns the entire church. If we wish to serve God with His word we must possess this basic revelation. Otherwise, we may teach the Bible but we cannot supply Christ. A minister of the word is to serve people with Christ. This work of imparting the Lord to others requires us to have a revelation of who Jesus is. Without this revelation the church is without foundation.

What happened to Peter, Matthew, John, and Paul in the early days must happen to a minister of the word today. We have some brothers who do not possess much Bible knowledge; nevertheless, they have a special experience, that is, they have been brought by the Lord to such a place as to be prostrate before Him. They know Jesus of Nazareth is God's Christ who surpasses all works; they know Jesus of Nazareth is God's Son who transcends everything. And when they begin to preach from the Bible they are truly ministers of the word, because they know Christ. Do remember that the ministry of the word is based not only on familiarity with the Bible, but also, and more importantly, on the knowledge of Christ. This does not dismiss the preciousness of knowing and expounding the Scriptures. It only emphasizes the fact that there can be no ministry of the word through touching the Bible outwardly without an inward knowledge of Christ, for the ministry of the word is founded upon an inner revelation—not on many fragmentary revelations of different passages in the Bible but on one basic revelation of Christ.

Five

Who is a minister of the word? He is one who translates Christ into the Bible; that is, he tells people of the Christ he knows in the words of the Bible so that in those who receive the Bible the Holy Spirit will translate it back into Christ. This may sound strange, yet this is the fact. The Christ he knows is a living person, and the Bible is also full of this living Christ. He sees the Lord Jesus through the mercy of God, yet he sees Him in the Bible too. When he speaks on the Bible he translates Christ into the Bible.

We know that as far as heaven is from earth, so far is the distance between a word with a translation and one without a translation. Some in their speaking move from the Bible to Christ, since they make the Bible the starting point; others, though, start with Christ and transform the living Christ into the word of the Bible. They put Him in the words of the Book and present this to the people. The Holy Spirit is then responsible for opening up these words and imparting Christ to the hearers. If there is no knowledge of Him the presentation will stop short, with just the words of the Bible being uttered; nothing will happen to the audience since only the Bible is being passed on.

Men need to know Christ. One who possesses a basic knowledge of Christ is able to send Him forth in the words of the Bible; subsequently the Holy Spirit will take up His responsibility. Man speaks and the Holy Spirit works. It is the Holy Spirit who breaks open the word and supplies the people with Christ. This is called the ministry of the word. We must be responsible in sending forth by words the Christ we know and possess, and then the Holy Spirit will be responsible to send out God's word. If we begin with the doctrines and teachings of the Bible the Holy Spirit will not be responsible for the supply of Christ. Speaking on the Scriptures alone does not supply Christ; it takes a knowledge of Him to make the supply. Only at that moment is the word of the Bible living and effectual.

A minister of the word is one who is able to impart the Lord through the words he speaks. As the words are given, the Holy Spirit works to enable men to touch and to know Christ. Only in this way can the church be profited. Do not say that the hearers must bear all the responsibility. We ought to know better: that the primary responsibility is ours. It has become almost habitual for people to hear some teachings or expositions of the Bible. Everything starts with the Book and ends with the Book. They are not shown the revelation of Christ behind this Book. And consequently the church becomes poor and desolate.

To translate the Christ we know into the words of the Bible and to retranslate, by the Holy Spirit, these words back into Christ in people constitute the ministry of the word of God. We need to translate the Personal Word into spoken word, and the Holy Spirit will translate the spoken word back into the Personal Word. A minister of the word is able to make the Personal Word and the spoken word one. When he stands up to speak, people see the Christ of God in his words. With his words the word of God is sent forth. The Bible is sent out and so is Christ, for these two are one.

The poverty of the church today is due to the poverty of the ministers. Let us therefore ask God to be merciful to us, that we may see how fragmentary are our revelations and how very external and superficial is much of our words and our expositions of the Bible. The Christ we know is not full enough; the dealings we receive are not sufficient and thorough. As a result we have little supply of Christ. We may tell people the words of the Bible but we cannot impart Christ Himself to them. But, brethren, if one day you are really under the mercy of God, you will be enlightened to see that "in the beginning was the Word, and the Word was with God, and the Word was God." The Son of God is the Word, and the Word became flesh; Jesus of Nazareth is the Word. The Bible is the word of God; and so is this Man. Being chosen of God to be His minister, you speak on this Book and you are speaking of this Man. As you give the words of this Book to men you give this Man to them, for you are preaching Christ.

True preaching is sending forth Christ. The supply of God's word is the supply of this Man. Unless one has been prostrated before God, saying, "Oh Lord, I am undone," he cannot be a minister of the word. By looking at a person's attitude we can safely judge whether he is a true minister or not. Who can listen to these hard words? It is not preaching about Christ, but preaching Christ. It is not delivering a message but delivering a Man. As people accept our words they accept Christ, because the Holy Spirit imparts Christ to them. This alone makes us ministers of the word.

This is an enormous task, a task which far surpasses human ability. Every servant of God must realize his incompetency. He should prostrate himself before God, knowing how incompetent he is in supplying Christ, even though he may be well able to speak on the doctines or teachings of the Bible. Let us look to God's mercy today. We need to re-evaluate everything. We must see how absolutely useless we are. We are utterly helpless without His mercy. To be a minister of the word is too serious a matter to be taken lightly. It is not an easy task which can be fulfilled just by reading the Bible so many times. A minister of the word must be able to supply Christ and help people to touch Christ by his words.

PART THREE

THE MINISTRY

10 The Foundation of Ministry

Having considered both the minister and the word of the Lord, we now turn our attention more fully to the subject of ministry.

As we have indicated before, in the ministries of both the New and the Old Testaments there is something of human element. There is a danger, though, if man, his ear and tongue not being instructed, were to mix himself in with God's word. Man could easily blend in his thought and feeling with the word of God if he were not a person who had undergone the dealing and cutting work of the Holy Spirit. God's word would then be contaminated and defiled by man. This is in fact a great danger. To obtain a pure minister of the word God has to so work in a person that his outward man is broken. Hence it is necessary for a minister of the word to accept the discipline and control of God; otherwise he will surely destroy God's word by the mingling in of his own undealt flesh.

But beyond this consuming work of the Holy Spirit we have seen that there must also be the constituting work of the Holy Spirit. We do indeed need the Spirit of God to apply the cross to us so as to rid us of all which we should not have, but we in addition need Him to incorporate the life of Christ in us. The Holy Spirit had so incorporated Christ in Paul that he became a very different person from that which he had been before conversion. This is not the changing of the flesh; it is the Holy Spirit constituting Christ in man. In Paul it had reached such a mature stage that when he spoke, the Spirit of God spoke too. Said Paul, "I give instructions, not I, but the Lord" (1 Cor. 7.10). This is ministry, and such a man as this is a minister of God's word. The human element must be so dealt with that when mingled with God's word it will not defile it. God's word remains pure. Not only is it not destroyed, it is even perfected. The Holy Spirit has been able to work to such a depth that when that man stands to speak, people hear the Lord speaking. You feel safe to let him speak, for the constituting work of the Holy Spirit in him is deep and thorough, so thorough in fact that his speaking is God's speaking, his judgment is God's judgment, and his refutation is God's refutation.

In considering the matter of the word of God we saw two important factors. First, that all latter revelations must follow the preceding ones. Since all the ministries of the New Testament words are based upon those of the Old Testament words, today's ministry of the word must be founded on the revelation of both the Old and the New Testaments. The Bible is therefore the basis of the word. God does not speak extraneously or independently; He speaks once again through His word and releases new light from the light already given. Today God does not give light independently. He imparts fresh revelation according to His past revelations.

Second, that it is imperative for those who would be ministers of God's word to have a fundamental encounter with Christ. They need to have this basic revelation before they can use the Bible as the foundation to their ministry. These two factors are not at all contradictory. On the one hand, today's ministry of the word must be based unquestionably upon the past ministries of the word—even as the New Testament is based on the Old Testament; on the other hand, we must also recognize the fact that all who minister the word must first have met the Lord and received the revelation of Christ before they can speak according to the word in the Bible. This latter point cannot be overlooked. For me to speak by my merely taking hold of the word already given in the Bible would be inadequate; I must first possess this fundamental unveiling of Christ before I can minister according to the word in the Bible.

Each Ministry Issues from a Revelation

When we touch the subject of ministry we should understand that there are two kinds of revelation; the basic, which is given once for all, and the detailed, which is given time and again. When you receive the revelation of Christ you obtain the basic revelation, the same which Paul once received. Later on, you discover from the Bible that what you have already seen before the Lord is this basic revelation. In seeing the Lord your total being has fallen down before God. You know that nothing you once possessed can now stand, not even your zealousness in serving God—much as Paul had once done. Let us realize that Saul of Tarsus was felled to the ground. This prostration of his was not that of sin but was that of work, not of coldness but of zeal. He knew the law, he was familiar with the Old Testament, he was more zealous than his contemporary Pharisees. He was so full of zeal that he laid aside everything to persecute the church. He felt that this was serving God, and he served in an absolute way. Setting aside his error for the moment, it must be admitted that his zeal was very real. Yet he instantly fell down when struck by light. He quickly saw that his past had been spent in persecuting the Lord, not in serving Him at all.

Many may be saved and yet still be blind in this matter of service or work, even as Saul was blind. Saul thought he was in the way of serving God, yet when he was enlightened by the Lord he cried out from the depth of his being, "What shall I do, Lord?" Perhaps this is a question which many have never encountered. They have never been moved by the Holy Spirit to address the Lord as Lord. They may only be calling "Lord, Lord," just as those in Matthew 7, but never have called Jesus as Lord according to 1 Corinthians 12. Here in Saul we see one who confessed for the first time Jesus of Nazareth as Lord and who also asked for the first time, "What shall I do, Lord?" He had fallen down—down from his work, his zeal, his righteousness. Upon his experiencing this fundamental seeing, the Bible became a new book—an opened book—to him.

Many people depend on instructions or references in studying the Bible; they do not know the Scriptures through meeting the Lord. But how marvelous: as soon as anyone meets the Lord and receives enlightenment the Bible becomes a new book to him. One brother, speaking out of his experience, once said, "When the Lord puts me under His light, what I get that day is enough for me to speak for a month." First you must have this basic revelation; and out of that, many more revelations will be given to you. When you have received this fundamental revelation you will discover God speaking here and there throughout the Scriptures. Day after day you will receive many fragmentary revelations which you can use in serving people. This is called ministry.

Ministry, therefore, is based upon our getting a word before God. We have met Christ, and we want to serve the church with the Christ we know; and for this we need to have revelation each time we serve. Ministry requires our seeing something before God and in freshness presenting this thing to the church. Revelations, we have said, are of two kinds: the basic and the detailed, the "once for all" and "the time and again." Without possessing the first it is impossible to have the second. Only after you have secured the basic is your spirit usable; only then is your knowledge of the Lord and that of the Bible usable, and only then too are you usable.

Even so, you still cannot simply go out and minister. It is true that this basic revelation makes you a minister, but when you do minister you need detailed revelations added to the foundational one. Ministry is founded on the basic understanding and revelation, but when God sends you out to speak today you must learn how to receive the particular revelation for that day before God. Not because I have once received revelation am I therefore able to speak. Each time I minister I need to receive special revelation for the occasion. Each revelation brings in service, each revelation gives a special supply, each revelation constitutes a ministry.

The basic revelation once given will not supply enough for a lifetime; it only serves as the basis for a fuller and continuous revelation before God. The first revelation brings in many more revelations. Without the first there can be no additional; but with the first, many more will be given. Not because a person has once received the basic revelation can he thereafter minister with that revelation for years or for a lifetime. If we need to depend momentarily on the Lord for our life, we in like measure need to do so for our work. Each revelation we receive gives birth to each new ministry. It requires many revelations for many times of ministry. Let us keep in mind that each revelation is only sufficient for one occasion of ministry, not for two. Nevertheless, all these detailed revelations are based on the fundamental one.

These foundational problems must be solved before there is the possibility of our being ministers of God's word. Revelation after revelation must continously be added; no one revelation can supply unlimited ministry. Each revelation affords ministry for one occasion; each gives one service. It never means having several sermons prepared in advance which we can use whenever an occasion arises. It cannot be that I have one sermon memorized on which I can speak at any time. We should understand that we speak *God's* word, not ours. You may have memorized a speech by heart, yet if you are going to minister God's word you need to have Him speak to you first. Continuous revelation begets continual ministry.

Spiritual Things Are Nurtured through Revelation

After you have received this basic revelation for the first time, you discover that the Bible is living. For example, you come to see that Christ is your holiness. You are especially clear that Christ *is* your sanctification, not that Christ sanctifies you nor imparts sanctification to you, but that Christ *is* your sanctification. The man who sees this is a man whose eyes have been opened by the Lord. He sees that his holiness is not a behavior but a Person, even Christ Himself. The same is true of righteousness. It is not the sum total of fifty good acts, it is rather Christ my righteousness. God has made Christ my righteousness; my righteousness is a Person.

Maybe two months later you go out to minister. You begin to tell the brothers and sisters that Christ is our sanctification, that sanctification as a thing and sanctification as a Person are two different matters. To do this, of course, you cannot merely depend on the revelation you obtained two months ago. You need to approach the Lord once more, saying, "What should I speak, Lord?" After you are shown that you are to speak on this topic, you then have the ministry of the word. Each time God wants you to speak this word He will rekindle the revelation formerly given so that you may see it once again in such freshness that it is as if you had never seen it before.

What is meant by revelation? It means we see something in Christ. The Bible is full of Christ, and revelation shows us what is in Him. Christ our sanctification is a fact already recorded in the Bible, but when we see it for the first time we feel the newness of it. Whatever is seen in revelation is the newest thing in the world, and it is full of life and power. Revelation is new, and it renews old things too.

We wish brothers and sisters to take note of this fact: that revelation not only makes the letter living, the old renewed, and the objective "subjective"; it likewise turns the subjective into a new thing. The original revelation transforms all the objective truth in Christ into subjective experience in one's life. Before that revelation, everything in Christ was objective; but the moment one receives that basic revelation, all these objective things turn subjective in him. Nonetheless, when one comes to minister Christ, he needs to have God renew that particular thing to him.

Let us remember that all spiritual things must be nurtured by revelation. God desires to have all things concerning Christ maintained livingly and nurtured through revelation. Only God's revelation can ever make an old thing new in us. Whatever is in Christ must always be kept in revelation; the absence of revelation will deaden everything. You may assume that since you have seen it before, surely you can speak on it today. But the result will be that you are unable to give people anything. The same thing can be applied to preaching of the gospel. You well recall how the Lord is your Savior and how your sins were forgiven. And in preaching the gospel you sometimes do touch this reality; but at other times the longer you speak the less you sense it, like a paste which has lost its adhesiveness. The one is in revelation while the other is not. Only what is in revelation is fresh, living, and powerful. Remember, death comes to all spiritual matters if separated from revelation.

Consequently, when we go before people to minister the word we cannot depend on our memory, we cannot draw on the experience and word which we once had. It may have been good during that first time, but not for now. For if you speak in such a way as this, you will sense that something is wrong. You have not touched the thing; it is at a distance.

The wonder of revelation lies here: that it is not teaching. Many people make a fundamental mistake. They think they can always teach. But let us realize that mere doctrine or teaching is useless. Never think because you are able to preach, that that is good enough. You may preach the truth and others may tell you how much they enjoy your preaching, but you should be your own judge, because inwardly you will sense that something is amiss. Many people are often vaguely, dimly helped; hence do not be elated if people tell you they have been helped by you. They may say so, yet it may not really be that they have gotten something. You yourself, though, will know whether the word has been near or far, old or new, dead or living. If you have received revelation from the Lord then you shall surely touch the thing when you speak. You will have touched the living reality. You will know it was living, and that solves every problem. So do remember that each time you minister, you need to have a new revelation.

In 1 Corinthians 14 the question of the prophets is raised. All the prophets can prophesy, but "if a revelation is made to another who is seated, let the first keep silent" (v.30). Here are some prophets, and one of them is speaking to the brethren. While he is speaking, one sitting by receives a revelation. He asks the brother speaking to let him speak, and so the first becomes silent. He who receives a revelation is the freshest, the most powerful, having greater fullness of life; hence he is to be allowed to speak. Though all are prophets, yet whoever is given a new revelation is the most living. Therefore ministry is based upon getting revelation time and again. The lack of it deprives a person of good ministry.

Let us never entertain the thought that because I spoke once on a given message with the anointing of the Lord I can speak again with the same anointing. Never take for granted that many will repent this time just because many were saved last time when that message was given. The same message with the same delivery may not produce the same result; only the same anointing will. It takes the same revelation to emit the same light; sameness of word does not necessarily produce the same light. How easy for a spiritual thing to become dead in us, as lifeless as stagnant water. Because I am still able to deliver the same message as three years ago does not mean that I still have the same light I once had. I need once more to receive the same revelation as three years ago if I am to speak that same message. The ministry of the word depends not on whether I have spoken the message before but on whether I have received new revelation.

The greatest trouble in the church today is the false assumption that with several messages in hand one can repeat them with the same result. We strongly attest to the impossibility of this. It is a fundamental error to stress messages instead of revelation. Even if one should use Paul's or John's message he would not secure the same result unless he had received the same revelation. Hence the ministry of God's word is not a matter of word but a matter of revelation. We serve on the basis of revelation, not on the basis of the word alone. The ministry God acknowledges is a ministry which comes out of revelation. We should distinguish between doctrine and revelation. What God spoke yesterday is doctrine, what He spoke the day before yesterday is also doctrine, but what He speaks today is revelation. That which we remember is doctrine, whereas that which we see and experience is revelation.

We know the prophets do not deal with the past but only with the present and the future. Prophetic ministry reveals the mind of God for today and for the future. Hence the Bible calls those men prophets or seers. A prophet is one who sees first. He is a seeing one. In the Old Testament there are many prophecies, yet what many prophets said actually did not foretell the future but foretold God's current mind towards the people. Take the case of Nathan. Nathan the prophet of God spoke to David following the incidents surrounding Bathsheba and Uriah the Hittite. Aside from a little prophetic message foretelling something about David's wife and child, Nathan's main burden was to declare God's current thought concerning the matter in hand. The highest ministry of God's word in the Old Testament time is to prophesy. Let us keep well in mind that if anyone admires this which is the highest ministry of God's word, he will need to see what God is after for today as well as for the future. He must possess God's current revelation; he cannot linger in the old word. Many are in possession of things seen several years ago, or seen several days ago. They lack today's revelation, and accordingly they are unable to be ministers of the word.

The Two Different Realms

We ought to recognize two different realms: one is that of doctrine (which we can learn in school through textbooks and instructors), and the other is that of revelation. The first can be attained with a little effort, a little cleverness, and a little eloquence; the second, however, is beyond human ability. We must see that in the ministry of God's word men are absolutely helpless if God withholds His revelation. If God does not speak, nothing can be forced out. If God does not give revelation, nothing can be done. With revelation there is ministry; without it there is no ministry. Each time we minister we have God's present revelation as our foundation. In this realm we have to be rightly related to God, we have to be before the Lord; otherwise we cannot stand before men. But in the other realm, that of doctrine, men are able to do something. Memory, cleverness and eloquence will all help. Yet in the realm of revelation you cannot minister if God does not speak. This is known by all those who have learned before the Lord. They can easily discern in what realm one is speaking. The ignorant person mistakes eloquence and cleverness as the criteria. He thinks preaching is strictly a matter of eloquence. However, the Bible shows us that prophecy is a matter of whether or not there is revelation; it is not a matter of eloquence. Preaching without revelation can only edify people's mind and thought; it does not produce revelation.

The difficulty can be explained quite simply: without the basic revelation there can be no further revelations. He who has not received the first unfolding is unable to obtain many other unfoldings afterwards. He may deliver many good messages but he cannot give people revelation. Since fruits are produced according to their respective realms, then after people have heard such a speaker their life and their flesh continue to remain undisciplined by his word. The word spoken in one realm can only produce the fruit of that realm, never that of the other realm. Within that one sphere the whole thing is merely doctrine and interpretation. It can produce nothing but what belongs to its sphere. Not so in the other sphere. If you continue to have revelation before God after you once have received it your speaking will impart revelation to others. Only revelation begets revelation and only light begets light. Only the word of God provides opportunity for the Holy Spirit to work in man's life. Knowledge produces knowledge, and doctrine, doctrine; revelation alone can beget revelation.

It is not enough just to deliver doctrine to people; nor is it sufficient to pass on the revelation of bygone days, for what is doctrine but the revelation of the past? The word in the Bible was once living, but it will not be living in each person today unless the Holy Spirit speaks again. Many who read the Bible today touch merely the letter of the Bible, not the living word of God. We need to have the Holy Spirit speak anew. Only the person to whom God is speaking can really hear. A hundred people may be listening to the message, but perhaps only two are helped. Maybe God is speaking to the two but the ninety-eight do not hear. If the Holy Spirit is silent, the word in the Bible becomes doctrine. Let us not forget that all past revelations are but doctrines. Even though God spoke to you and revealed something to you in the past, nevertheless that word and that revelation are merely doctrine today if the Holy Spirit does not anoint them. It can only produce the fruit of doctrine, not the fruit of revelation.

The challenge confronting us today is that while doctrines are handed on from generation to generation, there is no revelation. For instance, a believing father cannot beget a believing son. Through the working of the Holy Spirit the first generation may be born again; in like manner so may the second be saved; the third generation and the fourth generation, however, may not believe; yet the fifth generation may be born anew by the Holy Spirit. Each regeneration requires the work of the Holy Spirit. This is not so with natural birth. Generation upon generation of men are born without any work of the Holy Spirit. These are two different ways. One way is the preaching of doctrines, and these can be passed on for several hundreds or even thousands of years without any difficulty. Doctrine produces doctrine. The preaching of it will communicate it to the succeeding generation. It is like natural birth, not requiring the work of the Holy Spirit. Not so with revelation and the ministry of God's word. Each time the word of God is ministered it requires the anointing of the Holy Spirit. Each time a soul is born anew it needs the fresh working of the Holy Spirit. Each occasion of ministry of the word demands the revelation of the Holy Spirit. Whenever the Spirit ceases to reveal, the word turns into mere doctrine. When the anointing fails, there is no more seeing and hence no ministry.

Therefore let us pray to the Lord: "Oh Lord, I am here, utterly helpless. Lord, as far as Your word goes, if I do not fall down before You, if I only press close the way most others do, but do not touch You, then I can do nothing." Many today fail to realize how helpless they are in God's word. Many are like professional preachers. They can speak on anything: doctrine, teaching, truth, the Bible. It is just too easy, really too easy!

The ministry of God's word is something beyond our power.

Unless the Holy Spirit works, none can be regenerated. You may be able to communicate doctrine to others, but you need the revelation of the Holy Spirit in order to be a true minister of the word. In this realm, it never comes down to whether I am willing to speak or not; the entire matter is in the Lord's hand. It is not as simple as we think. God is truly looking for ministers of His word. He wants men to be his mouthpieces. Let us seek His face and confess to Him, "I am completely helpless, Lord, for I cannot speak." Man's flesh is useless here. Only the foolish can be proud, for they do not see the helplessness of men in spiritual things. They do not realize that neither human hands nor human eloquence or talent can touch this ministry. It belongs to a different sphere, and men are entirely excluded.

Beloved, God will bring us to the place where we realize the absolute uselessness of man. We have no way to beget a born-again child. Parents are able to beget a child in the flesh, but they cannot produce a regenerated one. According to the same principle, you may pass doctrines on to people, you may hand the interpretations of the Bible down to the next generation, but you cannot choose by yourself to be a minister of God's word. To be a minister of His word needs the speaking of God. If God does not speak, it is ineffectual merely to explain the Bible. Only after God has spoken to us are we able to communicate it to others. Oh! it is beyond us. Many can tell stories, many can preach doctrines; but who is able to speak the word of God? If God is merciful, we can speak. If He is not, we cannot. This then is completely beyond our power; we are helpless before it.

Is it not true that God desires to do a work, that He looks for ministers of His word? God has chosen you to be His minister, and yet you are completely incompetent. It is God who is merciful to you and gives you revelation so as to enable you to preach the word. You must have that basic revelation, and then your spirit must be so disciplined and controlled by the Lord that it is always open to Him for further revelation. May the Lord so work in our lives that we bow before Him saying, "You do it Yourself, Lord. For without Your mercy I am helpless."

We have seen how ministry is based on the revelation of the word, which in turn is based on the revelation of Christ. Let us remember that in spiritual matters such as the word of God and its ministry, there can be no reserve. None can boast that he has so much that he can hand out endlessly. Each time we must come to God with an empty feeling so that we may be filled and poured out. Any who are self-content are unable to be ministers of God's word. On each occasion after the word is given, you once again feel empty like a newborn child. You know nothing before God–so you wait for another filling, for more word and more revelation that you may pour it out again to others. When you return after serving, you are once more completely empty. You need to be poured out in this way time and time again. In being emptied is your ministry. In this spiritual realm God alone can work; men are helpless. Never be so careless as to speak the word of God casually. For this belongs to another sphere. Except the Holy Spirit does this peculiar work once again, we are undone. May the Lord be merciful to us that we may learn before Him how utterly useless we are. May we not be fools. Pride makes us fools, and our failure to see the basis of spiritual things also makes us foolish.

11 | Revelation and Thought

The starting point of the ministry of the word is revelation. When revelation comes to us, it is God enlightening us; we seem to receive a little light by which we are able to see something. Nevertheless this light appears to be fleeting. If we claim to have seen something it may be that we have not actually seen anything; but should we say we have not seen anything we seem to have distinctly seen something. We see it one moment and then we do not.

This is how it is with enlightenment. When we are first enlightened we seem to be very clear inwardly, and yet we cannot express what we have seen. We understand it so perfectly within us, but no matter how hard we try, we are unable to explain it. Inwardly we are most clear; outwardly we are still dull. We act as though we are two persons—as lucid as can be, yet as confused as before. Then after a while we forget everything except that God once shone upon us. Perhaps a little later God again enlightens us. Light comes for the second time and we seem to see something once more. What we see may be exactly the same as before, or it may be a little different, or it may even be completely different. But because we have had the first experience, we try the second time to hold the light so that it will not escape us again.

The Nature of Light

Light has the peculiar nature of easily fading away. Light seems to move very swiftly. It comes quickly to us, stays but a short while, and moves just as rapidly away. It seems reluctant to stay. All who minister the word share the hopeful thought of how good it would be if only the light were to stay longer so as to enable us to see more distinctly: that until we have a full grasp of the thing, may the light remain. But the strangest thing is, there is no way to hold the light.

This is the experience of many of God's servants. Countless matters can easily be remembered, but light is hard to recall. What we have seen may not be what we remember. We sense the greatness and the severity of God's light, yet it quickly passes away. How can we recall it? The greater the light, the less the memory. Many brethren confess that it is extremely difficult to remember the things they have read of spiritual revelation. So we do acknowledge the difficulty in remembering light. Light is for eyes to see, not for memory to fix upon. The more light we see, the less we are able to recall. Memory cannot hold the light, because the nature of light is for revelation, not for memory.

Let us observe the nature of this light. When light first shines upon you it seems as though it will swiftly fade away—and so it does. It requires many times of enlightenment to form a revelation. Perhaps all that remains of the first light which has passed is the mere fact that you have seen something. You may not even remember what you have seen. Aside from the fact that you have seen, your memory holds no other content. The second instance the light comes, however, you may remember some of the content; yet the light moves so swiftly that it is very difficult to anchor it down. But on the third occasion the light may linger longer and you may be able to see more distinctly; nevertheless you still have the same trouble holding on to it. Whenever you receive enlightenment the feeling is present that light quickly disappears; it easily fades and rapidly becomes something of the past. You know you have seen something, yet you cannot tell how you have seen it or what you have seen. Sometimes the light comes directly to your spirit; it is independent of any other channel. At other times it comes by way of the Scripture; that is, when you are reading the Bible light enters into your spirit. According to our experience enlightenment usually is given directly to the spirit, although there are occasions when it comes through the reading of the Bible. Whether light comes directly or indirectly, its characteristic remains the same: it easily fades away, making it difficult to retain.

Light Translated into Thought

We will now see the second point, which is, how to translate light into thought. When revelation comes, it is God who enlightens you. This is the starting point of the ministry of the word. God has shone in your heart; He has enlightened you. But this light has come and gone so swiftly that you cannot remember nor hold it fast. How can one utilize this swift-passing light in the ministry of the word? It is utterly impossible to do so. Hence something needs to be added to light.

This added element is thought. If anyone has been dealt with by God so that his outward man is being broken, that person will actually have very rich thoughts. Only the man with rich thoughts can translate light into thought. Only such individuals can understand the meaning of the light. It is similar to the idea expressed by some brethren who say, "Because I know Greek I am able to grasp the meaning more precisely and translate it more accurately for my understanding." In like manner, the light is the word of God, for it represents God's mind. If our thought life is poor we will not be able to know the meaning nor understand the content when light is given. But if our thought life is rich and strong enough, then we will be able to interpret the light we see and translate it into something which we understand. After we have translated light into something we can understand, we will be able to remember what we have seen, since we can only remember thoughts—we cannot do so with light. To put it another way, the light which is remembered is that which has been translated into thought. Before it is translated into thought we have no way to know it or to call it back to mind. After being translated, however, we are well able to recall the light.

How important is the thought life—the mind—in the ministry

of the word. How very essential is our understanding! As we learn to be a minister of the word we will see the significance of "understanding" as mentioned in 1 Corinthians 14. That chapter draws our attention especially to this matter of prophesying. Why pay such special attention to it? Because prophesying involves understanding. Why is not speaking in tongues emphasized in this chapter? For the simple reason that it does not involve understanding. Verse 14 points this out: "If I pray with a tongue, my spirit prays, but my understanding is unfruitful." Continuing on, verse 15 says, "What is it then? I will pray with the spirit, but I will pray also with the understanding; I will sing with the spirit, but I will sing also with the understanding." And verse 19: "In the assembly I desire to speak five words with my understanding, that I may instruct others also, rather than ten thousand words in a tongue." (Darby) Accordingly, in the ministry of God's word man's understanding plays a major role. God desires that light may reach the understanding of him who is a minister of the word.

Light first shines into the spirit, but God does not purpose to have the light remain there. He wishes this light to reach the understanding. After light has reached the understanding, it no longer passes away but can be fixed. Revelation is not permanent in nature; it is like lightning which flashes and passes away. But when light shines and man's understanding takes it in and knows its meaning, then the light is *fixed* and we know its content. When the light is only in the spirit it comes and goes freely, but once it enters our thought and understanding it becomes anchored. From then on we are able to use the light.

Let us realize that when the light is only related to our spirit we cannot use it, because it has not reached that place where we can use it. To God, man is a "living soul" (Gen. 2.7). Unless something reaches our soul we cannot use it, that is to say, it is not controlled by our will. We are *not* spirits. We have spirit, soul, and body. When the light of revelation is in our spirit we cannot yet claim it as our own. The light of revelation ought not to stay put in our spirit, it should reach our outward man. Yet it should be clearly recognized, too, that the outward man is unable to receive revelation; only the spirit can. Even so, revelation must not remain in the spirit; it has to reach the understanding of man.

This work of translating light into thought varies with different individuals. Whether one's thoughts before the Lord are rich or not makes a big difference. If one's thoughts lag behind God's light, then the light will suffer loss. If the vessel is unfit or insufficient, then again loss will be incurred. When God's light comes upon a person, if his thoughts are not scattered or otherwise occupied, he will be able to fix the light. A scattered mind cannot fix God's light, neither can a preoccupied mind do so. You may be conscious of the light, yet you are unable to translate it into your thought because your mind is burdened with other matters. Or perhaps your mind is neither scattered nor preoccupied, but is dull. If so, then when light shines in you, you are unable to discern what it is saying. A basic requisite for all ministers of God's word is that their mind must be renewed.

The difficulty with some lies in the fact that their thoughts are too many and too confused. They are not able to translate God's light nor understand its meaning. With others the problem may be that their thoughts are too low and mean, for they are always minding things of low degree. How, then, can they fix God's light or apprehend its meaning?

God is light, for light is His nature. God's light is as great, rich, and superior as God Himself. If our thought is small, poor, low, or confused, we will unquestionably miss much of God's light when it comes to us. God never intends to give us small revelations. If He grants revelation, His revelation is big; its scope and content is rich. How can anything inglorious come forth from the God of glory? The normal portion God gives man is a cup running over. God is forever rich, great, and all-inclusive.

The problem today is the incompetency of man's thought to contain the light which comes from God. The thought of man is small and low, wholly inadequate to hold the great light of God. Beloved, how dare we expect to fix God's light with a mind which is scattered and confused from dawn to dusk?

Even were God willing to give you light, your mean and low thought would be completely unable to translate, understand, and hold God's light.

Let us remember that before there can be ministry of the word there must first be revelation from God. But since God wants to use man as His minister, there is also the human element which must be considered. The light of revelation enters into man's spirit and afterwards is translated into human thought. Should our spirit be defective we will be incapacitated from receiving revelation or light. If our mind is incompetent the light will not be able to reach the outward man nor be translated into thought. The light has shone in our spirit, but it demands a sound and rich mind to interpret it in our understanding and later translate it into words. If our mind is pressed with care all day long or oppressed with the problem of food or family, then where will we secure the extra strength to think of spiritual things?

Man's mental strength acts like his physical strength. If his arm can only lift fifty pounds of weight, then he cannot handle anything heavier, not even one additional pound. So is our mental strength limited. If we exhaust its energy on other things we will have nothing left with which to spend on the things of God; and hence we will not be able to translate God's light into thought.

Some brethren set their minds on eating and drinking, on their families, or on worldly pursuits; they have very little thought left for God. Their minds are filled with these earthly matters and are oppressed by them all the time. It is not that their spirit is unable to receive light; for even if they do receive light, what is received will be wasted because they do not have a steady mind with which to anchor the light. Enlightenment must be coupled with a mind free to receive it. It takes a strong and rich mind to fix the light. When one's mind is occupied with other problems he seems to be wandering in a labyrinth, unable to extricate himself so as to discern the light. You know the light has shone into your spirit, but there it has been blocked.

God's light follows a certain way even as God's word follows its certain way. If God's word is going to become a ministration through us, then it must pass through certain prescribed stages in us. If we desire to serve God with the word, we must allow the word of God to go through these required stages. Any defect in the mind can block the light in the spirit from being translated into words.

It is rather strange that when light shines in our spirit we usually do not apprehend its meaning. It fades away before we are able to understand it. Our mind often proves inadequate in deciphering the meaning of the light. We have seen something, yet we do not know what we have seen. There is therefore the need in this case for a second or third enlightenment before we can fix the light. Yet if our thoughts are rich, we can easily hold the light when it first shines. If our mind has no other burden or is unoccupied with other affairs, we shall be able to perceive distinctly what is in the light.

All experienced ones will agree with us in this: that when our mind tries to translate light, it would appear the light is always fleeing; hence our thought must clear our mind swiftly or else the light will escape us. The quicker our thought, the easier the translation. Should the light escape, it may be that in God's mercy the light will come to us the second time. But if not, we have missed something precious, and all because of the inadequacy of our mind. Often we feel our thought is not keen enough. And oh! how frequently after we behold a light we try so hurriedly to translate it into words as though we were snatching something out of the fire. We may, indeed, be able to fix some of it, but the best escapes us. Light never stays put long enough to allow us to think slowly and to digest it gradually. Swiftly it comes and swiftly it goes.

Brethren, you will realize how inadequate your mind is when you find you cannot hold the light. Before you attempt to link your thought with God's light, you may consider yourself to be quite clever, you may even boast of your keenness. Nonetheless, you shall discover your mental weakness when you are unable to translate God's light into meaningful words. The feeling will be the same as an interpreter who finds himself at a loss for words to translate a message into knowable language. In the case of interpretation, the speaker can wait for the interpreter. Light, though, never waits for you. If you cannot follow, it just fades away. We know not why it should so act, but we are fully aware of the fact. Whatever of the light becomes fixed, stays; the rest disappears. If the light should return again, we may have another chance to anchor it down. Thank God for that. But should it never return, we suffer loss and the church suffers with us. The church will lose a precious ministry of the word.

Who, then, makes the choice of a minister? It is God. Nevertheless, if our thought lags behind the light we shall lose an opportunity to minister. Hence let us realize the importance of our mind in respect to God's word. How foolish for some to think it requires no amount of thought to be a minister of God's word. I Corinthians 14 plainly indicates the need for understanding in those who minister. No one can be a good minister of the word if he has neither understanding nor thought.

The Breaking of the Outward Man

Perhaps some will raise the question as to how we should regard the Scriptural teaching that in spiritual things man's wisdom should not be employed. This question points to the need for the outward man to be broken. If our thoughts, like a servant standing at a door, are waiting for enlightenment so as to understand the meaning of what is revealed in the spirit, then they become the best of servants; without them, there can be no ministry of the word. But if our thoughts, instead of trying to understand the light, tend to advocate their own ideas, then they turn into the worst master.

There is a great difference between thoughts as a servant and thoughts as a master. When thoughts assume the role of a master, they try in themselves to conceive God's light, create God's thought, and manufacture God's word. This is what we call man's wisdom. For a man to think independently is human wisdom, but it is condemned by God. Such independent thought needs to be broken. Our thoughts ought to wait at the door as a servant waiting and ready to be used by God. Do not think to conceive light; it is God who shines in our spirits. Instead, our thoughts should be prepared to fix the light, to understand and to translate it.

We may say that in the ministry of God's word thought is an indispensable servant. What a difference there is between conceiving light and fixing light. Anyone who has truly learned before the Lord knows immediately whether the thoughts of the person speaking are master or servant. Whenever man's thought wedges itself into the things of God and usurps the place of a master it becomes a distraction to God. Therefore, the outward man needs to be broken. When one's thought has been broken, it is no longer confused and independent.

Simply realize that the power of thinking is increased instead of destroyed once the outward man is broken. To have the thought broken means to have that thought which initiates and centers upon itself broken. Afterwards it will be more usable than before. For example, one whose mind is taken over by one thing and is made to think on that one thing day and night will soon become obsessed. In such a mental condition, how can he ever understand the Bible? Yet from God's viewpoint, our thoughts too are more or less like an obsessed person's, because they always revolve around ourselves. There is no strength left to think of the things of God. Brethren, do you see the seriousness of this matter?

One important requirement for the ministry of the word is that a minister have a fine mind and an unfettered understanding for God to use. By the outward man being broken we do not mean to say that our mind is so destroyed that we can no longer think. It only means that we will no longer think in and of ourselves nor will we be occupied with external matters. After the wisdom of the wise is destroyed and the understanding of the prudent is brought to nothing, then our mind becomes a usable instrument, for it ceases to be our life and master.

Some take great delight in thinking. They aspire to be one of the wise. Their thought becomes their very life, and they thrive on their own ideas. You would be demanding their life if you were to forbid them to think. Their mind revolves incessantly from sunrise to sunset. Because of their continued thinking, the Spirit of God cannot enlighten their spirit. Even if He should, we wonder if their mind could accept the light. Let us know that it requires objectivity to see. He who is subjective cannot see.

Here is a man whose life is in his own thought. How can he ever perceive God's light? It is impossible, because he is too subjective. For a mind to be a useful organ it needs to be dealt with by God, it needs to be smitten—this is the breaking of the outward man. If your thoughts are central to you and if you are always thinking of yourself, then your mind is totally unusable when God's light shines on your spirit. You do not know what God intends to say, nor can you understand what He says. The road to ministry is blocked. It fails to produce the ministry of the word because the word is blocked by thought. The word must pass through you; you must be God's channel. God employs living persons as His channels. Water flows, but if one of the channels is blocked, it stops flowing. Many possible ministries of the word are cut off by this failure in thought.

Brethren, do not think the wasting of thought is something inconsequential. How many waste their thoughts! They think on unimportant matters from morning till night. Such waste in thought blocks God's way. We thus do not mean to suggest that thought is useless. On the contrary, revelation needs to be completed with man's thought. Whatever is given by God is useful. Our mind is created by God, hence its thought cannot be reckoned as useless. It is only when thought becomes one's center of life, issuing forth in many ideas, that it becomes unprofitable. It ought to be God's servant. It serves with profit if it remains a servant, but it becomes God's enemy if it attempts to be master. It can be a formidable foe to God.

"Taking every thought captive to the obedience of Christ," says 2 Corinthians 10.5. God does not intend to smash our thought; He only desires to lead it captive to the obedience of Christ. The whole problem rests with whether man's thought is under control or not. Should you take pride in your wisdom, considering yourself able, God will have to break it down completely. Do not misunderstand the meaning of "breaking." Such action does not destroy the organ, nor does it eliminate the function; it merely breaks down the life, that false center. As an organ and a function the mind will be used by God. There is a vast difference between the soul as life and the soul as a human entity. God forbids our thought to be the life which controls, but He employs it as His servant. The soul as man's life must be broken, but the soul as a servant of the spirit is very much needed.

"For the law of the Spirit of life in Christ Jesus has set you free from the law of sin and of death" (Rom. 8.2). How are we set free? By the law of the Spirit of life. How do we acquire this law? By walking according to the Spirit. If you walk according to the Spirit the law of the Spirit will be manifested in you; but if you walk after the flesh instead, the law of sin and death will be manifested. Whoever walks after the Spirit overcomes the law of sin and death.

Yet who is he that follows the Spirit? The one who sets his mind on the things of the Spirit. He who minds the Spirit is he who walks according to the Spirit; he who walks according to the Spirit of life is he who overcomes the law of sin and death.

What is the minding of the Spirit? It is to think on the things of the Spirit. If one's thought is scattered and confused the whole day long, naturally he belongs to the flesh. If he is always thinking on matters strange and alien to the Spirit, he of course is of the flesh. If one is brought by the Lord to the place where he can think on the things of the Holy Spirit, he will be a spiritual person, able to understand spiritual things. How can one whose mind is fully occupied with earthly matters live by the law of the Spirit? This is impossible. None can live by the Holy Spirit if his mind is set on the things of the flesh throughout the day and night.

Just remember that our thought ought not be the center of our being. It should be a servant listening carefully to its master's voice. Otherwise, we are not listening attentively to the Holy Spirit, but are thinking of many things according to our own desire. And the natural consequence is that we fall into that which we think. With the breaking of the outward man, though, we no longer make our self the center, nor do we think as we wish. We learn to hear God's voice, waiting before Him as an obedient servant. As soon as God's light flashes in us, our spirit catches the light and our understanding apprehends its meaning.

Never is the ministry of the word to be merely a matter of knowing doctrines. If such were the case, Christianity would be a carnal religion. But Christianity is not a carnal religion; it is a spiritual revelation. Our spirit knows the things of God, and our mind reads and interprets what is spoken to our spirit. Accordingly, our thought cannot afford to be scattered. A scattered mind is unable to fix the light of God, nor can a low mind hold God's light.

Different measures of understanding produce varying degrees of apprehension. For instance: God has revealed to us the matter of justification. This is quite common and elementary. But notice when people rise to speak on justification how differently they speak. The ministry of the word is based on God's light in man's spirit, yet the minds which read the light are so very different. Some touch the light with a low mind, others touch the same light with a noble mind. What is touched is influenced by the varying levels of the meaning of justification, and the nobler its representation in words. Though this one or that one may be given light on justification, if his thought is low he will apprehend it with only his limited mind and will deliver it with restricted words. It *is* the word of God, but how the word has suffered in him.

There is human element in the ministry of God's word, and the first and primary of these is man's thought. God's word shall suffer loss if our mind is not under strict discipline or if our thought is at a low level. One major problem in the ministry of the word is the adding of unsuitable words and unfitting thoughts to the word and to the light of God.

Brethren, do you realize the greatness of your responsibility? If your thought has been dealt with before, it will help the word. And then the adding of your element will bring in more glory to God's word. Paul, Peter, and John were all used in this way. Here was Paul. He had his character and personality. When the light of God shone on him and the word came forth from him, we saw Paul as well as the word of God. This is most precious. God's word is completed by man, and man perfects God's word. Instead of being a problem man adds to God's glory. It was so with Peter too. When God's word flowed through Peter it was the word of God, yet it had the flavor of Peter. God's word was perfected through Peter. It was not damaged in the least. Today's ministers of the word must be governed by the same principle as were those in the former days.

The question therefore narrows down to this: when God's light passes through our spirit and mind, how much is it damaged or how much is it perfected? We truly need the mercy of the Lord. If our mind lacks the dealings of the Lord, it will fail to read and interpret fully God's light. The result will be that the word of God will be presented weakly. Our words cannot be strong if our thought is weak. Our ministry will be weak because our thought is weak. We are God's channels, and channels determine the volume of water passing through. Channels can be leaky and defective. Either we deliver the word of God strongly to the brothers and sisters or we defile God's word and present it in damaged form. How serious is our responsibility.

We shall always stress the necessity of having the wounds of the cross upon us. We insist on having the outward man broken because we are fully persuaded that without brokenness there can be no ministry. This is so very basic that we simply cannot overlook it. If you wish to be used of God as a minister of the word, your outward man must be broken. If you expect to supply others with Christ, with God's word, your outward man needs to be dealt with drastically. Again and again we come up against the problem of man. It is unavoidable. If we are suitable we will be used; if unsuitable, then we shall not. The issue is man.

Training Our Thought

We have said that we cannot afford to waste our thought. We must preserve every ounce of our power of thinking. The stronger and fuller our thought, the higher we climb. By all means let us not use up our mind on unprofitable things. If we examine how a person uses his life we can fairly well judge how useful he is in the ministry of God's word. If he has already expended all his thoughts on other matters, what is left to apply to the things of God?

We have also stated that a subjective person is useless, because he continually thinks what he wants to think and sees what he desires to see. As his mind revolves around these things, he loses control over his thoughts. How can one wait on the Lord if his thinking is so loose, so profuse, and so confused? What is left for God if one's brain is set on lower things, that is, on the things of the flesh?

The ministry of the word requires thought. If our mind were renewed we would be able to hold and to fix the light whenever it shone in our spirit. Light tends to escape. How often we regret that our thought fails to catch up with God's light. If our thought is preoccupied with other matters God's light will escape us. Our mind needs to wait at the door like a faithful servant. This is the way of ministry.

Remember, light travels fast and is rich in its contents. A sound, noble, and rich mind can take hold of and fix much of the light, though no one can hold all of it. It is a strange experience to know that there has been a word and yet to be unable to remember what it was. If the best mind is incompetent in regard to God's light, how dare we waste our thought on unprofitable subjects? It is not good for us to engage our thoughts carelessly. Light needs to be fixed by thought; only after it is so fixed can it be profitable. Light is spiritual. It takes rich and strong thought to hold it. God is so infinite that when his light comes to us we cannot fathom what he wishes to communicate. Our thought must be rich. How often we have come to the Lord confessing the inadequacy of our thought. It is so poor that it tends to lose many things. We have lost much light. How, then, can we exhaust our mind on insignificant matters?

We must daily train ourselves in regard to our thoughts. The way we use our mind is closely related to the measure of our ministry of the word. Some are barren in ministry because they have wasted so much of their thought. They are like the man who has spent so much of his energy in walking down the wrong road that he has little strength left to walk in the straight path. Many exhaust their brain power on other subjects so that they have nothing left for the enlightenment of the Holy Spirit.

Do not be ignorant, brethren, of the relationship between thought and the light of the Holy Spirit. These two are intimately bound together. It is true that thought is no substitute for the enlightenment of the Holy Spirit, yet it is able to apprehend the Holy Spirit's enlightenment. Therefore let us waste none of our thought. The reason for poverty of thought lies in thinking too much. Learn to conserve your thought, not waste it. We do not suggest you should not exercise your mind; we only advocate that you do not exhaust its energy on insignificant things. So much brain power is spent on unimportant matters that when one really wants to understand God's word, he finds his power already used up. Do not spend your mental powers on some minor questions in the Bible. It matters little whether you can explain them or not. Neither waste your thought on spiritual problems, because these are not solved by thinking but by God's light. There are some who expend their precious mental powers on Bible questions and on spiritual problems, and thus dissipate their mental powers in reasonings and doctrines. Even if they have thought the thing through, they can only give thoughts to others. Their greatest loss, though, is in their inability to fix God's light. Real usefulness of thought lies in the power to hold God's light when it comes.

One important lesson to be learned by the minister of God's

word is to know how to engage his mind most profitably and most efficiently for God's enlightenment. Do not waste your mental faculty where God has not enlightened. No one can see anything by thinking. Do your thinking after God has shone upon you. Do you now see this way? You do not know the Bible through thought. No, you see only after God has shone on you and your thought has succeeded in translating the light into words. Your mind is open to God and so is receptive to God's light. This is the first step in getting God's word.

Let us ask God to raise up ministers of the word. Without these ministers the church is bound to be poor. Men must be raised up to supply the church with God's word. The issue which confronts us today lies in man, in incompetent channels. When God's light comes to us, it must pass through our thought. Light enters into the spirit, but it passes through the mind. How can we expect strong ministry if the light has suffered loss in the mind? This is very basic. May God show us this way of ministry.

12 | Burden and Word

In addition to having the light of God's revelation and in addition to fixing this light, a minister of God's word must also have burden in his heart. The Hebrew word "massam" has two different usages. One is that of a burden to be lifted or carried, as suggested in the Pentateuch. Examples are Exodus 23.5; Numbers 4.15,19,24,27,31,32,49; 11.11,17; and Deuteronomy 1.12. The other usage of "massam" is to convey the idea of an oracle or revelation to the prophet, as found in such prophetic writings as Isaiah 13.1; 14.28; 17.1; 19.1; 21.1,11,13; 22.1; 23.1; 30.6; Jeremiah 23.33,34,36,38; Nahum 1.1; Habakkuk 1.1; Zecheriah 9.1; 12.1; and Malachi 1.1. This indicates that the oracle which comes to the prophet is the burden he gets. This matter of burden plays a very important part in the ministry of the word. The prophet carries out the ministry of the word through his "massam," that is, his burden. When there is no burden, there is no ministry of the word. Therefore, a minister of the word must possess burden.

How a Burden Is Formed

We have already mentioned that the starting point in the ministry of the word is enlightenment. The light which shines in our heart is a sudden and somewhat elusive revelation. If our mind has been dealt with before God we are able to fix the thing which comes from God and translate what has shone in our spirit into meaningful words. Such enlightenment and fixing constitute the burden in us. There is no burden while the light is absent, neither is there burden when the light fails to be translated into thought or when the light dissolves into *mere* thought. A burden is formed by adding thought to the light. Light alone does not create a burden, nor does thought alone form a burden. It must be light together with the thought which comes from the light. *The light must remain after it has been translated.* This gives burden to those who minister before God.

Why is it called a burden? Because inwardly we have touched a thought while yet under enlightenment and so we feel heavy within, uncomfortable and even pained. This is the burden of God's word. Such burden as the prophets have can only be discharged in words. Without appropriate words this burden cannot be lifted.

In learning to be ministers of the word we cannot overlook the relationship between light, thought, and word. First we receive light, then we have thought, and finally we get the word. The usefulness of the word is in the discharging of God's light. From God's side it is light turned to thought in us; from our side it is thought precipitated into word. When we try to share God's light with others we seem to be discharging a burden upon them. The light and thought in us are like a burden upon us. Under this burden we cannot breathe freely, for we feel heavily pressed even to the extent of pain. It is only after we deliver this burden to God's children that our spirit is once more lightened and our thought is once again free. The burden upon our shoulders seems to have been placed elsewhere.

Discharging Burden with Word

How can we discharge the burden in us? We need words to discharge it. Just as physical burden is laid aside with hands, so spiritual burden is shed with words. If we do not find the proper word our burden remains heavy. In getting the appropriate word we lift our burden and feel released. All who have ministered God's word have the same experience: thought alone is inadequate: there must also be words in order to preach. Thought cannot singlehandedly bring people to God. If all you get is thought, then the more you speak the more confused your speech. You circle round and round, finding no way to get through—as though lost in a labyrinth.

But when you have the words, the more you speak the clearer your message. That is why sometimes a minister of God's word with a deep burden within may still find himself severely weighed down even after he has been delivering the message for an hour in the meeting. He carries away the very load which he earlier had brought to the meeting. If it is not because of not finding the right audience, then it is due to the lack of words. It is not that you have not spoken (perhaps you have said too much!), yet the burden within you remains untouched. This is because of a deficiency in word, not in thought. Were you to have *the* words, how different the result would be. Each sentence would help to lessen it until the whole burden were lifted.

This is how the prophets discharged their burdens. Their prophecies were their burdens. Their work was to shed those burdens. How did they discharge their burdens? Through their words. A worker unburdens himself with words. When words are missing, he has no way to shed his burden. Though people may praise you and say they were helped, you know that what was in you has not been released. They have heard the voice of man but have not heard the word of God. Referring the Corinthians to his ministry of the word, Paul has this to say: "Which things we also speak, not in words taught by human wisdom, but in those taught by the Spirit, combining spiritual thoughts with spiritual words" (I Cor. 2.13). Hence no one can be a minister of the word without having God-given words. The utterance of the words so given discharges the burden within.

Every worker must learn how to discharge his burden, but those workers who work with their mind or according to mental knowledge do not know this way. Whether the load is discharged or not depends not on your words or thoughts, but on God-given words.

It is imperative that we learn to receive words from God. The light which comes from God to our outward man becomes thought, and thought in turn is rendered into words which are delivered as the word of God. Thus we need to know how our thought is turned into words within us, and how these words within become spoken words. In this matter of discharging burden we should learn to know the difference between the words within and the words without. The words within are what we receive inside; the spoken words are the utterance by which the inward words are delivered.

The Relation between the Burden and the Words Within

Let us first consider the words within. When we receive light from God and get a thought, a burden is formed within us. Yet the way of discharging the burden is still missing. Light and thought are sufficient to create a burden but totally inadequate to discharge it. They must first be transformed into words within us; then with these words we may be able to utter the burden in an audible voice. Thought as such we cannot articulate, for we can only voice words. Neither can we transform our thought into words extemporaneously; it must first be converted into words *within* us before we can express it outside us. This is the difference between the ministry of the word and ordinary speech. Ordinarily we are able to speak out our thought, for what we speak is based on our thought. Not so with the ministry of the word. We must first convert the thought we have from God into inward words before we can speak.

The Lord Jesus on earth is the supreme minister of the word. But notice that He is not God's thought becoming flesh; rather He is God's word becoming flesh. Hence a minister of the word should seek words. Only after you have succeeded in converting the thought you obtain from God into words will you be able to minister. Suppose you receive a thought but try to utter it with your own words; you have missed an intervening step and will fail in ministry. This is a fundamental principle. There must be light, thought, and words within. After you have fixed the light of God as thought, you should learn to seek before God for words. You need to be watchful, praying and seeking for words.

What enlightens my spirit is revelation, for without revelation there can be no enlightenment. Enlightenment is God's work, but fixing the light as thought is the work of one who is instructed of God. Following the translation of light into thought there must be the conversion of such thought into words. To interpret the light with my thought and go no further is to serve my own purpose, but to interpret thought by converting it into inner words is to minister to others. For my own use, thought is enough; that is as far as it must go; yet to help others, thought needs to be turned into words. Light void of thought almost appears to be abstract to me, though spiritually it is quite real. It becomes concrete in me only after it is transformed into thought. In a similar manner, light becomes concrete in others if thought is converted into words.

Before any ministry of the word there must be the process of changing light into thought and thought into word. Now of course the thought mentioned here does not refer to ordinary thought but refers to what is revealed. My thought follows what I have seen. I cannot pass on thought to others. I can only pass on words. It is therefore necessary in the ministry of the word to translate God's thought into God's words. Light is given by God. It is fixed by the thought of one whose mind has been disciplined. The words which express that thought, however, must as usual be granted by God. This shows that sometimes revelation occurs in the spirit, sometimes in the word. Let us now see what these two are.

Revelation in the Spirit vs. Revelation in the Word

What is revealed in my spirit is the enlightenment which I have received. Such revelation does not linger; the light has to be fixed by my thought. But if my natural mind is incompetent and fails at the moment of enlightenment to convert the thought into word, what should I do? I should ask God for another enlightenment. But the second enlightenment will not shine into my spirit and from that give me a thought; instead, this enlightenment gives me a word, the spiritual thought being transformed into words within me.

Here then we discover two different types of revelation: one in the spirit and the other in the word. That which is in the word comes when God gives us a few words. To illustrate. Perhaps while you are praying you receive a light within you which is clear and distinct. You are also able to hold that light and translate it into thought. When you go out to tell others of this revelation, however, you find you cannot express it clearly. It is clear to you, yet it cannot be made clear to others. You yourself understand somewhat, yet you do not possess the words to make others understand. So you commence to ask God to grant you words. You pray watchfully and thoroughly. Your heart is open to God without prejudice, and your spirit is likewise free before God, unencumbered by other burdens. As you are in this state, something happens: God gives you a few words to fitly express the thought in you. These words unveil the revelation which had previously been given to you. They fix God's light for the second time.

There are therefore two ways of fixing the light: first, I use my thought to fix God's light; or second, God gives me words to fix His light. My mind holds fast the light shown me in my spirit or God grants me words to hold His light. The revelation I get in word is one with the revelation I get in my spirit. In my spirit I see for a split second. The time for seeing is so short, yet the thing beheld is timeless. What is seen in one second can never be expressed in one second, for in my spirit I have seen a great deal in that split second. If my understanding is strong and my mind is rich, I will be able to fix more of God's light. When God gives words, however, He seemingly gives only a few words. God employs a few words to transfix His light.

These words may be few in number yet inclusive in content, because they contain the whole revelation. In ordinary speech, if there are eight or ten words you are finished after those eight or ten words. Worldly speech is measured by counting words or counting time. Words of revelation, however, are enormously different. Perhaps there are but a few words, yet the words of revelation are as rich as the revelation of God. What is revealed is rich, what is enlightened in a split second is rich; so are the few words given by God rich in content. Just as God can reveal so much in a second, so He is able to show that much in a word. Just as what is seen in a second may take several months to unveil, so what is shown in one word may require several months to deliver too.

Here is the distinction between the words within and the words spoken without. The words within are never long but are rich in content. They do not come in long messages for us to deliver, since we are usually given only a few words. But what spiritual wealth is hidden in those few words! When they come, they come with one distinctive characteristic; which is, that these few words are life-releasing.

What is meant by life-releasing words? When God imparts revelation He gives nothing less than His life. He accords us life through His revelation. In a minister, such revelation becomes a burden. If this burden can be discharged, life is released; if not discharged, life is detained. The heavier the burden, the greater the power when discharged. But if the burden remains without any means of being discharged, it will grow heavier. Here, for example, is a leather bag full of water. It is very heavy in your hands. Suppose you puncture a hole in the bag and let out the water; you will not feel the weight any more. So it is with the word. If you have a burden in you, you need some words to express just how you feel. This is like puncturing a hole which releases the water. Such words of revelation are words which release life. Life is shut up unless it is released through burden; it takes appropriate words to let out the pressure within. How can life be released without words from God?

However heavy the weight, you must wait before God, for His words shall come to you. Sometimes you may have to pray for days before the words are given. At times you are able to fix the light with thought but you have no way to express it. At other times words flow with the thought: as soon as the burden is felt, appropriate words are given. We cannot decide when we will have the words. God may impart them immediately after you have seen the light, or He may wait until your burden becomes nearly unbearable.

In any event, the words when given are most appropriate. They hold the light which you have seen. The entire revelation seems to be completely uncovered by these few words. The revelation is rich, and so are the words. It is like unscrewing a cork—the entire contents of the bottle can be poured out. You must seek to have these few words granted to you. These we designate as the words within. They are God's, and they contain the whole of the revelation you have received. God hides what He has revealed in these few words, and through these same words His revelation is also unveiled. In the delivery of these words of revelation, God's enlightenment is also delivered.

Let us understand beyond a shadow of a doubt that there can be no ministry without enlightenment, no ministry without translating light into thought by our understanding, and no ministry without having the words of revelation to express the thought. This is what Paul means by "combining spiritual thoughts with spiritual words" (I Cor. 2.13). The Holy Spirit grants us words. He imparts not only revelation but the words of revelation as well. It may be only a few words, yet these few puncture the vessel and let out life. You may say many words, yet without these few God-given words life simply will not flow.

God's life is released through revelation. Take the crucifixion of the Lord Jesus as an example. The Lord has in truth already died for the whole world. Yet why is it that not all the people of the world have life? It is because not all have received this revelation. One can endlessly recite the sentence that the Lord Jesus has died for all, but if a person has no revelation he will not be in the good of the death of the Lord. Another person who has received the revelation can thank and praise God from the bottom of his heart, for such seeing has given him life. The Holy Spirit quickens us through His word.

Today God desires to supply the church with His words. He intends to give Christ—the life of Christ—to the church. And this life is released through the discharge of the burden in us. It requires appropriate words to puncture a hole so that life may flow. A person could be speaking for two hours and life would still not be released, or a person could merely commence to speak and life at once begins to flow. It all depends upon revelation and words. Each time revelation is given, a few appropriate words must accompany it; otherwise life will not flow. With such words, life is given. Without them, life is not even touched.

If God accords you a burden, He must also grant you words to discharge that burden. These two are both imparted by God. He who gives burden is also the One who gives words to release the burden. It is God who gives you burden, and it is God who helps you to discharge it. He will supply you with words. With these few words life is released. Hence do not go away still ladened with your burden; learn how to release life or else you cannot serve God. Do not merely bring the leather bag to your brethren, but puncture it so as to give them water to drink. The way to let the water out is to obtain some words from God. Frequently we meet a brother who speaks much but says little. He speaks with great effort, yet he is not able to bring out the thing within. He is going around in circles, always missing the spot where the water can be let out. If only he could add a few right words, life would flow; however, he does not possess the words within. He cannot be a minister of the word if he does not know how to secure these necessary words. The longer he talks, the farther he drifts.

How essential for us, therefore, to wait before God for these words. It is best if we have the words the moment we are able to fix the light with thought. But if no word is forthcoming at that moment, we must ask God for it. The day will come when we will realize how incompetent is our own eloquence. Is it not all too true that before we begin to learn to be a minister of God's word, we think very highly of our eloquence? Let us admit that man's natural eloquence is good for anything else except for the things of God. Man's eloquence is futile in the affairs of God; no amount of it will impart life. The words of life are only found in revelation.

We must acknowledge that Paul is naturally eloquent, yet he asks in Ephesians 6.19 "that utterance may be given to me in the opening of my mouth, to make known with boldness the mystery of the gospel." Paul requests the Ephesian believers to pray for him that he might be granted words to proclaim the mystery of the gospel. In things spiritual, natural eloquence is useless. God must give words; and these words come from within. The difficulty with many is that they talk a great deal but cannot express their inward feeling. Do not try to find words while on the platform; have them within you beforehand. Find the words and afterwards speak. A minister of God's word must learn to know the words within. May the Lord make us those who have the appropriate words. We need burden—plus the words to discharge it.

In toto, what is meant by burden? It means the enlightenment in the spirit, plus the fixing of the light in thought, plus the words within. These three constitute a prophet's burden. Our concern must be to impart God's revelation to others, and this can only be accomplished through the words of revelation. Oh that we may see the relation between burden and the words within!

How to Obtain the Words Within

Under what circumstances can we obtain these words within? They are usually acquired at the time of Bible reading and waiting before God. You have received an inward enlightenment and your thought, being powerful and active, is able to hold God's light. These two steps are sufficient for your own benefit, because the revelation you receive has already become a fruitful, substantial thought in you. Even so, you cannot impart your thought to others; as a minister of God's word, you can only supply people with words. Such words do not come from man's own thinking. They are revealed by God and granted by the Holy Spirit. They are not given to you for you to enjoy, but given to you for the sake of others that you may be a minister of the word of God.

One thing is quite plain: we are members of the body of

Christ: hence the light God shines upon us never stops in us, but is for the ministry. To obtain the words within we need to wait before God and read the Bible. Our experiences may vary from time to time. On some occasions it is very special; on other occasions it is fairly ordinary. In ordinary days God will grant us a few words as we are waiting before Him and are studying the Bible. He may give a few words today and a few words tomorrow, but what words we receive during Bible reading can sufficiently express what we have seen in the spirit. These words will release life when they are spoken.

Hence we must wait on God and read the Bible, asking Him to grant us the words. When the words do come, we are instantly assured of what we should speak today. We have learned the secret of utterance. We are able to express the light we have seen and the thought which is within us. Before we secure the words, however hard we try, we simply cannot speak forth the inward revelation. There is no way to release the light of revelation other than by the words of revelation. He who has the revealed light but lacks revealed words should not attempt to release his light. The greater the lack of revealed words the longer should be the waiting before God. Pray, commune, wait, and lay the Bible before God. This is not an ordinary waiting, nor ordinary prayer and communion. This is waiting before God with the Bible, praying to God with the Bible, and communing with God over the Bible. It is a convenient time for the Lord to speak, and so it is relatively easy to obtain the words of revelation. As soon as you receive a few words you are able to win sinners to Christ and to help the believers. These few words are God's words, not the word written much earlier, but God's most recent word. These can be used for life. Whenever you use these words, if your spirit is right the Holy Spirit will honor them. They are God's words; the Holy Spirit is at the back. They are not common words; they are extraordinary and powerful.

The Relation between Burden and the Spoken Words

The ministry of the word requires three steps: enlightenment, thought, and words. Words are of two kinds: the words within and the words without (that is, the spoken words). For the sake of convenience, we may consider them as four different steps.

What are the spoken words? And what are their relation to the words within? Their relation to the words within resembles the relationship between thought and light. These are spiritual facts which cannot be shaken. In the same way as the inward enlightenment tends to fade away if it is not held firm by thought, so the few words within need the spoken words without for delivery. Inclusive as are these few words within in regard to what God desires to say at that particular time, they cannot be understood by others if they alone are spoken. It takes many spoken words to deliver these few words within. So powerful are these words within that people simply cannot assimilate them. To speak out the words within, it may take perhaps two thousand spoken words, or five thousand, or even possibly ten thousand. It needs *our* word to deliver *God's* word. This is the ministry of the word.

We find here the blending in of the human element. Human element is first involved in the process of the mind trying to hold the light. Some minds are usable while others are incompetent. Human element comes into the picture the second time when spoken words are added. Some ministers possess sufficiently good words to express God's word, but others fail in this respect. The effect is tremendous.

The Words Within Need Spoken Words for Delivery

The words within are most "concentrated," hence hard to receive; the spoken words are relatively "diluted," therefore easy to receive. We are responsible for the outward spoken words. We are responsible for diluting the concentrated words of God so as to make them acceptable to men. The words within are few and concentrated, while those spoken without are many and diluted. The first of these is beyond man's assimilation; the second is able to be assimilated.

In the Bible we do not find much difference in the words

which the various people received directly from God, for they all are God's word. But when the word of God is delivered through Peter it carries with it a Petrine flavor. This is equally true in John and in Paul. If we are able to read directly in Greek we can easily detect which book is written by Peter, which by John, and which by Paul. Why? Because the outward expressions are varied even though the inner words are the same words of God. Peter is different as a person from John and Paul, and vice versa. When God's word is deposited in Peter and delivered through him, the doctrine is God's but the taste is Peter's. The same holds true with John or with Paul. In the ministry of the word God uses the human element. God looks for those whom the Holy Spirit can use to deliver His word. God imparts words to men, yet these relatively few God-given words require man's words for communication. Whoever is more instructed in God has more instructive words to communicate.

Let us return to the principle of tongues. Why do we pay attention to this matter? Because in the New Testament Paul compares tongues with prophetic ministry. Why is not the speaking in tongues forbidden? Because it is profitable to the one who speaks in tongues. Yet why is it useless in the ministry of the word? For the simple reason that there is no human understanding and no human element involved in tongues. To speak in tongues depends entirely upon the Holy Spirit, that is, the person speaks with his own spirit as God's Spirit gives him words. But it is nothing more. To our thinking, tongues may be better than prophecy, for is it not better to speak in God's own words or in the words of the Holy Spirit? Nonetheless the Bible views tongues as being inferior to prophetic ministry. God places the latter above tongues. A prophetic ministry includes in it God's word plus the prophet himself. In other words, the living water in the words flows out from the depths of the prophet; it does not pour down from heaven. This is a very fundamental principle in the New Testament.

God is concerned more with man. In studying the Scriptures carefully you can easily conclude which book was written by

Peter, by John, or by Matthew. Each of them has that particular person's traits, diction, and grammatical construction. God does not desire to dictate His word. The doctrine is God's but the words are of man. How great is the responsibility of the minister of the word. If the man is not right, what could he not add to God's word? It is therefore imperative for the man to be broken. Do not be mistaken as to the nature of God's word. It is not that God's words are supernatural and that is all there is to it. God first gives man a few words and these in turn are delivered through man's many words. It depends very much on how man dilutes these few God-given words.

In speaking, we should remember that behind the spoken words we already have three other things: enlightenment, thought, and the words within. Whether we are speaking on the platform or conversing privately with individuals, what is it we must do? We must hold on to the one or two sentences which have been given to us that they may be, as it were, the inspiration for all the other words. Due to their intense concentration, we must dilute them to make them receivable by people. It is like hammering a big rock into many bits. As we speak, we break and grind the strong words within us into small pieces, and then deliver them little by little. This is the way to present the word of God.

The finer the inward words become, the better; the fuller the words spoken, the stronger. It is not well if after two hours' talk the one piece within remains untouched. It is futile to deliver God's word with one's own words. There seems to be some discrepancy here, and yet the fact remains true. On the one hand, man's words are useless; on the other hand, they are precious. To speak the truth of God with one's own words is absolutely vain, no matter how clear or intelligent you are. But having God's word within you, it takes your words to deliver God's words; otherwise the latter will remain intact. Through your words the word of God is presented progressively. Your outer spoken words are for the sake of releasing the words within.

We discover that these four factors are inter-related in

functioning. As a minister of the word, you first receive the words within, then you try to present them with outward spoken words. But what really happens is actually not that simple. The mind needs to think. How can you speak if you do not think? Yet your mind does not think of the words, but rather of the revelation. You think of what you have seen in your spirit. The Lord gives us two bases from which to move: the enlightenment in the spirit and the words within. We use our mind to hold fast the revelation but use our words to send it out. There are all together four factors: two within and two without; two belong to God and two to us. When these four join hands we have the ministry of the word.

How we have suffered in these respects. Often we have spoken according to the words within, but our inner revelation is lost. The words have come today, but the revelation is missing. Or sometimes we have seen something inwardly, yet for months the burden is unlifted because there are no words. Hence we need to have words given us by the Lord but at the same time have our gaze fixed on the revelation while speaking.

Brethren, let us see these two sides. Sometimes there is a revelation and thought, but no word. We understand inwardly though we cannot express it. Thoughts may be all around, yet words be completely lacking. Who can apprehend thoughts? At other moments we have words but the revelation in the spirit has faded away. When people hear us they are as though chewing overnight manna; the taste has changed. The sending forth of the words does not seem to coincide with what is seen within. Thus it is essential both to have words which express the thought and to not lose sight of the light.

Our mind is very important; even so, it is not an organ for revelation. For receiving revelation all our wisdom is void. How the church of God will suffer if our intent is to receive revelation with our mind. We cannot do it with our mind. All four factors mentioned above are indispensable. There must be the words within as well as the spoken words without. They are like the double rails; the absence of either one of them will derail the train. They run parallel. The words within are sent forth through the spoken words without. Should we have the enlightenment and thought but lack the basic word, we will be like an ox at the grinding, moving in circles but without any let up of burden. If we have the words within but not the spoken words without, we will not be able to proceed further on just the one rail; the word of God is stuck. There can be no preaching with the light of revelation alone, nor with the inward words alone. These four factors—of revelation, thought, the words within, and the spoken words without—must be joined together before the glorious ministry of the word begins.

Speak According to the Scriptures

We must pay attention to the words of the Scriptures while preparing for the spoken word. We ourselves do not have many words to say, and our own words incline to travel in one direction only. The words within are strong and concentrated, but when we speak, our words are so poor and inadequate. If we repeat ourselves over and over again, people will become tired; on the other hand if we deliver only the few inward words they will be unable to appreciate their preciousness. How utterly ineffective is man's eloquence in speaking spiritual things! We may speak eloquently on other matters, but when it comes to preaching, our eloquence is quickly exhausted. Even after we have gone round and round, the words within still go unexpressed. For this reason we need to read the Bible diligently.

God calls us to be ministers of His word. He knows the inadequacy of our words. Accordingly, He speaks "in many portions and in many ways" to us (Heb. 1.1). We must spend time to read the Scriptures. There is much of doctrine, knowledge, and teaching in the Bible which can be added to our speech. We must have Scriptural basis, Scriptural teaching and truth, to make what we say acceptable to God's children. There needs to be a ground for acceptance. Upon receiving inward enlightenment with its corresponding thought and words, we will think of quite a number of similar experiences and similar subjects recorded in the Bible. We remember them and use them to bring out our message. We may ourselves only have a few words, perhaps ten-odd sentences, for what we say must be based on our experience. But if we are familiar with the Bible we can use the words there to help complete the delivery. This is not expounding the Scriptures objectively. It is on the contrary a highly subjective approach to the understanding of the Bible. We are not talking about the Bible but about the revelation we have received. We use the Bible because we find in it things similar to our experience. Something happened to Peter and to John; something was recorded in Genesis or in Psalms. These fit in perfectly with what we intend to say, and thus we clothe our message with them. We have noticed how Paul, how Peter, how David, how Moses, and how the Lord spoke about certain matters. When we are now given a few words concerning a particular matter, we clothe them with the words of Paul, Peter, David, Moses, and even our Lord. We still base our speech on the light and burden we have received from God, so that in speaking, the light shines out and the burden is discharged.

We do not read the Bible merely for the sake of expounding *it*. How vain for people to talk about the Bible! The words in the Scriptures are provided to release our inward burdens. We find the appropriate words in the Bible for the discharge of our burden. Such words may have been spoken ten to twenty times and in many different ways. When we are burdened, we use the Scripture words to relieve this burden. Is your burden heavy in you? If it is, try to find more passages in the Book. If your burden is not as heavy, then less passages may be sufficient. Try to use these varying ways to lessen your burden. Perhaps after you have tried five different ways your burden will be completely discharged. The ministry of the word means that the weighty words within are delivered through the words of the Scriptures. The Bible is consequently the best instrument.

Having said this, though, we must raise a warning: never deem the words of the Bible alone to be sufficient. The words of the Scriptures by themselves become mere doctrines. The basis for ministry is revelation—the words within delivered through the words of the Bible without. If one is lacking in inward revelations and merely tries to expound the Bible, his source is of a very low degree. We should not only talk about Paul's experience; we must *see it ourselves* before we have the ministry of the word. With revelation and words within, plus the words of the Scriptures without, the burden is released. With words inside yet without the words of the Scriptures, the burden will remain heavy.

The Test for the Ministry of the Word

How do we know if we have spoken rightly? See whether your inward burden is lessened, unchanged, or increased. This is very important. You do not need to step down from the platform before you know. Even as you are speaking you know. With the utterance of each sentence there should be a corresponding lessening of your burden; for the burden is to be discharged through the words spoken. If the spoken words fail to lessen your inward burden you know something is wrong. If after having spoken for a few minutes you discover your burden unchanged, then you know you have used the wrong way of delivery. It is better to stop than to continue for an hour. Confess to the brethren that you have taken the wrong direction and begin afresh.

Such difficulties will gradually be eliminated through practice. You must learn how to lessen your inward burden. You should come with a burden, but after you finish speaking, the burden should be gone. You should not begin speaking with a burden and a half hour later still have your burden. Nor should we have the rather peculiar experience of coming with a burden, but because our words are partly right and partly wrong discharge only a part of it. This too is wrong.

The whole thing is of course more complicated than we think. Sometimes your preaching not only fails to lessen your burden but even increases it. Perhaps a wrong illustration adds to your burden. Or you may carelessly bring in an untimely joke which arouses uncontrollable laughter from the audience. Or a sudden thought may increase your burden. For the above reasons, your eye must be single. You speak to lighten the burden, not just for the sake of speaking.

A basic principle to remember in preaching is to keep your eyes on how to discharge your inward burden. In the physical realm, we know, no one carrying a load to a certain place wishes to carry it back again. He expects to unload it there. The same is true in the spiritual realm: every burden which reaches the heart needs to be released through appropriate words. If, in speaking, the burden is increased, then cease speaking. Failure to find appropriate spoken words creates a real problem to the ministry of the word. If your burden is lessened with each sentence, you know you have said the right thing. You may say it in different ways a few times till your burden is wholly discharged. Actually, you have only a few inward words; all other words are there to dilute and to deliver these few words.

May God be gracious to us and grant us accurate words, words which bring out life and words which touch the height.

13 | The Discipline of the Holy Spirit and the Word

Whence come the words when a minister arises to speak? He need not churn up his brain in order to find the many words, for his words come from a different source. After he has decided on the source, he is clear what words are unsuitable and should not be spoken as God's word. We have repeatedly mentioned the intimate relationship between the ministry of the word and human element. It is God who gives just a few words which are later developed into many of our words. All the latter words are derived from the former. Our speech is based on the inward words. We simply speak out what God has spoken to us inwardly. Human element is definitely involved; hence we must pay much attention to what sort of person the speaker is.

The kind of person determines the kind of words spoken. Sometimes God acknowledges as His word what is spoken; sometimes He denies that it is His. The entire question seems to revolve around what kind of man the speaker is. Here are two persons. They receive the same inward enlightenment as well as the same inward words, but when they stand up to serve they present a profound contrast. Why? Because they are widely different persons. Ministry varies according to the person. Where, then, does the word come from? The word comes primarily from revelation, but it is influenced by human element. If the person is right his words will be right; if he is not right, neither can his words be right. The words of an unfit person are bound to be of lower quality—weak and immature, humanly clever and persuasive but not spiritual at all. That of a fit man will naturally be spiritual, accurate, of higher quality and able to touch God. In looking for the source of the spoken words we must pay attention to the person himself. What kind of man one is determines what sort of words he speaks.

The Words Differ According to the Constituting Work of the Holy Spirit

Were God through His Spirit to incorporate something of Himself in you—that is, were the Spirit of God to do some work in you by touching and breaking down your outward man so that your character undergoes a change and you were thus able to touch spiritual reality—then you naturally would speak out the words of the Holy Spirit. What you utter would follow what He has constituted in you. Without the Holy Spirit's constituting work there can be no Holy Spirit words. It is beyond us to utter His words unless He rearranges and reconstitutes us. We are like a house entirely renovated and even rebuilt after many years of the Lord's working in us. Take note of this: that the Holy Spirit's words are founded on the Holy Spirit's work. If we have not been reconstituted our words will remain the same old words. Only after we are reconstituted and become new can we speak new words.

We may learn from Paul in 1 Corinthians 7. The Holy Spirit is so successful in remaking Paul that to him revelation becomes natural. He has advanced to such a spiritual state that he is unconscious of his having received a revelation. Revelation is no surprise to him. He receives enlightenment so often that he finds it hard to distinguish between enlightenment and his own thought. The reason men today are so far apart from God's revelation is because there has not been a sufficient reconstituting work of the Holy Spirit in them. How strange the words of 1 Corinthians 7 sound to us. A brother is here brought by God to such an advanced stage—the Holy Spirit has done such a work of reconstitution in him—that his own feeling is not much different from God's feeling, his own thought is closely similar to God's revelation. He no longer senses anything special when he receives the revelation of God. The human element has climbed so high as to touch God Himself. Paul thinks these are his own words, for the Lord has not spoken to him. Yet there is such a large measure of spiritual constituting in him that he is able to conclude by saying, "and I think that I have the Spirit of God" (v.40).

Here we recognize the close relationship between man and the word. A man is here speaking the word of God. He has not received any special revelation, yet he is already speaking God's word because he has reached a very high spiritual level. The principle illustrated in Paul comes to this: if the person is right, the words spoken by him will be right. Out of the constituting of God within him flow from him the words of God. We must therefore be especially careful in this respect that we may be dealt with to the extent of such purity as to enable the words of the Holy Spirit to come through our lips.

Due to the difference in God being constituted in men the words come forth differently. Two persons may be equally usable, both having attained to a high degree of spirituality, but the constituting work of the Holy Spirit in them may not be alike. They may have received the same revelation, been given the same inward words, yet speak differently due to this variation in the Holy Spirit's working. Both are ministers of the word, yet each has his distinctive speech because the human elements involved are different. John is different from Paul, so is Paul from Peter; hence their spoken words are quite different. They are all greatly used by God though they speak so differently from one another. Within Paul is God's word, on his lips are his own words, and yet what is spoken is reckoned as the word of God. This is true of Peter also. Both of them have undergone a deep reconstituting work; as a result they can speak the word of God. Judging from their outward spoken words, however, they appear to be very dissimilar.

The Formation of the Word

Just as God's word is a Person in the Lord Jesus, so it must today be personified in us. The Lord Jesus is the Word become flesh; thus God spoke in the flesh. Today God intends to have His words become flesh once more, that is, He still wishes to speak through human flesh. That is why He deals with this flesh of ours, hoping that through it His word may come forth. To arrive at this goal there must be the constituting work of the Holy Spirit in us. By the indwelling Spirit God is able to incorporate something in us so that when we think and speak, the word of God comes through. What is incorporated in us by the Holy Spirit converts God's word into our subjective words. A minister of the word must allow the Holy Spirit to so reconstitute him that he may have this kind of subjective words. His thought must not only *agree* with God's thought but is to *be* God's thought. His words become God's word, not just coincide with God's word. This is the result of the Holy Spirit's incorporating work in us. And this is New Testament ministry. The man is there, and so is God. Man speaks, and God speaks too. What dealing must that man go through if the word of God is destined to come through him!

Let us see just how God does this constituting work in us through His Spirit. Words must be created within us by God. They are formed through the daily trials which God arranges in our circumstances. We may perhaps go through various trials these few days or months. Sometimes we are victorious, at other times defeated. We may seem to be getting through, and yet we seem to be bucking against a wall. All these are actually arranged by the Lord. Days pass and we begin to learn a little. Perhaps we start to have a few words. These few words give us clarity as to what is happening to us. They enable us to talk, for they are words imparted to us. God has created a few words in us. This is how words are formed. They belong to us as well as to God. It is vital that we know where and how to learn to have words. For instance, in the early stages of chastisement you may be puzzled because you have no word. You may be quite perplexed over God's dealing. But after a while you begin to understand: "Oh, *this* is what the Lord is after. He has been dealing with me that I may possess this thing."

Yet things are really not so simple, for you do not come to a definite understanding all at once. You seem to be clear and yet you are still unclear. It is as you are going through this ambivalence between clarity and obscurity that you gradually become clearer. When you are clear to a certain degree, you have the corresponding words. What you are clear about becomes your words. Sometimes the Lord accords you a very severe trial. You cannot get through. At times you think you may get through, you really believe you may, but you do not. Even so, in this process of getting through and not getting through you unconsciously finally do break through. And your coming through brings out words.

By this, then, let us understand that God is forming words in you as He puts you through this dual process of clarity and obscurity. In our trials, in the dual process we go through, God is creating words in us. We appear to be getting through but nevertheless are stuck; we appear undone, yet not completely beaten. After some days the Lord finally carries us through. This carrying through constitutes God's word. The farther you get through the clearer you become and the more words you possess. This is how words are formed. The word of the ministry is not something thought out but rather created. How different are thought out words from created words. You are groping in the dark; you faintly see something; it becomes a little more definite. By adding together these times of clarity, you secure the word. What you have passed through becomes your word.

A minister of the word ought to be attentive to how he speaks. The words he speaks must come through discipline, since God creates the words for us through His disciplining us. The measure of discipline determines the amount of words. Our experience before God gives us a corresponding degree of words. We should now understand that the Lord is chiseling this flesh of ours that we may touch the word of God. Out of a chiseled flesh emerges the word of God. How much you can speak depends upon how much you have learned inwardly. Your words are based upon experience before the Lord. God's aim is to unite you with His word. It is more than your preaching His word; you as a person must be so chiseled and tested by Him that the word which comes out of you is God's word.

Let us proceed a step further. Where do you see the light of revelation? Most likely you will say it is seen in the spirit. Why then do you not always see it in the spirit? Why is it that your spirit sometimes receives revelation and sometimes not? When is it that your spirit receives revelation? It is when you are under discipline. Perception in the spirit is governed by the dealing upon us. In the time of chastisement the spirit sees light. The light of revelation is seen and obtained as we experience the discipline of the Holy Spirit. When the discipline of God is rare the enlightenment in the spirit also becomes scarce. We receive light in a definite place and at a definite time. We get light in the spirit, and it comes at the time of discipline. Consequently each time of dealing supplies another opportunity for revealing.

Missing a discipline means forfeiting the possibility of receiving a revelation. When we accept a dealing by God we may receive a revelation, a new revelation. We should recognize the hand of our Lord. Frequently His hand is upon us, touching us and dealing with us in point after point; and so we yield little by little. Or He may have to touch us many times before we consent somewhat by saying, "Lord, now I am willing to yield and to strive no more." Then and there we receive enlightenment. The Lord continues to deal with us and so we gradually yield to Him. Each yielding brings enlightenment to our spirit. Thus we see light, and in this light we receive the word. Through testing, God gives us word as well as light. The words we use in preaching are not something we ourselves conceive; they are created through God's discipline of us.

In your various times of ministering, therefore, watch to see if your words grow. If there is progress in this respect you know you have been progressively dealt with. The first times you speak for God you will have only a few words. No matter how clear you are, how good your memory is, and how much information you have received from others, when it comes to speaking you find yourself wholly inadequate. In order to grant you word the Lord has to deal with you, time after time and in point after point. Each chiseling brings forth some words. God is giving words, ever progressive words. After many such dealings you are not wanting in words when you stand on the platform. But do notice how these words are formed—they are formed through the discipline of the Holy Spirit.

Paul tells us in 2 Corinthians 12 that he has received a very great revelation, a revelation of the third heaven and of Paradise. The third heaven is the highest heaven while Paradise is in the lowest part of the earth. One is the heaven of heavens, the other is the center of the earth. Paul received a revelation which includes both. Naturally such a revelation tends to elate Paul. He is so afraid that anyone should think too much of him that he refrains from speaking of it. Further, a thorn is given him in the flesh, a messenger of Satan, to harass him. Three times he asks the Lord for its removal, and the Lord's answer is: "My grace is sufficient for you, for (my) power is perfected in weakness" (v.9). This new revelation is not something mental but spiritual. Hence Paul can say, "Most gladly, therefore, I will rather boast about my weaknesses, . . . for when I am weak, then I am strong" (vv.9-10). He had indeed received a new revelation and a new knowledge. Perhaps this is a part of the wonderful revelation he has received. He may find more help in *this* word than in what he has seen and heard in the third heaven and in Paradise. We have never been to Paradise; no one has ever been told of what is spoken there. Nor have we been to the third heaven; we have no idea of all the things which will occupy us in that realm. But for almost two thousand years the church has received more help from what the Lord told Paul—"My grace is sufficient for you"—than from the apostle's experience of the third heaven and of Paradise.

Whence comes the ministry of the word? In the case of Paul it comes from the testings and trials he underwent in being brought by the Lord to such a state that his boast was that whenever he is weak then is he strong. Paul has the ministry of the word when he recognizes that God's grace is sufficient for him. In this very manner is his ministry produced. It comes through discipline. Such revelation as found in 2 Corinthians 12.9 results from the discipline of the Holy Spirit. No discipline, no revelation; no thorn, no grace.

The thorn upon Paul's flesh is a severe one, and not an ordinary thorn but a messenger of Satan. The word "harass" means to buffet, to beat, to oppress, ill-treat, make painful. Paul has gone through a lot; he is not one who is afraid of sickness yet he is being sorely tried. If *he* says it is painful, it must be very painful indeed. Paul had a thorn, and Satan sends his messenger to harass Paul by making use of that thorn. Under such a severe trial God gives him grace: "My grace is sufficient for you." Paul thus receives a revelation. He recognizes the grace of God as well as the power of God. He also knows his own weakness. Countless saints there are in the church of God who have been carried through trials and testings by means of this revelation of Paul's. If we only know how utterly weak we are! As soon as weakness leaves us, power likewise departs. Where there is weakness, there is power. This is a spiritual principle brought in by discipline. We receive light through discipline; we also receive word through discipline. We learn to speak time after time, not unlike a child learning to speak.

God puts you through trials; He allows you to be tried at the hands of many of His own children. As you begin to learn, you begin to have a word. In the measure of your yieldedness is the measure of your word. Immediately you yield, you gain the word. This word is obtained from obedience; your obedience is the word. As you fall and prostrate yourself before God you have the word. It is written in your life; it is engraved in your very being. God allows His children to go through many and varied trials. Sometimes you may be the very first one to be put through a trial, before the others. You are tried first and the others afterwards. The trial you go through perfects the word in you. You are able to rise up and speak the word tempered through trial to your brothers and sisters who are now being tried and seemingly unable to get through. The word you speak becomes light and life and power to those who are in the same trial. Once more you have ministered the word.

Let us realize that the minister of the word must be tried first. Without any trial there can be no word. If other brothers and sisters should enter into trial before you, you have nothing to help them. Even if you should try to say something, it falls as an empty word. What use is an empty word? Word is formed in fire. The church must go through fire herself; thus God leads His ministers into fire first that they may be burnt before the rest. He who is burnt first comes out with the word. As you are burned you possess the word. Time and again through burning and yieldedness words are added to words. And subsequently you possess the word to help those who are equally tried.

We therefore declare that a minister of the word ministers with Spirit-taught words. Not only does the Holy Spirit speak words of wisdom with my lips; He teaches me how to speak. I am instructed by the Holy Spirit; I have learned in the fiery furnace; I have the word. Otherwise, all which is said is merely empty words. How basic this is: that we need to learn in each dealing. Our words must be burned into being through fire, else they shall be ineffective. *We* cannot comfort those who are sorrowful. What is merely external is futile. In order to be truly useful, we must be those who have been dealt with by God.

How is it that the church has been helped for two thousand years by this word in 2 Corinthians 12? Thank God, it is because of the thorn in Paul's flesh. Had the thorn been removed the help would have vanished. The power of that chapter is manifested in this thorn. If there were no thorn in Paul's body there would be no spiritual value. That power of life is manifested in the thorn. Only the foolish tries to reduce his thorn. When the thorn disappears the word disappears, and the ministry fades away. The power of our word lies in the thorn we endure.

Hence the ministers of the word are those who are chosen by God to be dealt with first, to be tried first, and to know the Lord first, so that they may minister Christ to God's children. Because they have endured beforehand, therefore they can help others. Due to their much endurance they are able to give to many. Unless we do not care to be a minister of God's word, we must be tried in advance and endure much more than ordinary people are called to endure. God has established us to be ministers, and not to a few but to the entire church. We are called to supply the needs of many. We must therefore endure before others do, and more than the rest. Otherwise, how can we help the many?

Whether a minister has abundant words or not depends on how much he has been tried by the Lord. We should not expect God to deal with us slowly and fragmentarily. What we endure must provide for the needs of many; thus we must endure all which the others will be called to endure. Why are some brothers easily depleted in words? It is because they have not received very much dealing from God. One must be dealt with in a great amount before he can become a minister of the word. If an individual has received much dealing, then he will have a word for different brothers in various needs.

A minister should be rich in words. Richness in dealing produces the richness in word. Fiery trials yield abundant words. A wide range of testings enables one to meet the diverse needs of man. Accordingly, it is the one who "has" who can serve; it is also the one who has "much" who can serve. Merely having is inadequate to supply the various needs of the man. We need to have rich reserves, or else we are unable to solve people's problems. Thank God, Paul's ministry is a comprehensive one, because he has come through a great deal. What he has experienced makes up his comprehensive ministry. If we expect to have a big ministry we should be ready to receive more dealings.

The Aim of the Supply of Words

What is the aim of our supplying people with words? Is it solely to help them through their difficulties? There is a specific purpose in the supply of words, even to help people to know the Lord. All revelations are the revealing of Christ; the absence of this reduces the value of revelation to nothing. The ultimate end of the supply of words is to bring dead men to knowledge of the Lord. God places us in such an environment that we will meet difficulties. Our great need drives us to seek the Lord. We must realize that the discipline of the Holy Spirit indicates our need to us each time. The Holy Spirit shows us our need through His specifically arranged circumstances. There is no way to get through except by an intimate knowledge of the Lord. How can people know Him if they have no need? Paul would not be able to know the grace of the Lord if he did not have the thorn. When one is tried in fire it is more than just a matter of how to get through; he ought to know the Lord through this trial. Paul does not bite his lips and say, "All right! I will endure it!" Instead he claims: "I have known grace." This is the way to know the Lord.

For this reason God consistently uses the discipline of the Holy Spirit to make us realize a need which none but the Lord Himself can supply. Each need enables us to know a particular facet of our Lord. Paul's knowledge of the power of the Lord comes through his weakness. In suffering he apprehends grace. The thorn makes him weak, but it also shows him grace. The Lord puts him in weakness that he might know power, puts him in suffering that he might know grace. Need brings in knowledge. Each particular need imparts a special knowledge.

To be perfect in the knowledge of the Lord naturally requires many trials. How can one know the Lord perfectly if his trials are few? You may be familiar with many of the facets of the Lord, yet you may still be lacking in the knowledge of a particular side of Him. If you desire to know Him, then know Him perfectly. Any lack in receiving the discipline of the Holy Spirit results in a deficiency in the knowledge of the Lord. If the discipline you receive is imperfect you will have no word to supply others. Let us ask God to discipline us. Let Him place us in various environments so as to be tried on all sides and yet allowing Him to carry us through them daily. As we live daily in such conditions the Lord will give us plenty of opportunity to know Him more. Each new dealing, each new discipline, awards us with a new knowledge. Thus our knowledge of Christ is increased day by day. We are able to supply the church with the Christ we know.

What then is the word? The word is Christ. The word one gets in trial and under discipline comes from one's knowledge of Christ. How very lacking is the knowledge of Christ among millions of God's children today. Many know the Lord in only one or two aspects. They need ministers of the word to help them towards a richer knowledge of the Lord. Due to their manifold trials these ministers of the word have come to know Him in His various facets; hence they do possess many-sided words. Their words are for the supply of Christ. Therefore, God's word is God's Son, God's word is Christ. What we recognize in the word is what we know of Christ. In the church some are deficient in their knowledge of Christ in one area, some are lacking in another area; but if we have received the mercy of God and have had experiences in these particular areas, we are able to use words to supply their needs. We can supply what they lack because we have learned the lessons. If our ministry is established on this foundation our word will be God's word.

Sometimes we make use of others' experience. But using the experience of others is not an easy thing because it tends to over-activate our mind if we are not careful. Many clever persons, having no experience of their own, are continually employing others' experience. They themselves are empty and useless before God. It is necessary for us to have our own dealings in the Lord before we are really able to utilize the experiences of other people. If we need to nurture our own experience in the spirit, we must cultivate the experience of others in the spirit. Only what is preserved in the spirit is living.

You can only make others know the body of Christ if you yourself know what the body of Christ is and also have nurtured that knowledge in your spirit. You are permitted to use the experience of others only if you have that thing in your own spirit. If you are an individualist, having no understanding nor possession of the reality of the body of Christ, you should not use the experience of other people. You yourself must be living in the body of Christ, and you must have nurtured this experience in your spirit before you can supply others with the words of reality. Otherwise, all that you say will be mere theories and of no avail. You might consider your speech as most logical and coherent, but you have not touched the real thing. And those who hear you are also unable to touch reality.

This same principle is applicable to the use of the Bible. Today you wish to use the Scriptures. You are touched by a particular point; immediately five or more verses come to you. You should nurture these verses in your spirit, not in your mind. What you thus reserve in the spirit is that which you can give to others. Having the thing but not nurturing it in the spirit is useless. The experience you had five years ago must be nurtured in your spirit. For only in this way can your spirit use it when necessary. Even Scripture verses, if your spirit is unable to use them, cannot be employed for ministry.

It all comes down to this: that our words must be created in us by God. They are not what we ourselves conceive nor are they learned from others; they are created in us by God. After many years of refining, a few words come forth. They are the product of years of chiseling. They are constituted in us by the Holy Spirit. These words are entrusted to us by the Lord. They are truly spoken by us; nevertheless they are still God's word. We have learned them through deep valleys. They are words which have been washed and purified by God. It is clear that the source of such words can be traced to what we have seen and learned before the Lord. Such enlightened words are based upon the discipline of the Holy Spirit. Even if we quote the word of others, it must still be based upon the Holy Spirit's discipline. In order to speak forth something from the heights we need to learn it down in the depths. Only what we have seen in the spirit can become light for others. The words we speak are all formed in the depths under pressure. Only the person who has passed through a special kind of trial and has learned its lesson is able to speak that particular kind of word.

Words are born in trial, suffering, defeat, and darkness. Let not a minister of the word be fearful of being led by God into such an environment. If one understands God's ways he can begin to praise the Lord, saying, "Oh Lord, are You giving me words again?" You may be ignorant the first few times, not knowing why you have been brought into such an environment, but thereafter you surely shall begin to understand. You should know that each trial produces some word. As the number of trials increase, so your word is enriched. You become wise in the way of obtaining word. A minister of the word must walk before the church not only in words but especially in trials. If you fail to walk ahead in the discipline of the Holy Spirit, you have absolutely no word to supply the church. This is a most serious matter. You must walk ahead of the church in trial if you would desire to have something with which to serve the church, else all your words are empty. You are deceiving the church as well as your own self. That beautiful hymn, "Let us meditate on the story of the vine," climbs higher and higher in its sentiment till it points out at the end that he who forsakes most has most to give. If you have forsaken nothing, you have nothing to give. The ministry of the word is founded on the words from within. There is the source of our word.

Finally, let us not forget that fundamental law which Paul tells us of in the first chapter of 2 Corinthians: "We do not want you to be unaware, brethren, of our affliction which came to us in Asia, that we were burdened excessively, beyond our strength, so that we despaired even of life; indeed, we had the sentence of death within ourselves" (vv.8,9). What does the sentence of death work out in him? He tells us by saying that God has a definite purpose, and that this purpose is that under the circumstances he may be able to rely not on himself but on the God who raises the dead, and that he may be so comforted by God that he may also be used to comfort others under the same trial: "Just as the sufferings of Christ are ours in abundance, so also our comfort is abundant through Christ. But if we are afflicted, it is for your comfort and salvation; or if we are comforted, it is for your comfort, which is effective in the patient enduring of the same sufferings which we also suffer; and our hope for you is firmly grounded, knowing that as you are sharers of our sufferings, so also you are sharers of our comfort" (vv.5-7)

This explains the underlying principle of the ministry of the word. We are tested first in all sorts of trials so that afterwards we may supply others with what we have learned. We ourselves are comforted, so we may comfort others with our comfort. Dare we speak on a lower level? We ought to speak with words which are learned through many refinings. Many words and many illustrations we cannot use, for in using them we will lessen the power of our speaking. We must learn to speak accurately in our ordinary conversation. The Lord will refine us until our words run fairly close to the words in the Bible. Learn to use the words and phrases God uses. The words of a minister of the word must be inwardly refined.

Since our words have their source in discipline, how can we despise the discipline of the Holy Spirit? Whatever does not come from His discipline is empty words. They can never give supply to the church. Brethren, do not despise the chastening of the Lord, but learn the lessons of these fiery trials.

14 The Word and Memory

Another thing of which a minister of the word must take note is memory, the power to remember. It occupies a much larger place in ministry than we usually think. We have much to learn in this respect.

Need for Memory

When one is ministering he invariably senses the inadequacy of his memory. He may be endowed with a strong memory naturally, but when it comes to ministry he discovers his incompetency. This incompetency affects the outgoing of the words, seems to keep such outgoing covered as by a veil, and so hinders the burden from being discharged. We can only say what we remember, not what we do not remember. How does the inward word uphold the spoken word? How does the former flow out? Without the support of the inner word there will be no spoken word. If the inward word is absent, the spoken word must change its subject, for the subject is in the inward word and not in the spoken word. The second needs the backing of the first, or else it will wither away. Here then is the significance of memory. It is through recall that the inward word is transported to the outside. Whenever our memory fails, our burden ceases to be discharged.

A strange experience common to all the ministers of the word is that the more you remember doctrine the less you recall revelation. You may understand teaching, be quite clear on it, and remember it well. But with revelation it is different. You receive an inner revelation, you see the light, and succeed in fixing that light; you are also given a few words with which to express what you have just seen. Strange to say, though, you find it difficult to remember these words. They may be simple, perhaps only five or ten of them. Humanly speaking they should be easy to remember. Yet to your amazement, the truer the revelation and the greater the inward seeing, the harder (in actual fact) for you to remember the words. When you rise up to minister, you forget the words within a few minutes. Frequently you mix up the order of the words; occasionally you leave out some of them; and at other times you are able to recollect them with great effort but forget the thing itself. Thus you begin to realize how difficult it is to preserve God's revelation in man's memory. You start to learn to pray, "Oh Lord, be gracious to me that I may remember."

You have to support the spoken word with the inner word. Due to the inadequacy of memory, however, you often fail to have the supply ready. The longer you speak, the farther you drift away from the inward word. After you finish delivering the sermon you find your inner word remains untouched. You came with a burden, yet you return with the same burden. You have not been able to discharge it. This is a great suffering to you. Perhaps you say, "I will write it down in my notebook; then I will remember." This may or may not help, for an unusual thing happens: as you read your notes you recognize every word of them, but you cannot recall the thing behind the words. How totally inadequate is your memory. If what you have is mere doctrine or teaching you are well able to deliver it. The more doctrinal it is, the easier you remember. But it is not easy to recall revelation. In attempting to communicate your inward revelation you must come to realize that you cannot remember what you have just seen. The words you may remember, yet the thing itself is forgotten. Our problem on the platform is that we forget the thing we have seen. We may say many words, yet none communicates the thing we see. The ministry suffers loss. How necessary it is to have memory.

The memory we need is of two kinds: the outward memory and the Holy Spirit memory. A minister of the word needs both.

The outward memory points to the memory of the outward man, that which is produced in a man's brain. It occupies a very important place in testifying the word of God. The Holy Spirit memory is what the Lord Jesus mentions in John 14.26: "But the Helper, the Holy Spirit, whom the Father will send in My name, He will teach you all things, and bring to your remembrance all that I said to you." This is the Holy Spirit memory, for it is the Holy Spirit who brings things to your remembrance, not you yourself.

The Holy Spirit Memory

In our spirit we see something; we are able to fix it in our mind and we are also given inward words. These inward words contain the thought we have as well as the light we receive. God gives us a few words which are called words of revelation. Revelation means seeing, lifting the veil so that light shines and we see the thing behind the veil. When we see that inner reality we at first cannot express it. God grants us sufficient mental power to hold the light and translate it into our own thought—as though photographing the thing. He also grants us words to embrace all the meaning of the revelation. The words God gives include the whole meaning of what is behind the enlightenment. Such words of revelation are therefore seeing words. They are more than words, for they speak of our inward seeing and inward revelation. These words in us are simultaneously a seeing.

What actually are these inward words? They are the utterance of the revelation in me. They are more than simply five or ten words; they utter what I have perceived within. Seeing originally was the function of my eyes, not of my lips. I may be most clear inwardly but unable to utter what is within me. Now God gives me words to embody that light as well as to enable me to utter that which I have seen.

Such words need memory to accommodate them. I must remember two things: the words and the light. Let us call the recollection of the words the outward memory, and that of the light the Holy Spirit memory. Wherein does our difficulty today lie? It is that often we remember the words with our outward memory, but lose the Holy Spirit memory—that is, we cannot recall the light. Words we recollect, but sight we forget. There is no such problem in the realm of doctrine or teaching, because we can memorize and deliver every word and so our task is done. Doctrine stops at the outward. The ministry of the word, however, is to touch life. The more doctrinal, the easier to be remembered and to be uttered. The more full of life the inward seeing is, the easier to be forgotten. We may recall every word but lose sight of the reality. This is due to some defect in our Holy Spirit memory. Only in this way will the words be living. Whenever these inward words are separated from the Holy Spirit memory they change from spiritual to material. All spiritual things can turn material if care is not exercised.

Inward words may easily plunge into outward death. Spiritual words may quickly be materialized. To insure their effectiveness spiritual words must be kept alive in the Spirit. Words of revelation need to be nurtured in the Holy Spirit or else you may recall the words but not the revelation. It is relatively common, for example, to know the uncleanness and the repugnancy of sin. Some see this on the first day of their faith in the Lord; others are awakened to it at the time of revival. The first ones see the repugnancy of their sin immediately upon hearing the glad tidings, whereas the others live such a loose life that it may not be until three to five years later that they are revived by the Holy Spirit to be convicted of it.

Once a certain brother was convicted of his sin. He was so overwhelmed by it that he rolled on the floor from eight in the evening until dawn. Others had long left the meeting hall, but he remained there rolling as though he had come to the gate of hades. "Even though I go to hell," he cried out, "it still is less than I deserve!" During that night the Lord showed him the repugnancy of sin. He saw it in his spirit, and he was able to tell others of the hatefulness of sin. As is written in a hymn, he saw sin as black as smoke, and nothing is darker than smoke. With just those few words he was able to utter his inward revelation.

Many were helped. Even so, after two or three years his revelation gradually grew dim. The words "sin black as smoke" were still with him, but when he rose to speak, the picture was no longer there. The revelation of the Holy Spirit had faded away; it was no longer as distinct and powerful as before. Formerly when he preached on the blackness of sin it was with tears in his eyes; now he spoke with a smile. The taste was different. The words were the same, but the Holy Spirit memory was absent.

One day the Lord may show you the sinfulness of sin as found in Romans 7.13—"that through the commandment sin might become utterly sinful." You see the sinfulness of sin and you are terrified by the word "sin." It is possible, though, that within a few days afterwards you may still recall the words "sinful beyond measure," and yet the picture is missing. At the time you see the sinfulness of sin before God sin is present and is the image before you. When you subsequently stand to speak on that subject, however, the words may remain with you but the picture has disappeared. We call the picture the Holy Spirit memory.

As a minister of the word you need the Holy Spirit memory which enables you to recall not only the words but the picture also. Hence each time you rise up to speak you should ask the Lord to grant you the Holy Spirit memory so that when the words are uttered the reality may also be sent forth. Otherwise, after you have spoken ten or twenty times on the repugnancy of sin you yourself may become confused. Only when you once again see the sinfulness of sin in the Holy Spirit memory are you able to present the picture as well as speak the words. That is the word of God. *Words plus the picture.* Brethren, do you realize that God's word needs to have that picture? Words alone cannot be considered as God's word. There must be the reality behind them.

Let us use another example. Suppose you are preaching on the love of the Lord. While you speak you have the picture with you. You speak according to the picture; and it is effective. Frequently, though, you speak of how God loves you yet you yourself do not quite sense that love. How then can you expect others to believe? You are in need of the Holy Spirit memory. It is He who gives you that picture, that reality of the Lord's love. As you present the reality to others, the more you speak the more that reality is touched and the more abundantly life flows. Without the Holy Spirit memory, words are only words—correct, yet not real. Therefore when you preach the word of God you must look for the Holy Spirit memory to enable you to recall both the revelation and inward words God has given to you. Speaking according to the inward words will bring out life, and people will see what you have seen.

Probably many have been saved through the words in John 3.16. But suppose you merely recite the words, even to the tenth time; do you think they will be effective? To make it once more effective it requires the Holy Spirit to recall from your memory what you saw in that verse when you were saved.

Many feel the preciousness and loveliness of the Lord after their sins are forgiven. They receive an inward revelation which distinctly shows them how very precious the Lord is, for the one whose many sins are forgiven loves much. He has seen the Lord and he has the words as well as the thought in them. He can speak for an hour or two, pouring out what is within him; and those who hear feel the anointing and are helped. After some days have passed, he may once again speak on this subject. He remembers the words perfectly; they are just the same; yet the more he continues speaking the less it seems to be the real thing. He has forgotten the reality. The words are there, yet the love is missing. He lacks the Holy Spirit memory. All revelations must be kept in His memory.

Hence the one who desires to be a minister of the word needs to be one who has a good Holy Spirit memory. The better that memory the richer the ministry, because there will be much that is living in the minister. If our Holy Spirit memory is faulty, many of our revelations will have to be re-revealed. This is a very pitiable condition. Before God such a one must not only have the revelation of the Spirit, he must have it again and again in ever growing measure. Thirty years ago when you were saved you received a revelation from the Lord. Later on He gave you more and more revelation. In other words, revelation grows. What you saw at the time of salvation is the basic revelation which must grow progressively. A minister of the word nurtures all the revelations he has received in his Holy Spirit memory. And consequently all that he has is living.

Let us use the hatefulness or abhorrence of sin once again as another illustration. Such abhorrence must be fresh in your memory when you speak; otherwise you may talk about it but it will be totally ineffective because you are serving overnight manna or even last year's manna. Many brothers rise to preach the gospel; some, you notice, have the Holy Spirit memory; others do not. This is something beyond pretension. Its presence or absence is unequivocal. However high and deep is the revelation, it must be kept alive in the Holy Spirit memory. How strange it seems that even at the very first delivery of a word we may have already forgotten the reality of what we have beheld in the spirit. It may be forgiveable to have forgotten the abhorrence of the sin which you saw ten or fifteen years ago, but what about forgetting the revelation you received only last night? A revelation must therefore be remembered in us by the Holy Spirit.

We can use still another example. Some years ago a brother saw the big difference between touching the Lord and pressing the Lord, between that which is spiritual and that which is merely objective. He saw it most vividly at that time and he was full of joy. A few days passed. He went to visit a sick brother. He tried to share with that sick brother what he had seen, but he was simply circling around. He tried desperately to recall what he had seen; he even perspired; yet the more he talked the less meaningful it felt in him. This is because he had not learned to nurture the revelation in the Holy Spirit memory. Only when the word of revelation is nurtured there can you use it when you minister.

In addition to revelation, thought, and inward and spoken words, there must also be the Holy Spirit memory. Its absence affects both the inward and the outward spoken words. No one can depend on his natural strength. Whoever you may be, your natural strength is incompetent in the ministry of the word. Only the fool is proud of himself. How can you boast if you cannot recall even what you saw yesterday? You may try to recollect till your head aches, nonetheless you still do not remember. To supply spoken words with the inward words of revelation requires the Holy Spirit memory. This alone enables you to speak what the Lord wants you to and to use spiritual words instead of merely objective words. If this is not so, your spirit will fade out at your speaking.

It is therefore evident that when the Lord is working in us, to be a minister of the word is easy; but when He is not working, nothing is harder than being a minister. God's demand on a minister of the word is exacting. May He be gracious to us that we may have His memory so that we may remember the revelation together with the words. As we speak we will have the reality with us. To lose sight of the thing while speaking will upset us. The longer we talk the more confused we will become. We will not know what we are talking about. Brethren, let us acknowledge the futility of our natural brain.

The Outward Memory

Next we shall consider the outward memory. This may or may not be employed by the Lord, as He pleases. We are not able to explain why this is so; we can only mention the fact.

Frequently your condition may be as follows: you have the inward words, the words of revelation; you also have the Holy Spirit memory. But the latter needs the help of your own memory. The Spirit will bring things to your remembrance, but He does not create another memory for you. Review what John 14.26 declares: "and bring to *your* remembrance all that I have said to you." The Spirit of God in you is living, and the revelation God gives is nurtured in the Holy Spirit. Before you go to preach, God gives you two words, two key words. If you are able to remember these two words the Holy Spirit memory can also recall the revelation. If you forget these two words the Holy Spirit memory will also be lost. To protect yourself from forgetting you may write down these important words. Often at the sight of these words your inner picture reappears and you again see the revelation.

The outward memory is therefore at times used by the Holy Spirit. However, what you have written may sometimes fail to bring back the picture. That is why this outward memory may or may not be used of God. If only the outward memory remains and the inward revelation is gone, then of course nothing can be done. Usually the more revelation you receive the more effective is your outward memory. As the Holy Spirit memory increases in you your outward memory is correspondingly purified. The purer the thing the easier to be remembered, both inwardly and outwardly. At first your inward memory may not be able to compare with your outward memory. Do not be discouraged. For as your experiences multiply you will find these two memories getting closer until they become one. Hence we must humble ourselves before God. Pray much and wait more. After you are clear within, go out and preach. The inward words must be in the revelation of the Holy Spirit before we can ever speak.

Occasionally people praise you after your preaching, but you yourself know you have not been able to recall the thing. Your inward memory was disconnected from your outward memory. What you have said was perfectly right, but the revelation was dim and blurred. As ministers of the word we need to learn before God to have both the Spirit memory and the outward memory. The Holy Spirit memory must be placed between revelation and the word so that it may supply the inward words; while our own memory must be placed between the inward words and the spoken words so that it may support the spoken words.

We have noticed three steps (leaving thought temporarily aside): first, enlightenment; second, the inward words; and third, the outward words. Put the Holy Spirit memory between the first and the second, and our own memory between the second and the third. Between enlightenment and the inward words stands the Holy Spirit memory, for it uses the enlightenment to supply the inward words. The inward words need to be supplied with the enlightenment of the Holy Spirit. Without that, the words are dead—merely objective and unspiritual. Through the Holy Spirit memory, light shines on the inward words, which in turn live in the enlightenment. Our own memory then supplies the outward words so as to make us articulate.

But let us be reminded that this outward memory can never be a substitute for the inward memory, since oftentimes the Holy Spirit memory does not take up our outward memory.

A warning needs to be sounded here. Our outward memory may sometimes strongly obstruct the Holy Spirit memory. Our inward words may be full of light and life as the Holy Spirit enables us to remember that enlightenment, but if we cannot recall outwardly those few key words then they are blocked from going forth. Nothing is wrong inside; the problem is with the outside. If you are busy with many things throughout the day and evening, naturally you are unable to recall many words. Or if your thoughts are loose or you have many cares, the three or five words which the Lord gives you will soon be forgotten. It may be a help if you write these words down so that you may restore the thing and revitalize your inner revelation.

Each time you minister the word the Holy Spirit has many words to say. You need to be careful not to over-emphasize one part while overlooking another. For example, the Holy Spirit may have three things in mind but you may let two of them slip from your memory. These will become a load to your ministry. How can you minister well if you lose something? Within a certain revelation God may want you to mention two or three problems. If you forget and let some slip by they will make you feel very uneasy. Hence in taking down any word be sure that these few words cover all the things to be mentioned, lest you skip over something. It is bearable if you miss the last point, but it is disastrous to forget the first point. The entire ministry would then be spoiled.

How serious is the ministry of the word! Let us not offend the Holy Spirit in this. Do not think it does not matter if you skip over only one of the five words. If you skip over what you should have said, you will come to feel heavier and heavier as you drone on. This is because you have failed to give the words which the Lord intended for His children.

A minister of the word must not fail here. Mention three things if the Lord wants you to speak on three things; five if He so wishes. Any failure will intensify the load. If everything is said except the one thing which ought to be said, the light of that one thing will overwhelm you and make you miserable. Let us therefore exercise our memory. We must guard against any defect in it. May God show us the way of ministry. Our outward memory is only a slave to the Holy Spirit memory. Yet if this slave fails, it impedes the usefulness of the Holy Spirit memory. May our memory be renewed for the use of the Holy Spirit. That is why our thought life must be dealt with. Our memory must be disciplined until it is usable. How important recollection is in the ministry of the word. Its failure means the end of a revelation.

Memory and Quoting the Scriptures

As we deliver the word of God we should be like the apostles—that is, we should quote the Scriptures. They quoted the Old Testament, but we quote both the New and the Old. What we say must be based on the written word, on the Old and the New Testaments. A difficulty is present with us today, however. If we are less careful, we may run away with the Bible—we may speak on the New Testament as well as on the Old Testament but fail to discharge the burden of the day. If so, our burden will become heavier when we arrive home. We frequently have no control over our memory at the time of speaking. We can easily be carried away by a passage in the Old or in the New Testament. We return home deeply reproved in our conscience because we have spent all our time in talking about the Bible, in preaching on the doctrine, whereas we have not discharged the burden which God laid upon us.

Consequently all the while we are speaking we should check

to see if our burden is being discharged. We speak one word or many words; we quote from the Old or the New Testament; nonetheless all of these are only engaged to draw out the word which God has given us for today. Otherwise, people may as well gather and read the Bible together; why should we come and speak? We must say not only what the Old and New Testament say; we must also utter the words God gives to us.

The ministry of the word is a most subjective thing in a man. We have words to speak which God gave before, and we have words to say which God gives today. We must let out not only the words of the Old and New Testament but our words as well. We speak the word through the Old Testament and through the New, and afterwards with our own words. Our words should be strong and rich. As they are delivered they should pierce and cut so as to let out life. As life continues to flow, the burden is gradually discharged. By the time we cease speaking, the burden is entirely released. Even if our words are not as we wish, so long as the burden is lifted the job is done. There will be fruit. One thing is very certain: if a burden is discharged God's children will surely see light. Under such circumstances as these failure to see light is due to some difficulty in the audience, not to the speaker. But if the burden fails to be discharged the difficulty lies with the speaker, not with the audience.

Let us learn something important before God: the minister of the word has a burden, words are used to discharge that burden, and the Holy Spirit memory is necessary for this discharge. But even with the Holy Spirit memory, care should be exercised lest we be carried away by the truth we find in the New or in the Old Testament. Always keep in mind that our responsibility is to bring God's current words to men. We are not to teach the Bible and forget what God has shown us. If we forget the word given to us, then no matter how much we say and though strange as it may seem, we will continue to have that one thing pressing in on us. It is possible Satan is trying to obstruct. Our thoughts must be rich and our memory strong as we give our very best for the discharge of the burden.

15 | The Word and Feeling

As was mentioned earlier, a minister of the word must be attentive to four things. Two of these come from God: enlightenment and inward words. Two come from the minister himself: thought and memory. Moreover, in the process of speaking he is in need of two more things: a usable feeling and a usable spirit.

The Spirit Flows through the Channel of Feeling

In reading the Bible we discover that those who were used to write its words shared a common characteristic, which is that their feelings did not obstruct them. On the contrary, their feelings were *expressed* in their writings. One thing worth noticing is that whether or not the spirit is able to come forth is often determined by our feeling. If man's feeling is unusable his spirit has no way of flowing freely. The outflowing of man's spirit depends not so much on his will or on his mind as upon his emotions, for the spirit flows mainly through the channel of the feelings. If the feeling is blocked the spirit is obstructed. If the feeling is cold the spirit is likewise cold; if the feeling is dry so is the spirit; if the feeling is calm the spirit too is calm.

Why do God's children frequently mix up spirit and feeling? They can distinguish spirit from will, since that difference is great. They can also divide spirit and mind, because the distinction in this case is quite sharp. But to discern what is of the spirit and what is of emotion seems to be extremely difficult. Why? Because the spirit cannot come out independently; it often flows through feelings. What the spirit relies on in expressing itself is not man's thought or will, but his emotion. Hence many find it hard to distinguish spirit from feeling. Though these are two absolutely different faculties, nonetheless one is expressed through the other. Let us use an illustration. That which lights up is the bulb. Electricity and bulb are two entirely distinct things, yet they cannot be separated. In like manner is the relationship between spirit and feeling. They are two separate entities; even so, the spirit frequently is expressed through the feeling; they are inseparable. Yet this does not imply that spirit and feeling are one and the same thing. Only to those unlearned in the Lord's way does feeling seem to be one and the same with spirit and vice-versa, just as someone might consider electricity and the bulb as one.

When a minister is speaking, his inner man must be released; but this in turn depends upon his feeling. If the latter is unusable the spirit is stuck. No matter how much electricity may be stored in the power company, if there is no electric bulb there will be no light. And by the same token, no matter how excellent is the condition of our spirit, it will be severely hampered if our feeling is unusable. The spirit flows through the channel of emotion. A minister of the word must therefore have a usable feeling as well as a free spirit. If emotion refuses to listen to the spirit or fails to cooperate with it, the spirit is inevitably arrested. For the sake of letting his inner being come out freely, man must have a usable feeling. Now we shall see how a feeling can be useful.

We human beings have a will, but the will of man is rather rugged. So have we a mind, which, though more refined than the will, is nevertheless quite rugged too. But the emotion which we possess is the most delicate part in us. We may ruthlessly make a decision with our will, we may carefully think over a matter, but we touch the tenderest spot when something touches our feeling. Accordingly, in the Old Testament, especially in the Song of Songs, the Spirit of God employs fragrance or savor to express the tender feeling of man, for it can only be smelled with the nose. Smelling is a most delicate act. It represents man's tender feeling. "Nose" in the Scriptures stands for feeling. Man's feeling is most delicate, though it may or may not be useful.

Every time a minister speaks he needs to mix his feeling with the words spoken, else his words are dead. Before he speaks, he must have memory and thought; when he speaks, the first thing to be added is his feeling. If it fails to flow together with his words, he is finished.

The Lord Jesus told his disciples a parable. "To what shall I compare this generation? It is like children sitting in the market place and calling to their playmates, 'We played the flute for you, and you did not dance; we (wailed), and you did not mourn'" (Matt. 11.16,17). This implies that if there is feeling, one has to dance when he is piped to or has to mourn when wailed at. Even so, a minister of the word cannot afford to have his feeling different and separate from his words. Otherwise, this will disqualify him from speaking before God. You cannot speak mournful words without mournful emotion. If you do not possess the right emotion you cannot be a minister of the word.

Now of course the emotion we here mention is not a matter of performance. In any theatrical performance the feeling is something put on. A minister should never use human ingenuity in putting on a show while speaking. As he is speaking he must actually have the feeling of each word. He should have a mournful feeling when he uses sad words. How does a man's spirit give expression to its mourning? Through his mournful feeling. And when happy words are said his feeling should be one of happiness, for the joy of the spirit comes through a joyful emotion.

Let us understand that the coming forth of words alone is not enough; the spirit must also come out, and when it does it will do so together with feeling. If our feeling lags behind, our words are stripped of the spirit. If our feeling is too hard, it renders itself unusable. Feeling is the most delicate part of man. A little hardening will deprive the word of its spirit. To be useful, a certain kind of word must be accompanied by the same kind of spirit. If it does not agree with the word the latter is damaged and becomes useless.

In speaking, we must send forth the right kind of spirit with the right kind of word. Any discrepancy will render the word ineffectual and the ministry void. The word and the spirit must be one. Yet the spirit cannot express itself alone; it needs to be expressed through feeling. How, then, can your spirit flow out if you have a feeling other than that of the spirit? It is necessary for both our feeling and our spirit to be one with God's word.

Feeling Must Accompany the Word

Not because we have word can we therefore begin to speak. If there is any obstruction in the realm of the emotions it must be removed before our words can be effective. It presents a real difficulty if God's word requires one kind of feeling but we have in us another kind of feeling. Today we are not touching the feeling of the Bible from the outside; we are speaking the words of the Bible from the inside, out from our feeling. God's feeling is embodied in His word; He demands us to have the same feeling in ourselves. Then as we speak, our feeling will be one with our words. Thus shall we be able to impart our feeling to others. Hence our feeling goes out with our words and the Holy Spirit goes out with our feeling.

Where does our problem arise today? It is this: that we have both revelation and word and yet we see no fruit. Why is this so? Because our spirit fails to go forth. This in turn is due to the failure of our feeling. The Holy Spirit does not find the proper emotion in us upon which He "may ride." There can be no fruit if the emotion is unusable, even though we may have light and word. Bear in mind that feeling is most necessary in the delivery of the word. Before the delivery, we touch enlightenment, thought, inward words, memory, and spoken words; later, at the time of delivery, feeling must follow suit.

The Holy Spirit touches men through right feeling. We would repeat that trying to move men with only our emotion is a mere performance, resulting in a dead ministry. Yet we use emotion to move people as our spirit is released and as the Holy Spirit too is released. To put it another way, the going forth of the word is powerful only when it is coupled with a corresponding emotion, for then the Holy Spirit will work in people. The first hurdle for a minister of the word to overcome when speaking lies within himself—his own difficulty in the matter of feeling.

A brother may stand up to speak when he has a burden to discharge, yet he meets his first hindrance in himself. His word does not go far; it is obstructed; it is not free; it has no outlet. His main difficulty is himself. He may be speaking on the love of the Lord, yet he does not feel the love. The question is not as to whether he has seen the Lord's love but whether he senses the loveliness of the Lord while speaking. Or, to take another example, he may have seen the hatefulness of sin, but when he stands to speak on it he lacks a corresponding feeling. His emotion is not one with his word. The lack of feeling on his part will result in a lack of feeling on the part of his audience.

Just precisely what is the purpose of supplying people with words? Is it not because they are lacking in a particular feeling, thought, light? You have seen the abhorrence of sin; they have not; and you want them to see it. Even so, unless you have the sense of the abhorrence of sin as you speak, your words will not produce the same sense in others. You purpose to try to get through to their feeling that they too may see. How can you pierce their feeling, though, if you yourself lack this feeling or if your feeling is not usable?

George Whitefield specialized in the topic of hell. Once he was speaking on that subject at a certain place. Before he had finished his message some were found holding tight to the pillars of the hall lest they fell into hell. This was because when he spoke he saw sinners falling away into hell. As his words were sent out with his feeling, the Holy Spirit as well as his own spirit sallied forth to convict people of hell.

If you are careless about speaking you will not sense the inadequacy of your feeling, for everything is basically wrong. But if you truly come to minister the word you will see first of all that your feeling will not do. You will then know that the most formidable obstacle to your word lies in your own self. You may have a weighty word in you, yet you find yourself defeated as you speak on, since your feeling lags behind. Your words may be serious, nevertheless the longer you speak the less serious they become. You simply are lacking in that serious feeling. As you continue on you seem less and less concerned. Since your emotion does not correspond to the words, you try to raise your voice and shout. Many brothers shout with their voices. However, they shout not to be heard by others but to be heard by themselves. You are helpless, so you shout. You are aware that your feeling is inadequate.

Many spend half their strength convincing themselves while speaking on the platform. This is because their feeling is so unusable. We need to bring our own feeling into conviction before we can communicate God's word to others. Though our words seem to be directed at them we are actually speaking to ourselves, because we are the real obstacle to that word. How necessary it is for us to discover on the platform that we are the hindrance. We truly wish to deliver God's word; but we lack its corresponding feeling. Our feeling is unusable, with the result that we hinder the word from going out.

How absolutely needful a usable feeling is to a minister of the word. Any inadequacy there will hinder the outgoing of the word. This is most serious. Frequently the trouble is that though we have the word, our feeling is at variance with that word. We know quite well the seriousness of the word, yet our feeling is not so serious. In speaking, the feeling ought to come forth with the words; but our feeling fails to follow. Who will believe us if we speak without feeling it? We may raise our voice ever louder, yet all is of no avail. We ourselves sense how tasteless it is; we may even feel like laughing, for it appears to be a performance. How, in that event, can we expect others to believe in our words? Only when we feel our own words and believe our own words can we hope that others may do so also. Otherwise our words are powerless; neither the Holy Spirit nor our spirit is released.

How to Cultivate a Delicate Feeling

We need to know not only how to use our feeling but also how to secure a usable feeling. This leads us back to the foundational experience of having our outward man broken by the Lord. When we were on the topic of the minister himself we especially noted the significance of our outward man being broken. This alone insures the going forth of the Lord's word through us. If our outward man is not broken the Lord can use very little of us. Here too must we emphasize the necessity for the Lord to break our outward man that our emotion may be made ready for the ministry of the word.

For the one who is under His dealing God orders all sorts of circumstances by which to break him. Each stroke opens in him a wound which gives him pain. His feeling is automatically wounded, becoming more delicate than before. Man's emotion is naturally the most sensitive area of the soul. It is more tender than will and mind. Nonetheless it does not possess enough sensitivity to be useful to God. It does not possess the degree of tenderness which is demanded of God's word. If His word is to come through, we must be filled with the feeling of His word. We must match our feeling with that of God's word. Our feeling must be able to cope with our words. Whatever emotion the word requires must be fully supplied, else the word will not be strong in others.

Upon our having received much dealing we begin to see how very coarse our feeling is. Though it is the most sensitive facet of our soul it is still too rough to be employed by God. Because of the coarseness of our feeling the word of God which comes from our lips is unevenly backed with feeling.

When a painter mixes some paint the powder must be fine. If it is coarse it cannot be spread smoothly. With fine powder the paint can be spread over all surfaces evenly. In like manner shall this happen to a minister of the word. If his feeling is coarse he may speak ten sentences, but eight out of the ten are void of proper feeling. If his feeling is delicate each sentence will be accompanied by its appropriate feeling. The Bible figuratively uses fine flour to speak of the life of the Lord Jesus. This shows how very sensitive is our Lord's feeling. How terrible it is for a brother to say many words without communicating the corresponding feeling. His emotion is not usable. It does not follow the word. It is not delicate enough. Always remember, God's word will not be strong in its delivery if our feeling is not sufficiently responsive.

We need the Lord to so work in our lives that our feeling is brought to a delicate state. We will have to be broken before our feeling will turn tender. In reading the Bible we not only see the life experiences of the writers and the thoughts of the Holy Spirit; we touch many of their spiritual feelings as well. The emotions of those who ministered the word of the Bible came forth with their words. This ought to be the same with us.

Should our feeling fail to accompany our word, we cannot expect our audience to hear us attentively. If our outward man has not been broken by the hand of God our feeling cannot be tender and delicate, for there is no wound, there has been no suffering. Where there is tender feeling, there must be wounds and suffering. The grain must be ground and broken before the powder can be fine. Under pressure, the one grain of wheat is no longer a single grain. It has become three, five, seven, even a hundred particles. It now is truly fine. The more the wounds and the deeper the suffering, the finer the feeling. Never anticipate fineness in sensitivity if you expect no wound, if you experience no suffering before God. To have wounds you must be dealt with.

Suppose there is a brother here. He has learned something in life. He has advanced in the reading of the Bible and other matters. Yet he has not developed a delicate feeling. Before God he lacks something; there is an area which God cannot use. No matter how much he seems to improve in behavior or how much light he has seen, all which he has learned thus far is shallow and superficial so long as his feeling remains inadequate. He has not learned enough. One who has had the cross worked into his life has been broken by the Lord. His stubborn will is no longer stubborn; his big brain is no longer inflated. The Lord will deal with our will; He may use a great light to break us down. We consider ourselves clever and capable. The Lord will deal with that big brain of ours. With one sweep of brilliant light He may strike us to the ground.

Nevertheless, our emotion is not transformed by one enlightenment. A fine feeling is the result of many dealings. Before we face a problem, our feeling is not delicate enough. We are careless about that matter. The Lord accordingly arranges our environment so as to refine us in this particular respect. Time after time we are ground like wheat till we are sufficiently broken.

We need to have a broken spirit before God. What is a broken spirit? It means that in us there is a broken feeling, for the spirit is expressed in feeling. The Lord wishes us to live with a broken spirit because He wants us to have a fine feeling. This we will not have until we have been stricken. We must continually experience ourselves so broken as though we were just stricken. The meaning of being stricken will always be with us. Thus shall we have a godly fear, a trembling feeling. We will not dare to be careless or flippant. Each strike, every dealing, is for the purpose of making our emotion more tender and more keen than before. This is one of the deepest lessons in the breaking of the outward man. The breaking of feeling is not as dramatic and prominent as that of will or mind, but it certainly is deeper than either of them.

If we live with a stricken spirit we will have a wound in us and sense its pain. This pain in turn will create in us a godly fear and render our feeling delicate. After many such dealings you will be able in your feeling to express fully and exactly what your heart is. You will truly be glad when your heart is glad, and you will actually grieve when your heart is grieved. Whenever the word of God comes to you, and whatever the flavor of that word is, you will have the corresponding emotion in you. Your feeling is able to catch up with the word. How glorious this is!

The effectiveness of being stricken is shown in our oneness with God's word. What God intends to say is matched by a kindred feeling of yours. As soon as God's word comes, you immediately sense it. When God moves, you respond. Your feeling is able to follow God's word right up to this point. And as the Lord increases His dealings, you are progressively being ground until all your emotions are made suitable to God. After you have been so trained in the area of feeling, you will discover a marvelous thing, which is, that you not only speak God's word, you also begin to feel God's word.

With the feeling within there comes the expression without. Peter "lifted up his voice" when he addressed the audience at Pentecost. His voice was raised because his feeling was deep. Perhaps some have never once lifted up their voice while preaching, showing how inadequate were their feelings. The depth of emotion in Peter made him lift up his voice.

The word of God is full of emotion. It should not be recited verbatim in a mechanical way. It ought to be pressed out through deep feeling. Paul exhorted the church at Corinth "with many tears." Some may never have shed any tears in their preaching, for their sensitivity is inadequate. A loud voice is indeed nothing; tears too are nothing; but if one *never* lifts up his voice nor sheds tears, something inside must be wrong. There is no merit in a loud voice, neither is there any special credit in tears; but it is an indication of unbrokenness if one has never raised his voice or shed his tears.

One's emotion must be so refined that he can rejoice when God's word is joyful and wail when the word of God is sorrowful. His feeling follows the word of God closely. This is not performance. Please never learn to perform. People with discernment immediately recognize a performance that has been falsely manufactured by man. There ought never to be any human manufacturing because it invariably spoils the word of God. What we stress is the need for feeling. Whatever feeling the word of God has, we must have the same feeling. Joy and sorrow are two distinctive examples. When the Bible says rejoice, let us be joyful; when it indicates sorrow, let us be sorrowful. This is normal and proper. Some have been tightly bound in their emotion all their lives. They are so cold that they cannot dance when piped to and cannot weep when wailed at. Because their feeling lags behind, God's word is obstructed in its delivery.

Why is it that the emotion of many cannot be used? Why

must the Lord bring people through so many trials? This is all due to the fact that feeling is essentially the person himself. The issue with emotion is quite different from that of will or mind. The latter are more complicated; the former is simple in that it is used for one's own self. Most people's emotions are spent only on themselves. They can easily feel the things that concern them, but have no sensitivity for things which concern others. Some may be extremely insensitive to all things, yet when it comes to their own affairs they are most keen. A brother may be very rude to others, but suppose you are rude to *him;* he will deeply resent it and feel hurt. All the feelings of this brother are spent on himself. He just loves himself and lives for himself. If he meets any personal difficulty he will cry, though he has absolutely no feeling toward others.

Brethren, unless the Lord has succeeded in breaking down our feeling how useless we are in the ministry of the word. Often under the discipline of the Holy Spirit the Lord's hand remains on us until we can feel for others. We need to channel all our emotion into the ministry of the word. We have no time to spend them on ourselves. Our feeling must grow in its sensitiveness. It ought not be exhausted. Many people mistakenly believe only in themselves: they reckon themselves as the center of the universe: hence all their feelings revolve around themselves. God must deliver them out of such confines. Feelings are limited by their reserves. If we spend them wantonly we will have nothing left for the ministry of the word. God will strike and deal with us till we do not feel just for ourselves, till our emotion has become sensitive. The secret of a sensitive feeling lies in not making ourselves the center. The finer we are ground the more selfless we become and the more effective will be our feeling.

A minister of the word needs to possess a sufficiently fine and rich feeling for God to use. Simply bear in mind that the richer our emotion the richer will be our word, since the quality of the word is controlled by our emotion. The amount of feeling within determines the effectiveness of the words without. If we have more words than feelings, our words will be restricted by our feeling. A man's word is measured by his brokenness before God. A spiritual man is rich in all kinds of feeling. The more spiritual a man is, the richer his feeling. It is not true that the more spiritual a man is, the less is his feeling. The more lessons one learns before God the more enriched his feeling will be. Compare the feeling of a sinner with that of Paul. You will immediately see that Paul is superior in spirituality and so is he superior in feeling. Increased dealing creates more feelings. If our feeling is rich we can match whatever feeling the word requires while we speak. God's word has then found a way whenever the feeling keeps up with the word. Otherwise, no matter what we say it somehow is not good.

One who desires to be a minister of the word must receive thorough dealing. Any negligence here will disqualify him. We must be broken before God, else we cannot undertake any work. No discipline, no work. Even if you are the cleverest person in the world, it is of no avail. Only the broken man is useful. This is an extremely serious matter. Our affections and feelings must go through repeated dealings so that when we speak, our feeling is usable. Suppose the Lord, for example, has dealt with you in the matter of self-love. After several dealings, your feeling can follow the word if you should stand up and speak on self-love. There is no hindrance to the outgoing of the word. Or again, suppose your pride has been broken by the Lord. Your feeling can easily match the word as you speak on how the Lord resists the proud. In short, only after our emotion has been touched by the Lord can it flow together with the word which we speak. This is a necessary requirement for a minister of the word. Match the word with feeling. Equalize the amount of words with the same amount of feeling. The higher our words touch, the finer must be our feeling. May God be gracious to us that all our feelings may be used to support the word.

16 The Word and the Release of the Spirit

The Relation between the Spirit and the Word

We now turn to the subject of the word and the release of the spirit. Whether the word comes forth as a revelation or a doctrine depends on whether the one who ministers is able to release his spirit or not. Whether people receive life in these words or not is also dependent on the release of the spirit of the minister. Whether men see light and are thus stricken or only hear the words and remain the same is determined by this same factor of the emancipation of the spirit. If the word and even the feeling are right but the spirit is not released, then what men encounter is not God but only a perfect doctrine.

The word may come forth void of the spirit, or it may come out with a weak spirit. A most serious message becomes common if it is delivered in a weak spirit. When the inner man is strong the word will also be strong. If the word is already right, then it is a question of under what sort of spirit the word is given. A minister of the word may deliver the word with a weak spirit, a strong spirit, or even an explosive spirit. The quality of the word is decided by the kind of spirit which delivers it. The effect of the word on people is not determined by the word itself but by the spirit with which it is delivered. A minister is able to release his spirit or to check his spirit. He can let it explode or keep it weak.

The relation between the spirit and the word is most intimate. If the spirit is touched the word becomes touching; if the spirit is checked the word loses its impact. We cannot say how much the spirit affects the word. All we can say is that man's inner being is very delicate, something which should not be offended. In the preaching of the word you may be prepared in every other respect, but if your spirit is not ready your word has no way to be released. The word needs your spirit to send it out.

All who know how to preach God's word have this experience of the release of the spirit. Let us say that a storm rages outside; the wind blows hard and the rain falls heavily. It is also pitch dark outside. Now suppose a man tries to go out but is beaten back by the storm. In order to help him someone pushes him at the back, and out he goes. This is the way the spirit sends forth the word. When you stand up to speak you must push your spirit out, else the word will suffer greatly.

Frequently you are able to give your spirit a push, and so you have a strong word. People have not only heard the word but have also met the reality in you. They touch your spirit as well as your word. Sometimes after listening to a message you can remember every word of it. Yet when you pass on the message to others you can recite the words but cannot communicate the spirit.

The same applies to studying the Bible. Some merely read the words while others meet the spirit of the Bible. Some read the words of Paul without hearing his voice. Whether his voice is low or high, light or strong, sad or glad, they are totally insensitive. But some in reading the Bible know Paul's voice as well as his words. If Paul's prayer or word is sorrowful, they know it. Whether Paul speaks with wrath or joy, they can distinguish. They have touched the spirit of Paul. When one reads the story of how Paul cast out the demon from the slave girl (Acts 16), if he has not touched the spirit, then all he knows is that the demon is cast out. Paul may be speaking with a loud, shouting voice, nevertheless the reader has no knowledge of it because he has not touched that spirit. We must enter into the spirit of those who wrote the Bible if we desire to know what they have written. All their writings are the expressions of the release of their spirit. No one can be a good student of the Bible unless he can touch its spirit as well as its words.

Going still further, it must also be emphasized that at the time of preaching it is necessary that we be dealt with by God. This is the way to release our spirit. Should anyone be lacking in this discipline of the Lord or if this discipline is not deep and pure enough, his spirit will not be able to follow God's word and he will have no strength to push forth his spirit. Someone may be able to push out his doctrine but he will be totally unable to push forth the spirit behind God's word. Let us be clear as to the nature of preaching. Preaching is not simply delivering the word; it is in addition releasing the spirit. As a minister of the word speaks he simultaneously releases his spirit. Through the word comes his spirit, and of course God's Spirit is likewise released through the man's spirit. The Holy Spirit is released together with man's spirit. If the latter is not released then it poses a big problem, because the Holy Spirit is not able to come forth either. Do not forget that listening to a message is not simply listening to the words but trying to meet the spirit.

Let us take note of this principle: that if there is a ministry of the word there must be spirit as well as word when the message is given. As the word is released, the spirit is released as well. Those who listen not only touch the words, they also touch the spirit. If only the words were touched the message would be common and weak. Even in regard to God's recorded word, if a person does not touch its spirit it will seem common to him. When the spirit is touched, life is touched. "The words that I have spoken to you," declared the Lord, "are spirit and are life" (John 6.63). Only by touching the spirit can anyone know the meaning of that word.

Hence in preaching God's word we must learn how to release our spirit. This does not mean that a person is able to release it at all times, for to do so requires a heavy cost. Frequently the ministers of the word fail to pay the cost. The stronger our spirit is before God the more able we are to release it. We trust that all who speak for God have experienced something of its release. No person will be stricken just because of words; it is only when a person has come up against the spirit that he is stricken. Word alone can easily degenerate into doctrine; even words which come through revelation are no exception. We must deliver the words of revelation with our spirit so that people may meet not only the words but also the spirit. God's Spirit comes upon men through our spirit.

The Training of the Spirit

The exercise of the spirit in a minister of the word hinges upon two factors: one, the training of the spirit, and two, the willingness of the minister. Whether or not he is able to use his spirit and to what extent he can release it when he is ministering to the church depends entirely upon how much he has learned of these two matters.

Let us discuss the training of the spirit first. No minister of the word can release more of his spirit than he has learned before God. If he has little training in this respect he can exercise his spirit only a little. If he is deeply trained he can obviously use that much more of his spirit. No one can push forth a measure of the spirit which he does not already have. This is a lesson we must understand.

Accordingly, God spends much time on us in training our spirit to be usable. He so arranges our environment that our outward man may be duly broken. He places us in circumstances completely beyond our ability to cope with, circumstances as serious as those Paul describes in 2 Corinthians 1.8-9: "we were burdened excessively, beyond our strength, so that we despaired even of life; indeed, we had the sentence of death within ourselves."

The situation which the Lord orders is usually greater than we can endure. It is beyond our own strength. Whenever a thorn comes to us it afflicts us more than we can bear. We have no way to get through. Such divinely ordained circumstances produce a two-fold result. On the one hand the Lord uses them to break down our outward man. Sometimes it is our thought which is broken, at other times it is our emotion; and most often it is our will which is cast down until we wholly yield to the Lord and acknowledge out total inability. These, though, form the negative side. On the other hand, under the discipline of the Holy Spirit God works out in us something positive. As we are being broken, do we go down or do we get up? Are we overwhelmed by the thorn or do we overcome it? When we say we are so utterly, unbearably crushed that we despair of life itself, do we thereafter rely on God who raises the dead?

Let us keep in mind that the environment which the Lord has arranged for us is something beyond our strength. It does indeed give us the sentence of death and renders us hopeless. Yet in our extreme helplessness we learn a little of believing, of hoping, of trusting. In ordinary days, how easy for us to say we believe, we hope, and we trust; but only after we are placed in a hopeless situation do we begin to learn to believe, to hope, and to trust a little.

Herein do we touch something of God's grace, something of the power by which we are unconsciously carried along. You may feel your believing is in such weakness, your hoping is with such trembling, and your trusting is with such little confidence. You conclude that your faith, hope and trust are of no avail for they are so weak. To your surprise, with this little faith, hope, and trust you unwittingly touch a little of what grace and power are. You receive mercy in your circumstances and are carried through. And your spirit has received another time of training.

Yet it is more than having the outward man broken, since it has achieved the purpose of training the spirit. It is without a doubt the negative breaking down, but it is likewise the positive building up. You discover here a circumstance which you have overcome, or rather the Lord has caused you to overcome. The Lord has enabled you to rise higher than the difficulty and you have strangely solved the problem. Although Satan spends all his strength in the circumstance, your weak faith, hope, and trust have touched the power of God. With the result that you can say to Satan, "You have done your best; though by myself I cannot overcome, thank God, I *have* overcome. He has given me hope, for He raises the dead and strengthens the weak." By going through this kind of experience your spirit has gained a little more strength, received a little more training, become a little richer, and is accordingly made more usable.

The Lord works in our lives not just once, but many times. After these many dealings our spirit waxes stronger and stronger. He builds up our inner man as well as crushes our outer man. Each time we emerge from a trial it is due to the coming out of the spirit. The latter, having been dealt with and trained by the Lord, is able to emerge first, then the whole man follows suit. The Lord is daily building us up. When we enter into trial we are hard-pressed, but when we emerge we thrust the circumstance aside and transcend it. We enter in weakness, we come out in strength. We enter in death but we exit with resurrection life.

No trial can keep us in; and when we emerge from a trial we are not the same. A trial will either break us into an unusable vessel or make us more glorious. If it does not cause us to be better it renders us worse. He who cannot stand trial is unusable. He who overcomes a trial adds one more victory to his life.

Time and again the Lord brings us in and carries us over certain circumstances. He gives us victory upon victory. There is always the next time when He arranges some new circumstance, some new difficulty, so as to give us a new victory. In other words, our spirit has something new to learn continually. Each trial enables us to rise once more above our circumstances. It gives us more strength to deal with similar cases. In this manner the spirit keeps getting stronger. It emerges from each trial sturdier than before. The Lord uses the discipline of the Holy Spirit to break our outward man; and when this outer man of ours is broken, our inner man is strengthened to overcome all difficulties.

When a hammer falls on us it breaks our outward man into pieces; nonetheless it also is the same instrument which our inner man must overcome. The Lord puts us in a certain environment. This environment breaks our outward man, for that man cannot endure any trial. Every test which comes along causes the outer man to collapse afresh, yet it additionally gives the spirit within occasion to secure one more victory. Through this dual process of the environment overcoming our outward man and our inner man overcoming environment, we emerge from the trial. This is the way we go through difficulties. The Lord gives us a trial; He allows our outward man to be broken. Yet His work does not end here; our inner man must rise up and overcome the trial. The circumstance which overcomes our outer man is the same which our inner man must overcome. Each time this happens our spirit receives further training. And in this way our spirit learns what the grace of the Lord is. Our spirit waxes stronger than before. Through such training our spirit becomes more usable at the time of ministry.

Hence a minister of the word needs the Lord to break down his outward man on the one hand and to strengthen his spirit through training on the other hand. Both of these are done by the discipline of the Holy Spirit. Please note that each one comes out of a trial a different person—either he is stronger or he is weaker. You either murmur against God and go under or you emerge in victory.

2 Corinthians 12 shows us that when the thorn is on us God gives us grace to overcome it. True, we may have known something about grace before, but it is equally as true that we did not know grace over thorns. In each trial we fall through the thorn yet also learn to know the grace over a thorn. You may have known grace without trials before, but now you know the triumph of grace over them. Suppose a boat requires two feet of water in order to float. It can sail in a river which is two feet deep. But if a rock should jut up two feet from the bottom the boat cannot pass through unless someone were to add two more feet of water to the river. So is it with us too, we learn to know grace as never before. Our spirit is verily strengthened. Paul exclaims, "I will all the more gladly boast of my weakness!" When we experience this weakness we find new strength. As we minister we are able to draw upon this strength. To what extent each minister of the word can draw strength from his spirit varies from one to another, because what God has built up in each of

them is different. The word may be the same but the spirit is different. If we desire to use our spirits they must be firm. True, we have been trained. Even so, take note of the extent to which we are trained; this determines the usability of our spirit. We can only exercise our spirit to the limit of our training.

A minister of the word should know that God is building up his ministry through each trial and difficulty. Do not be so foolish as to deem it best to flee from trial. If no thorn, then no grace, hence no power and little ministry. You may speak the word but you do not possess the strength of the spirit to push it out. You need the word; you also need a usable spirit.

The Willingness of the Minister

As a minister of the word engages his spirit he also uses his life, for it actually requires his life. Ministering before God is not only a question of having a usable spirit, it is a question additionally as to the degree of willingness on the part of the minister to exercise his spirit. Each time a person ministers the word with his spirit he pours out his life—as the Lord Jesus poured forth His own. During the evening prayer at Gethsemane the Lord warned His disciples, "The spirit is willing, but the flesh is weak" (Matt. 26.41). On the part of the disciples it was a case of being merely willing, but for the Lord Jesus He not only had a willing spirit—He was in addition ready to pour forth His life. His sweat became like great drops of blood falling upon the ground.

Consequently, the exercise of the spirit is the outpouring of our life. We expend all our power in reaching out to the spiritually weary and dead. Each time the spirit launches out, it touches man's weakness and man's death. It goes forth at great cost. It goes out as a burden, with pain and privation. The giving forth of the spirit requires one to forsake something. Whether in private conversation or in public speaking, he encounters spiritual weakness in many people. So he allows his spirit to go forth, he pushes it out to meet these weaknesses so as to destroy them. It is as if the one ministering to these needs and lacks is wrestling with them. He senses spiritual death, coldness, hardness and barrenness in many people, and his spirit therefore goes out to suppress and overcome these deaths. He rises above them and swallows up death.

Or take the case of when someone has a word from God and sees those sitting before him full of darkness; his reaction will be to push his spirit out, push it out mightily in order to break through the darkness. As he preaches God's word he is continuously under the assault of darkness. The blindness of the darkness may consume his spiritual strength; its death and weakness may swallow up all his spiritual power. Yet he stands there pushing out his spirit to break through darkness and to overcome it. This is a very costly task. It is most tiring and demands a costly price. A minister of the word may not find it necessary to pay such a heavy price each time he ministers; nonetheless he must be willing to pay it if need be.

This exercise of the spirit is governed by just how much of it is usable, for we can only use that part of it which is trained. Above that, we are powerless. But how much of our usable spirit we *can* use depends on whether we are willing. Sometimes we are deeply pressed before the Lord, hence we are willing to pay a high price to get through. At other times we may not be willing to pay the price, with the result that we send out our spirit carelessly.

It is not an easy thing for a minister to spend his spirit to the limit. A brother who does it or nearly does it finds it most tiring. A minister therefore inclines to be a little lazy, being unwilling to stretch himself to the limit. Such a statement as that can only be understood by those who know the cost of exercising their spirit. Only those who know the heaviness of a burden can appreciate these words. How can one who has never borne a load of two hundred pounds know how heavy such a load is? Only the one who has had it on his shoulders knows how much power he must exert. Each spiritual ministry, each exercising of the spirit creates in him such a burden that it literally exhausts his strength. For this reason, there is a controlling factor in the exercise of the spirit; which is, how willing are we before God? If we are willing, we may push the word out with strength. Whether our words are strong or weak depends on how much of our spirit is released. During the time of ministry the spirit is controlled by the minister. He can either restrain it or send it forth. He can strengthen or weaken the message he gives. If anyone is willing to pay the price he can make the meeting strong; if he is unwilling, he makes it common. To the one who is unlearned the working of the Holy Spirit surprises him; but the one whose life has been wrought upon deeply by the Lord knows that the Holy Spirit works according to that one's willingness to pay the price.

If in a gathering you are not afraid to get tired, nor are you lazy, neither is there anything that keeps you back, and you are perfectly willing to pay the price, then, as one who has been dealt with by God, you are willing and able to push out your spirit firmly. As your words go forth your spirit goes forth, and so people meet forceful words. On the other hand, if you feel tired and are somewhat lazy, if you are not quite willing to serve or you merely intend to fulfill your duty, then you have held back your spirit. You may say the same words but with very little or no spirit. What people meet in that event are mere words, no spirit. They hear correct words, yet weak words nonetheless.

What concerns the ministry of the word is not simply how you should speak but whether you are also willing. Should you release your spirit, people will hear strong words. But frequently the words are rather flat, because the spirit is unable to break through. Only a breaking-through spirit has impact upon people. A brother may be praying and his inner man breaks through in his prayer. Whoever stands in the way of that brother's prayer will be swept off their feet. The same words are uttered, even so, due to the gushing forth of the spirit, no one can resist.

A worker must learn how to speak accurately, but he should not stop there. He should learn how to release his spirit. If at the time of preaching your spirit is wounded or you are troubled by something, then the words you deliver will be ineffective. The more you speak the less are you in it, and the less effective your words upon those listening. Your words are hindered by your wounded spirit. Under such a condition people will not easily see God's light. You are wounded; your spirit is not released; hence your words become empty and weak. Only words pushed out by the spirit are strong. Your spirit must be mingled with your words, for they are sent out through the spirit. As this is done, people will see the light and touch the reality.

Since the release of the spirit constitutes the spiritual content of the ministry of the word, a minister must try to push out his spirit in the strongest possible way. In sending out your spirit you must call upon every power in you. All of your emotion, thought, memory, and words must be there, waiting on the spirit. At that moment no discordant idea may be allowed. Every thought must be quiet and at attention. Thought, memory, physical senses, all must be concentrated. In a word, your whole being—all your memory, word, emotion and feeling—is waiting on tiptoe to be used by the Lord. All your own activities cease; only the spirit is in command; just as an army waits expectantly for the commander-in-chief to give battle orders. We will use our mind, but as a servant and not as a master.

The same is true with our emotion. Unless all the faculties of the being are called together to be commanded by the spirit, the latter will not have a free way. During the time of ministering, if a necessary word is forgotten the spirit will be wounded; if an appropriate feeling is missing it will also be hurt. It cannot be released.

There is no work which demands such a high degree of concentration as that of the release of the spirit. It requires the focusing of every part of the entire being, not in the sense of coming out independently of each part, but rather of following the lead of the spirit. The spirit must have at its command every word and all else that it needs, just as all parts of a whole army await the commander's orders. Whenever the spirit gives an order, that particular part is ready to obey. If the thought today is a little bit scattered, the emotion slightly confused, or the memory somewhat dull, the spirit will suffer and find it hard to be released.

A minister of the word must therefore learn not to let his spirit be wounded. Whenever he desires to speak, his whole being should be available. Not a single part should fall behind. Every segment should be readily waiting to be engaged by his spirit. This unquestionably demands a great price. For this very reason, a minister of the word sometimes fails to exercise his usable spirit to the uttermost. When he is willing, there is more release of the spirit; when he is unwilling there is less release. At the time of his willingness he is able to impart more blessing to others; at the time of unwillingness, he brings less blessing to people. The measure of blessing which people receive from us depends on the degree of our willingness to give. If we will to impart grace, we shall help people to grace; if we will to enlighten people, they will be exposed and broken. The question rests upon how far we ourselves have been brought by the Lord. The more our spirit learns before God the greater is our spirit usable. How much light people receive is governed by us; how low they fall before God is again up to us; how deep they touch spiritual reality is in our hand. The Lord has committed His work in us.

Push Out the Spirit

All who have truly been ministers of the word know what is meant by pushing out the spirit. While you are speaking, you receive the strength (but not the fleshly kind) to push out the spirit within you. It itself is strong in you, and you try to send it forth. As your words go forth, your spirit goes forth too. Only in this way will people touch reality. Whether the audience hears the word of God or merely hears a sermon depends on how you push out your spirit. If you are willing to extend it they hear more than a message, because they meet the reality behind the words. But if your spirit is not released, then they will not touch the reality behind the words. This explains why the ministry sometimes seems too common, too ordinary; for though there are many words there is little spirit. Words are spoken yet little spirit is released.

It is quite common to find in a message which lasts an hour or two that only during a small portion of that time is there a strong spirit pushing forth. This makes the ministry of the word rather ordinary. In a forceful ministry the spirit watches the word. They are equal in measure. As the words go out, the spirit is released. The words are delivered in the spirit. All who hear touch the out-going spirit as well as hear the words spoken. The strength of the words is wholly governed by the speaker. What he has learned is what he possesses, and his willingness measures out his gift to others. Some may possess something but they are unwilling to give; others may be willing to give but have nothing. We must have something and also be willing to give.

It is best if the words and the spirit collaborate. A special condition might exist when there is more spirit than word. This may happen in a certain special environment when God permits us to release more spirit than words in order to meet a particular need. This, however, is quite rare. Nonetheless, the ministry of the word means the release of the spirit. Hearing the word means meeting the spirit. Ministry is to serve in the spirit. As we speak, beyond merely uttering words we release our spirit. It is not simply a ministry of speaking, it is speaking with the spirit. It is not just opening the mouth and making sounds; it is sending out by the spirit what word we have in our heart.

Words without spirit degenerate into doctrine; this is not the word of God. How absolutely impossible for one to minister the word if he has no usable spirit. The ministry of the word is the release of the spirit. God does not wish people to hear the word alone; He wants them to touch the spirit of the word. The spirit rides along with the words. God desires men to touch His Spirit and not merely to touch His word. His Spirit goes forth in and with His word. Each time we speak we need to push forth the spirit.

Particularly in all strong ministry, the spirit is not merely pushed forth, it explodes. When the words are delivered the spirit is released in such fulness that it simply explodes. Under such circumstances, you find people prostrate before God. As your words flow forth you overpower many opposing spirits, many cold and hard hearts. Your spirit is exploding all along the way. No one, however strong he may be, can stand up against this from God. He must be stricken to the ground. Let us therefore note how much of the spirit is released while speaking. Your spirit cannot be stronger than what you really possess. Nothing can be forced. No word, no voice, no gesture can counterfeit the spirit. Never attempt to imitate the manner of speaking and the tone of voice, for people fall before God only when the *spirit* is released.

What, then, do we mean by the release of the spirit? We will now mention a few points for our consideration together.

1. *The release of the spirit is the release of the Holy Spirit.* The Lord commits the Holy Spirit to the church, for He has ordained the church to be the depths out of which the rivers of living waters flow (John 7). The church is the vessel of the Holy Spirit. We ought to know what the current task of the church is. It is the Holy Spirit's vessel. God does not pour His ointment at random on people; He keeps it in the church that through the church it may anoint men. As the vessel of the Holy Spirit the church is not merely a vessel to be used by the Holy Spirit; it is primarily a vessel to hold or contain the Holy Spirit.

But exactly how does God keep His Spirit in the church? His Spirit is not held in any part of our being save in our spirit. It is clear in Old Testament typology: (1) The dove which Noah let out of the ark cannot alight upon the old creation. It must descend upon the new creation. In our beings, the spirit alone is the new creation; hence the Holy Spirit can only dwell there. (2) Again, in Exodus it is written, "Upon the flesh of man shall it (the holy anointing oil) not be poured" (Ex. 30.31-32 Darby). No part of the flesh can contain the Holy Spirit. Man's spirit alone is the container. This truth is especially made clear by the words in Ezekiel: "A new spirit will I put within you;. . .and I will put my Spirit within you" (36.26-27). The "new spirit" is our spirit; the "my Spirit" is the Holy Spirit. Were there no new spirit in us there could be no Holy Spirit within us. To have His Spirit we must have a new spirit.

In view of what has been said, the meaning of pushing out our spirit is that the Holy Spirit goes forth with our spirit. All students of the Bible acknowledge that in many places in the Greek original it is impossible to distinguish man's spirit from the Holy Spirit. The place where the word "spirit" is used most is Romans 8. There, it is extremely hard to distinguish where is meant the human spirit and where the Holy Spirit. In the English versions we have the upper case "S" and the lower case "s", but in the Greek original there is no such distinction. Man's spirit is already united with God's Spirit. Due to the fact that the Holy Spirit dwells in our spirit, the more we are instructed by Him the more spirit we can release. When our spirit is released He too is released. So the coming out of the spirit points to more than our spirit; it likewise points to the coming out of the Holy Spirit. The amount He is released depends on the measure of our spirit's coming out. The Holy Spirit is limited by our spirit. Today's problem lies not with the ointment but with the vessel.

Brethren, do not be so foolish as to place the entire responsibility on the Holy Spirit. Today the Lord has placed the responsibility on the church. Matthew 18.18 shows us the influence of the church. The words of the Lord in John 20.23 and that portion in Matthew 18 are quite alike. If you forgive the sins of any, I too will forgive; if you retain the sins of any, I also will retain. How can this be? Because we have received the Holy Spirit. The Lord desires the church to receive the Holy Spirit. And after you receive Him, whom you forgive He will forgive, and what you retain He will retain. The power of the Holy Spirit is now given to the church to use. How tremendous is the responsibility of the church!

If God were directly looking after His own affairs Himself it would not matter if the church were incompetent. But He has committed His affairs to the church. How terrible it will be if she fails God. Were all authority in the hands of the Holy Spirit it would matter little whether or not the church were capable; but He is limited by the minister; if the minister is incompetent the Holy Spirit's way is blocked. Should God retain authority in

Himself, even though we all fail, it would make no difference. God does not hold the work of the Holy Spirit in His own hand; He instead commits it into the hands of the ministers of the word. When the spirit of the minister is released so is the Spirit of God released. If his spirit fails to come forth, God's Spirit is shut in too.

It pleases God today to commit His authority to the ministers of the word. Only the foolish can be careless. Let us remember that the problem today falls entirely upon the ministers of the word. Whether the Holy Spirit is released or not is a matter which rests in the hands of the ministers.

2. *The release of the spirit is the release of power.* Whether a stubborn person yields to the Spirit or not depends upon the amount of the power of the spirit you generate. If your spirit is robust he will yield. Except for those who close themselves tightly in, even the hard person can be overcome if your spirit comes out strongly. Never put all the responsibility on others. Probably nine out of ten times the difficulty is in you and not in them. Were your spiritual vigor greater you would conquer. The greater your spiritual strength the lower people fall.

3. *The release of the spirit is the release of life.* The release of the spirit means the release of life as well as the release of the Holy Spirit and of power. Whether people who hear you touch spiritual reality or not relates to whether you release or retain your spirit. If all you release is words, people will only touch a teaching and not the Holy Spirit. But when you are willing to push out the spirit, they will touch life as well as hear the words. Touching the outer shell of words or touching life depends on your ability or inability to push out the spirit.

4. *The release of the spirit is the release of light.* Light turns into words in you, but it reverts to light in others. Your words spoken in the spirit become light to men. Except for those who are so prejudiced as to be unable to see light, the responsibility

for not seeing rests with the minister, not with the audience. If anyone listening should close his eyes he alone is accountable for not seeing; but if there is no light before the open eyes, then this is the minister's responsibility. The other person is responsible for opening his eyes; the minister is accountable for bringing the enlightenment. Nothing can be done for that one who shuts his eyes tightly. If, however, he opens his heart and his eyes yet fail to see anything, it is the minister who must be held accountable. When the word comes forth it will become light to people if the spirit of the minister is strong and the Holy Spirit is willing to accompany the word spoken.

God's light is stored in God's word. If by the human spirit and the Holy Spirit the word is sent out, it will invariably become light to men. If after one has heard a message he kneels down and prays, "O Lord, give me light," it indicates he has heard the teaching but has not heard God's word, for the word of God is light. This is where Christianity fails. Doctrine has come forth, nevertheless the light is absent. We understand it all, yet nothing is usable. We can speak on it, but it does not work.

Let us understand that when people hear God's word they ought to see light. If they do not, the responsibility rests on the speaker. We often try to push it onto the audience. This is wrong. We confess that with the sole exception of those who have a special difficulty and shut themselves in, the speaker is wholly accountable for the enlightening of the hearers. After they have heard the word there is no need for them to ask for light, because they have already beheld the light. How must many ministers repent before God! They have no light to give; light does not shine from them. They are responsible for the lack. The brethren's responsibility is indeed to open their own eyes; even so, the minister is responsible to give them light. Whenever the spirit of the minister is released, light shines.

A minister of the word is able to decide how much light he will send out. If he is one who has received dealings he can push his inward revelation out through his own spirit. As it is released the light shines forth. He may not only enlighten people to make them understand; he may also slay them with the light. If his intent is merely to prepare others for understanding, then his ministry will end up in making them understand. But if he is ready to pay the price before God, he can push his spirit forth in such power that people will not only understand, they will also be overwhelmed. Light is able to strike people down. All this must be decided by the minister of the word himself.

5. *Pressure and the release of the spirit.* The release of the spirit follows certain laws. The degree of its release depends on two factors; first, how willing you are, and second, how much pressure you are under. When you come to the meeting you receive a burden from God. If the pressure is heavy and tense you know God wants your spirit to come out with an explosion. Owing to great pressure, your words fail to come forth. In order to relieve the pressure your spirit has to explode. Accordingly, pressure causes the abundant release of the spirit.

Suppose you are conversing with a brother. How very dark and blind he is, how proud and high-minded. You are greatly pressed in your spirit. It gives you great suffering. You are pressed till you feel angry within. You can endure no more. You open your mouth and speak. Words come out impetuously. Your spirit comes out. The amount of spirit released corresponds to the measure of pressure you have endured. Hence the current problem is, firstly, whether you are willing or not willing to speak this word, and secondly, if you are willing, how intense is the pressure within you. If the pressure is great, then as your spirit rushes out it will reprove that high-minded brother until he falls before it. And we should realize that after each exercise our spirit grows stronger.

Such was the case with Paul when he cast out the demon from the slave girl. She shouted for days—"These men are servants of the Most High God!"—till Paul had become so annoyed that he turned and said to the spirit, "I charge you in the name of Jesus Christ to come out of her!" And it came out that very hour (Acts 16.17,18). Many can raise their voices but not their spirits. This is utterly ineffective. The principle of miracles is the same as that of the word. Paul was annoyed inside; the pressure gradually built up; and finally he gave the charge and the demon was cast out. It is when the spirit within is deeply burdened that the word pierces and cuts.

The Lord Jesus came to Jerusalem. He saw a fig tree without any fruit. He said to it, "May no one ever eat fruit from you again!" (Mark 11.14) Such words were uttered under great pressure in the spirit, with the result that the fig tree withered away to its roots. A minister of the word is not able to say such strong words carelessly. You may rise up and speak only when you are pressed beyond measure. This is the principle of miracles as well as the law of reproof. When your spirit comes out, people will fall down.

The supply of the word is the supply of the spirit. When the spirit is released, power, light, life, the Holy Spirit, and pressure are all released. Only what comes from the release of the spirit is useful. All else is vain. To preach, you need to add the spirit to thought, word, memory, and feeling. When your spirit comes forth, then you can speak. Then and there you have the ministry of the word.

6. *The spirit needs to be cleansed.* There must indeed be spirit in the word. Yet in order to send out a clean spirit we need to learn to receive dealings from the Lord. A most important matter to bear in mind is that whatever kind of spirit there may be conveys the corresponding facet of the Holy Spirit; whatever kind of person one is communicates that particular aspect of the Holy Spirit. The manifestation of the Holy Spirit differs in various persons. When He comes to people He comes with the special character of the channel being used. He comes with the quality of the carrier. Hence the Holy Spirit is manifested one way in one person and another way in another person; consequently, there are various ministries. His manifestation through Paul is different from that through Peter. The manifestations are from the same Holy Spirit, yet in Peter it bears the characteristic

of Peter, in Paul, that of Paul. This is evident. The Holy Spirit never sets aside the human element. Nowhere in the Bible do we see that God annihilates the human factor. One individual may exhibit the filling of the Holy Spirit in one way, while the other may do so in another way. There is no such thing as uniformity in all.

Brethren, do you see our responsibility? If the Holy Spirit speaks through us without carrying along our particular characteristics, we have very little responsibility. If you merely pass the Holy Spirit on to others without you yourself becoming involved, then it is all right so long as you are able to pass Him on. But the experiences of many saints show us that when the Holy Spirit comes to men He comes with the special character of man. If so, then how our spirit must be purified, or else people will receive an abnormal thing.

We ought to know the significance of the human element. The Holy Spirit does not act independently, that is, He does not act directly and on His own. He always carries our characteristic with Him when He acts. "If any man is thirsty," said the Lord, "let him come to Me and drink. He who believes in Me, as the scripture said, 'From his innermost being shall flow rivers of living water'" (John 7.37-38). The Lord indicates that the water is first taken into man's innermost being and afterwards out of the depths flow the rivers of living water. J. N. Darby explains that the belly is the innermost of our being. From the depth of our being flows the Holy Spirit and He always carries us with Him.

We need to be dealt with. The cross never comes to us in vain. Each time when it comes, it cuts and carves us one more time, and so we are cleansed once again. Each difficulty which crosses our path increases our cleansing. Each fire brings in more purifying. The more difficulties we receive before the Lord and the greater they are, the cleaner our spirit is. Thus the Holy Spirit is able to carry a cleaner spirit (even ours) with Him. Frequently the dealing with our peculiar characteristic is not thorough enough; with the result that people meet both the Spirit of God and our own impurity. We all have met ministers of the word who have the word and are able to release their spirits, yet are too big in themselves, not having been sufficiently reduced. And when the Holy Spirit comes out, *their* peculiarities are mixed up in it as well.

How great is our responsibility, brethren. If the Spirit of the Lord made no use of man or if He were to reject every man who had some defect, things would be much simpler. It would be very easy to distinguish what is the work of the flesh and what is the work of the Spirit. The problem is compounded, however, because even though our spirit is not clean and even though the work of the flesh is in us, God nevertheless does not reject us outright. Instead, He uses us. This in turn causes many young and proud men to think that they are usable. They do not know that God often uses the weak. The more God uses us the greater is our responsibility. If He does not use us our problem is almost nil. Many times we know we are incompetent, yet God still wants to use us. The Holy Spirit always goes out with man's spirit; the Lord uses man with his characteristic. This is the deep law of the working of God.

Let us be careful of one thing: let us not forget our incompetency when we are utilized by God. Remember that our responsibility is great. If I am not right, then all my wrong will be mixed in with the word of the Lord. One day when we receive more enlightenment, we shall prostrate ourselves before God and acknowledge: "Never once in my preaching have I been competent." Anyone who receives light will see his utter helplessness. True, the Spirit of God works through you, but you are not a clean vessel, you are not a perfect vessel. You are an impure container in God's hand. You need more and deeper dealings. Hence you must seek for mercy before God, asking Him to be gracious to you that you may learn daily under the discipline of the Holy Spirit. Otherwise, your spirit will not be usable.

Perhaps the Lord wishes to make you a minister of the word; so He works daily in you. Each and every dealing, trial and environment is to increase your usefulness. All of these serve to make your spirit cleaner and more perfect so that when it comes out it may come with a clean quality and be more usable to the Lord. The Lord in His mercy may cause His Spirit to come through you. You consider yourself as one greatly used. You become proud, not knowing that you are only temporarily chosen by God.

Let us see that the training of the minister is a daily and lifelong work. You may not be able to speak better, but certainly your spirit can make more progress. You may say the same words as you did ten years ago, yet your spirit in saying them now is vastly different from that of a decade ago. Let not the young say, I can say the same thing as the elder has said. You may say the same thing, but do you have the same spirit? Do not ask, Can I say that word? Rather ask yourself, Do I have that spirit? To a minister of the word, word alone is inadequate. There must also be the spirit. "The words that I have spoken to you are spirit and life," says the Lord. Whenever a minister of the word rises to speak for God, his spirit as well as his words must be clean.

Therefore, the question is not whether I can speak or not, but with what kind of spirit do I send out the word? Some do not even have any spirit. Here is a fundamental distinction. They are of two different realms. In one realm, a person is competent if he is clear, eloquent and wise. In the other realm, he is inadequate without the chastening of the Lord and the discipline of the Holy Spirit. Words belonging to this second realm must be beaten into you by the Lord's hand. They are wrought in you and built up daily in you by the Holy Spirit. Not because you find a good sermon to preach, therefore you can preach. Not at all. You may say the same thing yet there may be no effectiveness in your words. Someone may preach a certain truth; you accept it and preach on it too, but where is the effectiveness? The word may be the same but your spirit is wrong.

The words which the Lord speaks are spirit and life. Hence your spirit must be disciplined before God. You yourself need to be carved and chiseled by Him. Then when the word goes forth your spirit follows suit, and, thank God, the Holy Spirit is also released. This is the way of the ministry of the word. Without this you will be like a scribe preaching the Ten Commandments. Everything will be reduced to doctrine, teaching, exposition. The spirit is missing. All is vanity. God must bring us to the point where, when our words go out, the spirit is released. Sometimes it needs to explode. Not every time, but occasionally the spirit should explode in order to facilitate the work of the Holy Spirit. Otherwise, the word we preach is not the same as the word the apostles preached.

Let us know what the task of the church is today. God has entrusted Christ to the church that she may impart Christ to men. God has committed the Holy Spirit to the church for her to give Him out. God has deposited revelation in the church that she may cause others to see. Today all the spiritual blessings of God are given to the church for her to dispense to the world. This is God's thought and design. The church is the body of Christ on earth. As the body of man expresses the thought of man, so the church as His body expresses the thought of Christ. The thought of the head is manifested through the body. Without the body the head has no way to express itself. In like manner, Christ has no way to express Himself without the church. In this dispensation God blesses men through the church. Her responsibility is therefore enormous.

Do not mistakenly think that everything today is in heaven. How can you forget Pentecost? How can you forget the cross? Today's situation is entirely opposite to that of the Old Covenant. In Malachi 3.10 we read, "Bring ye the full tithes into the storehouse, that there may be food in my house, and prove me now herewith, saith Jehovah of hosts, if I will not open you the windows of heaven, and pour you out a blessing." This is the Old Testament principle, for the blessing is in heaven. But in our age the blessing has come to earth and the Holy Spirit is to lift the church to heaven. The Protestant forgets the position of the church, while the Roman Catholic attempts to seize God's blessing in the flesh. We now ask God to open our eyes that we may see that every spiritual blessing is today vested in the church, and that it is the church which should dispense the blessing to men.

The church ought to be dispensing gifts. The letter to the Ephesians distinctly shows us that the blessing has descended and the church has ascended; all spiritual gifts are now in the church. What is ministry? It is the imparting of spiritual riches to men. The church is now in possession and enjoyment of the riches of Christ. She should share the Christ she possesses with others. A minister is to impart what he sees and has of Christ to men. Let us not be so self-degrading as to think everything is far, far away. Many are praying as though the Holy Spirit had never descended to earth and that the church had never been to heaven. That cannot represent the church. "The word is near you, in your mouth and in your heart" (Rom. 10.8). Brethren, you have light; hence the light of God can be sent out through you. You have God's word, therefore you can send it forth. The question is, are you willing to do so?

In these present years God needs clean vessels to send out His word. It does not mean that God will never use you if you are unholy. Over the past two thousand years countless carnal hands have touched the work of God and have spoiled it. Brethren, you know what you were ten years ago. You can only confess that even though you were of the flesh, God had still used you. You know what you were twenty years ago. You cannot but acknowledge that you were an unclean and sinful person, and yet God used you. Do not be so foolish as to think that because God used you, therefore you must be usable. We recognize more and more the greatness of our responsibility: "O Lord, when we are used, we mix ourselves in and defile and damage Your word. We mingle our sin and defilement into Your work so as to confuse the work of the Holy Spirit with the work of the flesh. Lord, we have sinned; we ask your forgiveness. Be merciful to us."

The Lord has committed Himself to the church; His way is upon us. He desires to dispense His riches through man's spirit. Accordingly, you should ask the Lord to make your spirit acceptable before God. You should not be proud of the work you have done. We have no reason to remain unclean or carnal.

Always remember that God has committed Christ, the Holy Spirit, the word, and light to the church. Today she is able to give light, word, the Holy Spirit, and Christ to men. The one difficulty is our uncleanness, our impurity. Let us see our responsibility. We must be made holy vessels if we wish to have the word, the light, the spirit, and the Holy Spirit all to be released.

If we see before God what the church is, then we will naturally know what a minister is. A minister is to dispense by word what God has entrusted to the church. Consequently, his responsibility is greater than the rest. Should we continue on in the mixture of the flesh, we have no way. We shall greatly impair God's work and make it suffer. God needs men, but are we God's servants and ministers? May God have mercy upon us. We must learn what this way is. When our words go out, light also shines forth. May we have sufficient words to give, that all who hear may see light and fall down before God.

17 Some Helps in Speaking

To be a minister of the word is a very new task to us. We have never done it before, just as a newborn babe has never learned to speak. Indeed, we have lived on earth for some decades now and have spoken much during these many years, yet we have never spoken this word. In order to speak this word, we must learn from the very beginning. We should not entertain the thought that since we have had experience in speaking, even in preaching, we can well make use of it. Such a concept is disturbing because the ministry of the word is something quite different from our past learning and understanding. We ought not be so careless as to draw upon the past and try to speak as we usually do.

Remember, in speaking for God, you are like a babe who has to learn from the start. Just as a babe learns to speak each and every word, so you also must learn all the way up. Speaking in the flesh possesses its characteristics; speaking in the spirit has its own qualities too. You are not able to make use of your past experience in speaking or in preaching. You will change the nature of the word of God if you do. You must learn at the start. Many words, many phraseologies, many thoughts have to be gradually learned; even how to exercise yourself while speaking needs to be learned afresh. This is neither engaging the old method nor replenishing it with a new way. It is something entirely new, hence everything in relation to this ministry of the word needs to be learned point by point.

When you deliver the word which God has given you, it is both easy and hard. It is not unlike prayer. You may consider it easy, yet even after a lifetime you have not succeeded in mastering it. But if you say prayer is hard, one who is newly saved can easily pray on his first day of salvation. Thus to be a minister of the word is on the one hand difficult, while on the other, not too hard.

Let us now consider a few of the things which we should be attentive to in speaking.

1. *Keep the spirit from being wounded.* We speak not simply to let the words out but to release the spirit as well. Our ministry will be a total failure if only words come out and the spirit is missing. Of course, it is equally impossible to release the spirit without the words. The spirit and the words are both necessary. When the words come forth they come with the spirit. It is the spirit that touches, moves, and makes people see. If the spirit is strong it may cast people down. The coming forth of the word is the coming forth of the spirit. Without the spirit no amount of words will be of value. Hence we must be careful lest the spirit is hurt and is unable to be released.

The spirit should not be offended. A least offense will hold it back and make what is left merely words. Sometimes we are not even conscious that the spirit is already wounded. It is most delicate, therefore easily hurt. The spirit is so intensely sensitive that it is far keener than our own feeling. Once it is wounded, it fails to go out with the words. We must accordingly be very careful in keeping the spirit from being hurt. A few things may easily damage it, and some of these we shall now proceed to point out.

(a) Your spirit is wounded and unable to be released if before speaking you unknowingly touch a little sin or defilement. Though we do not know exactly what sin or defilement can hurt the spirit, we do know that the mere contact with many sins and defilements (not to say committing these things) can wound it. As you commence to speak you find you cannot, because you are conscious that your spirit is hurt. Consequently, every minister of the word must seek for forgiveness and cleansing before he speaks. All known sins and defilement must be confessed before

God and forgiveness and cleansing asked for. Even for that which you do not know you must ask cleansing and forgiveness. In ordinary days you must learn how to avoid these things, you must learn how to carefully keep yourself from contacting them. The spirit is more sensitive than your feeling. It may take three to five days before you know what sin or defilement it was that your spirit had already sensed. Sometimes, when you speak, you feel the word is right, the thought is also right, but somehow you are not able to push your spirit out, as if it is unwilling to come forth. You have the sense of not finding the spirit. This is because it is wounded by the defilement of sin. It is thus immovable.

(b) The spirit needs to be waited on before it can come forth. If our thought is somewhat scattered and fails to concentrate on or to follow a certain line of thinking, the spirit is hurt. Our mind must wait watchfully on the spirit so as to be used whenever called for. Scattered thoughts make the spirit heavy. Some ministers of the word have their spirit wounded through their thought. We should keep our mind entirely for the spirit's use. It needs to wait wholeheartedly on the spirit as a servant waits on his master.

(c) To keep the spirit strong and unhurt you must not use the wrong word or words, wrong illustrations or divisions while speaking. If you misuse two or three big words, you know your message is spoiled. These few incorrectly used words have hurt your spirit and hindered it from being released. (Sometimes it is not that serious if only a few unimportant words are misused. Your spirit is not hurt and can still be released.) Or perhaps you may use an illustration which does not agree with the spirit's thought. The spirit can easily be wounded and refuse to go forth. Or you may simply tell a story which is not according to the Spirit; your spirit will also be hurt and held back. Or you may speak a whole section of words out of touch with the Spirit; you again will find the spirit hurt and withdrawn. In any case, let us realize that the spirit is easily wounded. If you are careless you shall find to your surprise that it refuses to be pushed out. You may want to release your spirit but you do not have the strength to release it. You are then clear that you have wounded it today.

(d) Our attitude may also damage the spirit. Many, coming to the meeting, are full of self-consciousness, and this easily hurts the spirit. Suppose you are speaking at a certain place and you are full of self-consciousness. You feel how awesome the people are who sit before you; you are particularly fearful of a certain few. As you speak you are conscious of yourself because of those people. This will stifle your spirit so as to hinder it from coming out. As soon as the soul commences to rule, self-consciousness begins to increase; as self-consciousness rises, the spirit loses its control.

We should know how different is the trembling of the spirit from the trembling consciousness of the soul. We need the first but not the second. When we come to a meeting place we should be filled with trembling, but certainly not the trembling of the soul's self-consciousness. Knowing our incompetency and lack of power, we come with trembling. This trembling enables us to look up to God, to believe and to trust. The soulish self-consciousness is not so. It looks at man. Spiritual trembling causes us to lift up ourselves to God, whereas soulish self-consciousness turns our eyes toward men. When self-consciousness which belongs to the soul arises, our spirit is immediately hurt. It becomes unusable and unable to be pushed forth.

An evangelist must therefore not have any self-consciousness. Throughout the ages, those who are used by God in preaching the gospel are those who are void of self-consciousness. The less self-conscious the evangelist is, the more powerful is his spirit. While he stands there he is not aware of the heaven he sees, nor the earth, nor the people. He speaks what is in his heart. He is conscious neither of the right nor the wrong attitude of his audience. Such total absence of self-consciousness is a basic condition for an evangelist. It will cause his spirit to rise up. Hence a minister of the word must learn not to be self-conscious. Should he rise up to speak God's word and be afraid of the people—afraid they will not listen to his words, afraid of this or afraid of that—such fear will invariably hurt his spirit and prevent it from going forth. His inner man is not sufficiently strong to meet the challenge. He will wither on the spot.

Suppose one who is preaching the gospel is all the time conscious that those hearing him are senior in age, higher in position, greater in learning, or more in knowledge than he is; how then can he succeed in his preaching? The more he speaks, the more withered he becomes. In preaching the gospel, if you make men a little bigger, you make the gospel somewhat smaller. But if you think primarily of the gospel, your consciousness of other men will soon be overwhelmed. The spirit of an evangelist needs to be released. He should not develop a consciousness of self-abasement, for this will reduce the power of the word of God as well as render his spirit weak and empty. The fear of man is not humility; it is a soulish feeling of self-abasement. Spiritual humility comes through our being enlightened by God to a real knowledge of ourself, whereas soulish self-abasement is the result of looking at man, comparing ourself with others, and being afraid of men. Under certain conditions such self-abased persons can manifest an attitude of pride. This is never humility. This hurts the spirit and makes it unusable.

Whenever you stand before men you must be in fear and trembling on the one hand and courageous and sure on the other. You need to have both; the lack of either will wound your spirit. A wounded spirit disqualifies one from being a minister of the word.

2. *The spirit and the word must not lose contact.* Perhaps you have four or five sections in your message or four or five verses in the Bible to read or four or five items to mention. Which you put first and which you put next can affect the release of the spirit. You have the word, but if you disturb the order which the spirit intends to take, your spirit will not be able to come forth as you speak. There is a real difficulty in speaking, in that our words tend to lose touch with our spirit. Some words should be spoken first, yet you put them at the last, and vice-versa. If such be the

case you will find that though you utter the words the spirit is restrained.

In addition, words sometimes need to pass from one section to another as the thought turns in a different direction. Things may happen during such a transition. The words may continue on but the spirit may not make the turn. The spirit may stop short and become separated from the word. Hence at the turning of thought, it is necessary to keep the spirit in touch with the word. Suppose you misuse a passage in the Scriptures. Your spirit fails to make the turn and as a result loses contact with the word. This becomes a very serious matter in speaking.

To those who have learned little before God the chief matter is the wounding of the spirit; to the more experienced, however, the main difficulty lies in the losing of contact between the word and the spirit. When one is just beginning to learn, he often wounds his spirit; it fails to come forth because he has hurt it. After a person has learned somewhat, his problem is no longer that of wounding the spirit; instead, it is the word and the spirit being mutually out-of-touch.

It is not an easy thing to keep these two constantly in touch. Sometimes the message begins on the wrong foot and this causes the word to lose contact with the spirit. On other occasions the order in the speaking is confused; the words are delivered but the spirit is shut in. The contact between the word and the spirit is most easily lost at the point of turning. When the word commences to turn, our thought may not be adequate, our spirit may not be sufficiently active, and our feeling may not be sensitive enough to follow; the consequence is that the word goes forth while the spirit lags behind. The contact is lost. How necessary it is for us to learn to let the spirit go out with the word. As soon as we sense a loss of contact we should instantly try to return the word to its former position.

Our spirit is keenly sensitive. At times, even after we have returned the word to its original place, the spirit still refuses to come along because once it is set aside it is wounded. How extremely delicate is the spirit; how very careful we must be in speaking! We need to look to God's mercy that at the time of transition our spirit does not lose the contact. As we speak to the brethren we must maintain each turn according to the spirit. If any mistake is made we must immediately withdraw our word. If the spirit still fails to be recalled, we will have to sacrifice that section of the message and try to locate where the anointing is, for there lies the direction of the word. The spirit will then be released.

Whether a minister of the word turns rightly or wrongly depends more on the mercy of the Lord than on man's own arrangement. It is quite difficult for us to control the strength of the word and the cooperation of the spirit with the word. It is not owing to our knowledge and experience that we are able to make the right turn. We may not know when we are right, but we certainly recognize when we are wrong. In a matter of a few minutes we shall know.

As soon as we realize that it is not right, stop going on. Never try to rescue the message. If you sense that the word has drifted away, return at once. At other times you may feel as if you are standing at a fork in the road; you do not know whether you are right or wrong. Yet if you continue speaking, you will know after a few more minutes. When the word and the spirit are divided, you realize you are wrong. Though you are speaking outwardly, your spirit remains immovable. How very sensitive indeed is the spirit; one slight error makes it immovable. You cannot push it out. In this case, you should return to the former position and start out afresh. How do you know whether your word is right or wrong? It is judged by whether your spirit goes out with the word. While you speak you are speaking the right word if your spirit is released; otherwise you are wrong. This is the restraint the Holy Spirit exercises over you.

How helpless we are in ourselves; how we must wholly look to the mercy of God each time we speak. We cannot help ourselves speaking in God's Spirit even for five minutes. We easily turn in the wrong direction. It is beyond the control of human wisdom and knowledge, and it is not under the control of man's experience. Hence, if in our daily life we receive mercy from God by learning to entrust ourselves to the God of mercy, then at the time of speaking, we will find to our surprise that everything is right. We say again that it is the mercy of God, because no one can maintain himself on the right course. It is something controlled by the Master, not by the servant; it is something we cannot do, only the Lord can. In spite of your knowledge, learning and experience, you should place yourself unreservedly at the mercy of the Lord; otherwise, you may be right for three or five minutes but then make the wrong turn.

The least that a minister of the word must know is that in speaking it is not so much the release of the word as the release of the spirit. The words are uttered in order to send forth the spirit. A minister's responsibility is not merely to discharge the word, it is more so to discharge the spirit. You have not fulfilled the work of a minister in only sending the word out, but you do accomplish the task if you discharge the spirit by the word. The acid test is the degree to which your spirit is released in your message today. The marvel is this: that the more the spirit is released the lighter you feel afterwards; you know the Lord has used you.

You need not be worried about the fruit, that is the Lord's business. Whether people are saved or not, helped or not, is in the Lord's hand and not in yours. The result belongs to the Lord, not to you. Success is His concern, not yours. To us servants there is but one subjective fruit, and this is, that during the time of speaking and afterwards, if I have discharged my burden I know the Lord has been gracious to me.

The joy of a minister of the word is not in the amount of words spoken nor in the nodding of people's heads, nor in the fact of people being helped, but in the release of the spirit in speaking. As the spirit goes forth the burden is discharged. When the spirit is released the heart is joyful. You know you have done your duty and have done it right. If the word is uttered while the spirit is retained, then you will come back with the same burden upon you. You may speak so loud as to make your throat parched and your body weary, yet you return defeated because your spirit is blocked. The reason for speaking is to discharge your burden, to let your spirit out. The more it is released the lighter you become and the happier you are.

With the release of your spirit comes the word of God. Without it, your word is not God's word; it is merely an imitation. Whenever God's word comes through you your spirit inevitably comes out with it. Only the foolish look for fruit and the praise of men. The fool admires his own words and touches not his spirit. If he is so foolish as to desire to stay in darkness he shall be satisfied with the excellency of his words. He forgets that a word void of spirit is entirely empty.

Consequently, watch as to whether the spirit is released in the word. Such watchfulness will help to maintain the contact between the spirit and the word. Failure to watch may cause the word to lose contact with the spirit. The negative rupture of contact is caused by unwatchfulness; the positive maintenance of contact is through the mercy of God. The spirit must go along with the word. Its release will make the word right and cause the word to reach high. You need to be watchful on the one hand and learn to look to the mercy of God on the other. You will be totally lost if you try to arrange your message and make your transitions yourself. If anyone should be proud about his preaching there can be only one result: though he can preach well, he has no ministry of the word. He may feel elated after his preaching but he will never be a minister of the word. Fools are proud. Do not forget that only by the mercy of God is the word in constant touch with the spirit.

3. *The spirit follows the word and the word follows the anointing.* There are two ways of speaking. One way is to push the word out by the spirit, that is to say, the spirit is put into the word spoken. The other way is to have both the anointing and the spirit beforehand and our word to follow the anointing. These are the two different ways in which our spirit and the word unite together in the speaking.

When speaking, there is the possibility that God wants you to release certain words. He will fill your spirit with these words. You put your spirit into the words and send them out one by one. You as a minister exercise your will to push out the words by your spirit. When your words are uttered your spirit goes out with the words. You use the spirit to push out the words, and your spirit goes forth with the words. As these words come to men the spirit also descends on them. By the mercy of God, such a way of speaking can be very effective. The words are strong and the spirit is high. The mouth utters the word while the heart pushes the spirit. This is one way.

There is another way: before you speak, the power of God is upon you—the anointing is on you. The anointing precedes the word. Under the influence of this power you speak according to the anointing. The anointing flows out, and your words follow after. Whenever there is some feeling in the spirit, you learn to speak accordingly. In such a way of speaking, your spirit goes out unceasingly. The special benefit is that you will never be wrong, because the anointing always goes ahead of the word.

Your way of noticing the audience will differ with these two ways. In the first way of speaking you watch the audience, notice their facial expressions, and observe their condition; in the second way of speaking you cannot pay attention to the audience because you must focus your whole attention on the spirit, waiting for the anointing. You are like a watcher standing at the door. As soon as you see the unction, your words immediately follow. You simply flow with the anointing, disregarding completely men's facial expressions, attitudes, and reactions. Under the power of the anointing, you speak word after word. In this way of speaking, if you were to turn your thoughts to the audience you would at once be interrupted and unable to flow with the ointment.

All who learn to speak in the spirit need to learn these two ways of speaking. Sometimes by the mercy of God you speak through your thought, and at the same time you put your spirit in the word and push it out. At other times the Lord causes you to gather up the strength of your whole being in patiently waiting on the spirit to which He gives anointing to lead the way. First there is the unction, then you are able to conceive the corresponding words to utter the feeling within. The anointing goes ahead; the words closely follow. As you speak you may see the faces of the audience, yet you sense nothing since your whole being is focused on the anointing. Such release of the spirit causes God's children to touch the spirit. A minister of the word should use both these ways of speaking.

The best condition for the ministry of the word is to speak according to the anointing but to push out the spirit at times of great importance. Speaking by the anointing serves as the mainstay. You send out words according to the anointing, completely disregarding any reaction from the audience. The anointing is with you, so you find the crevices into which you pour the words. But during that time you may add another way of speaking because you desire either to bless or to break the audience. You send your spirit out with the word. As the power of the anointing flows, your spirit as the content of the word flows simultaneously. Then and there you shall see the grace of the Lord. You are able to give revelation to the audience when you wish; you are able to bless or to break them.

Preaching to make people understand is the ministry of the word at its lowest level. When it is exhibited at its highest level, people shall see and shall fall. From making people understand to causing them to see and to fall depends on how willing and to what extent you are ready to pay the price. When you are ready to spend and be spent, people shall receive blessing. Under the anointing plus the pushing forth of the spirit people cannot but see and fall.

How much price you are willing to pay becomes a very significant factor here. The basic issue for a minister of the word is to exercise the spirit. We must pay close attention to this before the Lord. The outward man needs to be broken, because this is the only way to make the spirit usable. The breaking down of the outward man is the one thing which the Holy Spirit aims at in discipline. We must allow Him to work in us. If there is no disobedience or resistance to His discipline, inevitably He will break our outward man and make our inner man usable.

4. *The thought must be under the control of the spirit.* In speaking, the matter of thought is worth noticing. It occupies quite a large place in the ministry of the word. If your faculty of mind is efficient you are able to so arrange your thought that the spirit is released while speaking. Otherwise your spirit simply cannot be released. No minister should be careless in not keeping his mind from harm. It is as precious to him as two hands are to a pianist. In ordinary times we ought to let the Spirit of the Lord freely use our thought. We should not allow it to run wild. Things unreasonable and senseless should not occupy our minds, nor should subjects low and base be the objects of our mental exercise.

This does not imply that thought is the source of the word. If a minister speaks according to what he thinks, his thought should be condemned and totally dismantled. If anyone believes he has thought through the Bible and can therefore teach, he must be set aside. All notions except that in the spirit need to be destroyed. All messages which have their origin in thought are to be rejected.

This, though, is not meant to mean the annihilation of the function of thought. Every book of the New Testament is written with thought behind it. For example, in Paul's Letter to the Romans how abundant is the thought, yet also how noble. This letter does not originate from the mind; rather, it originates in the spirit; and the thought therein follows the spirit. The source must be the spirit, not thought. Ordinarily we need to take good care of our mind that it may be usable when God wants it. Let us not therefore condemn wrongly. We should condemn thought only as it becomes the source of speaking. If anyone speaks by his mind he is to be condemned. But for the spirit to use thought is normal and ought not be judged.

The more spiritual the message, the fuller must be the

thought. All spiritual messages are full of deep and noble ideas. When the spirit comes forth it requires full and rich thought. Our mind must take its rightful place in the ministry of the word. Which words should be spoken first and which should follow next is the work of our mind. What is first thought of will be spoken first, and so forth. Our speaking follows our thought.

Now we know that the spirit does not directly command the word. Were it so, it would be speaking in tongues. The spirit usually directs our words behind the understanding of our mind. This alone is called the ministry of the word. Hence our understanding must be usable. In case it is not usable the spirit is obstructed and loses contact with the word. That which connects the spirit and the word is our thought.

We need to carefully watch our thought before God. It needs to be daily renewed. Let us not permit our mind to be habitually occupied with mean and base matters, for this will disqualify us from being used by the Holy Spirit. We must keep our thought holy. We touch the reality of consecration in ministering the word. Consecration means presenting all of our being to the Lord for His use. It means the offering of all our thoughts to God. Daily must we be watchful lest they habitually take the lower level and are thus unable to reach the high level in time of need. Train our thoughts daily to meet the Holy Spirit's use; do not allow them to be a hindrance to the spirit. Let God so direct our mind that we may later think of the thing which should be first spoken, and so on. Our word is governed by our thought and our thought is directed by our spirit. In this order the word shall come forth.

5. *The peak of the word versus the peak of the spirit.* In speaking, it is easy to know when our words reach the peak, but it is not so easy to recognize the peak of the spirit. The peak of the word is known by our thought; that of the spirit is beyond the knowledge of our thought.

A minister of the word should take note of the difference between the peak of the word and the peak of the spirit. If our spiritual condition is right we are quite clear as to which special words God has given us; that is, certain words reach very high while the rest remain ordinary. This is something we know, so while speaking we aim at bringing in this peak of the word. However, the peak of the word may not be the peak of the spirit. Sometimes they coincide; sometimes they differ. This makes the ministry of the word more complicated. In case of a coincidence of these two peaks, the minister need simply watch that his words climb continuously towards the peak, for his spirit is released with the word, and is as strong and as powerful as the word. But sometimes the word has reached its peak while the spirit is strangely restrained, or vice-versa.

What should we do when the peak of the spirit and that of the word do not coincide? Bear in mind that this is the moment when our thought has some work to do. In ministering the word, our thought needs to be gentle and not rigid. Our thoughts must indeed be focused upon the word, yet they are to be used by the Holy Spirit. They should be gentle and flexible to the degree of being able to receive any unexpected thing. In ministering the word we often meet unexpected elements. God may wish to speak something else extemporaneously; He may want to add some words; or the Holy Spirit may desire to do something unusual. If our thought is hard and fixed as iron it is unable to receive the additional words of the spirit; and so, we are bound in our own words. We may reach the peak of the word, but we do not attain to the peak of the spirit. Our ministry will be common and ineffectual. It is rather difficult to explain such an experience, nonetheless we will certainly understand it when we encounter it. Simply remember that a minister of the word should have all his thoughts available to the word, while at the same time these thoughts must be gentle and active before God so that whenever the Holy Spirit indicates something else they are flexible enough to follow. Then shall he succeed in reaching the peak of the spirit in speaking.

Hence when you rise up to speak, your mind must be open and flexible before God and your attitude must be ready to accept any unexpected turn. Only in this way can you discover what God intends to do today. You should anticipate that unexpected things may happen. Accordingly, you should learn how to test your own spirit as well as the Spirit of God. If after saying a few words you feel released in your spirit, your thought should try to add more words to it so as to release more of the spirit. When you speak a word and the spirit flows copiously, you should follow this trend and add additional words. As you speak, your mind searches for the center of the spirit. Once it touches the center your thought tries for additional words that more spirit may be released, and so on and so forth. In other words, whenever your word releases the spirit your thought should not attempt to change the direction. Both your thought and your word must follow the trend. The more you speak, the more anointing you receive and the more the spirit is released and the stronger is the word. It touches the peak of the spirit.

The two peaks do sometimes coincide, as we have said; but not always. We can do nothing if the spirit reaches its peak before the word. But if the word reaches its peak first we are able to do something to greatly release the spirit. This can be likened to the attempt to locate a fallen pin. You use a magnet to search everywhere for the pin till the latter is attracted to the magnet. In the same way, you use your word to test the spirit. If one word fails to activate the spirit, try another word. Through experience you will know when the word has activated it. You can detect the very delicate movement of the Holy Spirit. You speak by your thought; you use your word to test if the Holy Spirit is pleased with the word. If He is pleased you will sense it. As you follow up with more words along the same line you will see that the spirit is being released. In such times your thought governs your word and follows up strongly, making no turn but proceeding straight ahead. Words will draw out words, the spirit will be more and more released until you touch the peak of the spirit in the time of ministry.

We must therefore learn how to try the Holy Spirit with this or that word, testing out which word will release Him to the peak of His speaking. When a word touches the right point, then the more you speak the more will the spirit be released and the more abundant will be the anointing and the more accurate will be your words. Gradually the word will lead you to the peak of the spirit which is the climax of your message. When you see the presence of the Lord's Spirit as well as of His blessing, you are assured of touching the center of today's message. If your spirit is strong you may be able to continue in the word for a longer time after the climax is reached. However, if your spirit is not sufficiently strong you will have to make a turn after a while or else your word will fall flat. The problem is now the strength of the spirit. The stronger the spirit the longer the peak is maintained. Nevertheless, you must not force yourself in maintaining the peak. Whenever the spirit is missing, though the word still lingers, it is time for you to stop.

To sum up, then, our mind should be focused and should be adjustable before God. It must be so focused as to think of nothing else, and yet so flexible as to be able to receive any unexpected thing. Be on guard against falling into any fixed position in your thought, for this will hinder you from touching the word or the unexpected peak which the Lord may wish to give you today. How necessary for us to exercise our thought daily in cooperating with God's word and the spirit's movement, that during the time of ministry our word can rise up to meet the spirit's peak.

6. *Memory must be perfect.* In ministering the word our thought controls our word. We speak according to what we think. But we need materials for our thinking. No one can think something out of the thin air. Our thought is based on our memory. What we have learned and thought of and experienced in our daily life, these become materials for the word. These materials are accumulated through the dealings of the Lord in our ordinary movements. How much the Lord has destroyed and built up in us serves as the material in reserve.

We spend a lifetime to accumulate experience, discipline, doctrines, and teachings of the Bible. One day, when we stand up to speak for the Lord, the Spirit of God exercises our mind, and our mind makes use of what is held in our memory. In other words, the Holy Spirit directs the thought which in turn regulates the word. Our thought supplies materials to our word, which materials are based on our memory. If we are lacking in experience we have nothing of which to remember later. One cannot recall what he does not possess. What things we store up in our memory supply our thought and in turn supplies our word. Behind the word is good and meaningful thought, based on our memory. Nothing is extemporaneous; all is spoken according to past experience.

Word depends on thought, thought on memory, and memory on experience. When you rise to speak, you select usable material from your life experience. Your life experience appears as a reservoir. The Lord has brought you through many things. He has given you many lessons and many truths. These are all laid away in the storage room of your experience. When you speak, your words are based upon these experiences. How does this come about? The words come from your thought, but your thought gathers its material from the storage room through memory. Only your memory can enter the storage room of your experience and select suitable materials from it.

Memory is like a storage keeper; it alone can bring out what you have learned and stored away in the past. Then your mind organizes these materials and presents them in order. Now you recognize the importance of memory. All ministry of the word begins with the Holy Spirit. When the Holy Spirit desires to speak, He uses our thought. For whatever word He wishes to say, He searches to see whether our thought is usable, whether we are able to supply the right word, whether we can follow the right order of the word to be spoken. More and more we discover the incompetency of our own brain. We cannot think of the word the Holy Spirit wishes to say; instead we conceive of words which the Holy Spirit does not desire to use. No minister of the word can be proud, because once he ministers he sees his own incompetency. It is like the gears of a machine, the teeth of which do not fit. Sometimes we feel we are in gear. Our mind is able to supply the word the Lord wants to say. But such is not our daily experience. Frequently our mind is not usable. Our thought is too dull to supply the Holy Spirit with the right word.

We should realize that the Holy Spirit directs the thought and the thought directs the word. Without being under the direction of the Holy Spirit our mind is utterly unable to direct our word. Yet when our mind tries to direct our word it depends on memory. Thought remembers what to say, it does not conceive what to say. These words are not to be conceived miraculously; rather they are to be recalled from storage. The Holy Spirit directs the thought, which in turn recalls from memory the word to be spoken. If the memory is good the supplies will always be at hand. While ministering, the Holy Spirit enables us to recall what we have learned in the past. Suddenly He recalls that particular thing from our memory and puts it in our mind so that there we may apprehend it once again and express it in words.

Many experiences are stored in the memory with perhaps just a few words. If our mind today is especially scattered we cannot recall as we should, and this affects the release of the spirit. The spirit is hindered if any one part of our being is unusable. One may still preach, yet the spirit is not released. For the release of the spirit a perfectly usable mind with a perfectly usable memory is necessary. If either our thought or our memory is just a little defective our ministry will be affected. This is very serious.

Let us suppose that the Lord wants you to say something today. It may be seven or eight words. You are somewhat fearful lest you forget these words. You try your best to memorize them. When you come to the meeting you remind yourself repeatedly that you must not forget these words. Your heart is fully occupied with them. But to your surprise the spirit does not come out when you speak.

It is useless to memorize simply with our brain. The words become empty, for the spirit remains inactive. The memory of a minister of the word must be very natural. If any rein is put upon it it becomes useless when the Holy Spirit wishes to speak.

Instead, the minister needs a perfect memory as well as perfect thought. Like an electric wire, if one end is broken the electric current is shut off; even so, the Spirit of the Lord fails to come forth if any point in the memory is broken. However, we are undone if we take memory or thought as the source of our ministry. It is only when the Holy Spirit becomes the source that thought and memory become useful. Under the enlightenment of the Spirit we realize how inadequate is our thought, our memory and our eloquence. We should therefore ask the Lord to transform our memory into the Holy Spirit memory that it may serve God's purpose. Whether or not we can recall those few words which the Lord wishes to speak will make a great difference in ministry. If they can be recalled, then the words shall come forth and the spirit will be released. If not, we will be suppressed as though we are under a heavy millstone; neither the spirit nor the words can come forth.

We must gather up everything which is to be used by the Holy Spirit. We must collect all we have learned, read, heard, and been shown through revelation throughout our life and make them available to the Holy Spirit. This can be likened to a man who manages to close all the windows so as not to be distracted by the noises and activities outside the house. He offers all he has to the Holy Spirit to be fully spent. In a relatively strong ministry, such a man gathers up his whole life to be spent by the Holy Spirit within five or ten minutes. Ministry is costly. Each and every release of the spirit demands a price. One's outward man must be closed up; all the windows to the outside must be shut. He gathers up all his memory and all he has so that it may be used by the Holy Spirit in time of need. This is strong ministry. There ought to be no interference, no scattering, no carelessness. Never in your life, it seems, have you gathered together so much to be spent all at once by the Holy Spirit. This is the time when memory does its work. In order to stock your memory with supplies, you need to learn many lessons before God and go through many experiences. The ministry of the word is based on the discipline of the Holy Spirit; without such discipline you have no material for the word. If you have stockpiled materials through the discipline of the Holy Spirit your memory can move them around as needed. If, however, you have received little discipline and learned very little, your memory cannot possibly have enough material in store to supply the need of the Holy Spirit.

Hence the richness of a ministry depends on the abundance of discipline and learning. In case of such an abundance, memory naturally has much to supply the thought, and thought has much to transform into word. There should be substance in our words. We are not to say empty phrases. We must put all that we have learned into them through our memory. Should the Spirit of God be in charge, all we have learned in life turns out to be useful.

7. *The feeling and the word must be one.* We need to use our feeling while ministering. The spirit will not be released unless it finds our feeling and our word in one accord. When our feeling has some reservation towards the word which the spirit desires to use, the word will be hindered and the spirit will be held back. Often we find our feeling has reservations. What are these reservations? Sometimes we have a shy feeling, or a feeling of fear lest others will criticize. We may sense people's coldness towards us and their opposition against us. All these curtail what we should say, for they prevent us from mixing our feeling with the word. We are afraid to let our emotion flow alongside our word.

Therefore, in speaking, we have to let loose our feeling. If we have any reluctance, the word cannot freely flow and the spirit will not be released. Should the word require us to shed tears, we simply must shed such tears. Frequently the word requires them, yet we refuse to shed them. Our feeling and our word simply are not one.

How very hard man's outer shell is. If man's feeling is held back the spirit cannot come out. One of the great benefits of the outpouring of the Holy Spirit is to free our emotion. The liberation of man's emotion may derive from two different causes: one comes from the outpouring and the other begins with brokenness. The liberation through the outpouring is an outward liberation, hence the person needs to let go of himself before the spirit can be released. Brokenness too causes one to let go of himself. Discipline enables one to let go even without outpouring. A young brother who has not yet received deep revelation needs the outpouring for his liberation, although he should not depend on such liberation. What is exceedingly precious is when his outer shell is broken after being disciplined daily. Then he is able to let go of himself not only at the time of the outpouring of the Holy Spirit but even when the outpouring is absent. In other words, if the Spirit of the Lord is upon us and we have had sufficient discipline to break the outer shell of our emotion, then whatever kind of feeling today's word requires we are able to release that feeling.

We must coordinate the word with our feeling. Should our feeling fail to accompany the word the spirit is frequently restrained. Why is it that when God's word requires the shedding of tears your tears do not fall; or when it demands shouting you cannot shout? The main hindrance is you yourself. Your feeling has been influenced by the people who surround you so that it dare not correspond to the word. Sometimes you need to shout in order to greatly release the spirit. The Lord Jesus cried with a loud voice: "On the last day, the great day of the feast, Jesus stood and cried out. . . ." (John 7.37). On the day of Pentecost "Peter, taking his stand with the eleven, raised his voice" (Acts 2.14). The pressure of the Holy Spirit was so heavy upon them—the Holy Spirit had given them such deep feeling—that they were pressed to lift up their voices. Their outward emotion and inward sense were joined together in one. After Peter and John were released by the Jewish leaders, they gathered with the brethren. They "lifted their voice together to God" (Acts 4.23-24). The situation at that time was exceedingly grave, hence they asked the Lord to look upon the threatenings and give to them all boldness to speak the word so that the Lord would stretch out His hand to heal, and that signs and wonders take place through His name. This happened to Paul when he saw the man who was lame from birth. He "said with a loud voice, 'Stand upright on your feet'" (Acts 14.10).

All these cases show us that in the ministry of the word the going forth of the word must be accompanied by a corresponding feeling. If our emotion is not released the spirit will be held back. The Lord Jesus Himself, the early church, Peter, John, and Paul—they all had sufficiently strong feeling to lift up their voice. To release the spirit demands strong feeling. Now we are not persuading people to shout in their preaching; we are simply stating that when the spirit is vibrant the outside voice is to be lifted up. If there is no inward feeling, even though our voice fill the whole building, it is of no avail. For some, the louder they sing the less the spirit; the louder their voice in preaching the less spirit they have. Whatever is artificial is useless. Artificiality has no place in the ministry of the word. What is within should be released. Never imitate outwardly. When our word comes forth let our emotion accompany it. For this, though, we must be broken. And after the outer shell is broken we may shout, rejoice, or cry as occasion demands. Such feeling arises from within, it is not artificially manufactured from without. If the Lord cannot penetrate the feeling of those who minister, how can He ever reach the feeling of others? How cold, how dry, how opposing *their* feelings are! We must thrust through their emotions each time we speak. If the Lord cannot make us shed tears, He cannot make others shed them either. If the pressure on us is not heavy enough to make us cry, how can we expect the others to cry?

The first stronghold the word must penetrate is ourselves. Frequently in preaching we sense the inadequacy of our feeling. Why? We have not been broken. The ministry of the word demands a high cost: the Lord must break us to pieces. If we are greatly affected by the word whenever it touches us, our reaction becomes the reaction of God. If a *crying* Jeremiah was unable to bring the Jews to tears, how much less could a *tearless* prophet bring the nation to tears? The prophet must cry first before the people of God can be brought to tears. God loves to see a broken man releasing his feeling in preaching. A minister of the word must therefore learn how to effect this oneness of feeling and word.

8. *The word should be clear and high.* All who minister for God should find out what the characteristics of God's word are. Only then can you know what your words should be like so as to be used by God. Simply put, the word of the Bible has two characteristics: one, it can be easily understood, and two, it is high in quality. God's word is so plain that even the blind will not lose his way nor will the cripple miss his step. The parables in God's word are never puzzles. God does not intend to make His word a puzzle, hence His word is clear and easily understandable. He who desires to minister the word must learn how to speak simply. In ordinary conversation he should cultivate the habit of speaking simply, never in long drawn out sentences. Watch whether people understand you or not. If they do not understand, try to say it differently. Always remember that God's word is for men to understand, not for them to become confused about. Matthew 13 is an exception. Due to their rejection of the Lord, the word of God was hidden from those Jews.

You should practice the power of speaking. If you are given light within the space of five minutes you should spend five hours to meditate on it. When you speak, try to ask the brother if he understands. If he does not understand, change to another way of speaking. You must learn to speak until people can comprehend you from the moment you begin. Do not speak for half an hour when people only understand five minutes of it. On the contrary, speak only the five minutes which they understand. It is better to speak less than to waste twenty-five minutes.

So in ordinary times you need to learn how to say simple words and cultivate the habit of speaking clearly. Never be tempted to speak at length. Always try to make people understand. Ask God to give you simple words or to to give you an appropriate illustration to bear out the thought clearly. To be easily understood is the nature of God's word. If your word is different in nature from God's, you will have trouble in speaking. In the event you do have difficulty in speaking clearly, do not save your face but humble yourself to seek the advice of your brothers and sisters. Learn to speak for five minutes so as to ascertain whether people understand or not. 'Tis better to be criticized than not to be understood. You are speaking for God, therefore the meaning must be perceptible and the word appropriate. God does not want His word to be a puzzle, like some Old Testament parables which can only be interpreted after much research. Do not be ashamed to ask the help of those who are more experienced. Ask them to point out to you where your words are unclear that you may improve upon them and make them understandably simple.

God's word is not only understandable, it is also high in quality. God never says anything superficial, that is to say, God never says anything which may be pleasing to men but lacking in spirit. A minister of the word must strike high before he can hit God's word. If one's word is of low quality he cannot touch God's word. Hence words must be maintained at a high standard. Once we change its quality we lose the touch of God's word. Since words are used to introduce the Lord of Hosts, they ought to rise high. If a brother quotes a verse from the Bible and then proceeds to explain with words of low quality, how can the word of God be released? There is no chance for God to come forth through our words. Now it is perfectly proper for you to say to a two or three year old child who is just beginning to learn how to speak and listen: "If you are a good child, the Lord Jesus will delight in you, and will buy a piece of candy for you tonight." But suppose you go to the platform and say, "If you all listen carefully the Lord Jesus will be pleased with you, and I will treat all of you tonight with sweets." Do you see the absurdity of persuading people in such a fashion? It is too low and immature, too childish in language and thought. God expects His servant to reach high. The higher you rise the deeper the interest of the audience.

Hence a very important point in ministering the word is to climb high before God. The higher we climb the more God's word is released. God rejects low thought, low-quality persuasion, cheap metaphors or words. Reach high and yet be clear. Sometimes we may have both light and a burden; we wish to speak with simplicity; yet the pressure is so heavy upon us that we just cannot be simple. If we find it so difficult to be simple after much trying, how can we ever speak simply if we never even try to learn? Let us cultivate the habit of speaking simply, clearly and understandably, at the same time reaching high that the word of God may come forth.

Making Constant Progress

It is harder to speak today than it was one hundred years ago, harder for us to speak than was the case for Martin Luther four hundred years ago. This is because the word of God is progressively released, touching higher and higher as it is opened up. Since God has already spoken up to a certain point, we cannot afford to go backward in speaking. Our speaking must go forward. Said the Lord: "My Father is working until now, and I myself am working" (John 5.17). God has never ceased working. He worked yesterday and He works today. His work of today is more advanced than that of yesterday, and His work of tomorrow will be more developed than that of the present hour—He never works for less and less, but always for more and more. His work is progressive, never regressive. Martin Luther discovered justification by faith, even so, during the last hundred years people understand that tenet even more than he did. This is not an assertion of pride, only an indication that the word of God is progressively revealed. Martin Luther received great insight into the Letter to the Galatians, but today's saints see much more in that letter. If the revealing of God's word has advanced, how can we retrace our steps and speak the thing of the past?

We know all truths are in the Bible, all bases for speaking are found there, yet the discovery of Scriptural truth, the release of God's word, and the insight of the church before God are steadily progressing. From generation to generation the children of God see something more. For instance, in the early centuries the church generally took the kingdom as God's heaven. Since the last century, however, this problem has been gradually solved. The kingdom is different from heaven. Today it is even clearer; the kingdom is not only a reward but it also has its aspects of spiritual dominion and authority. We believe all truths in the Bible were clear during the apostolic time. Since then they are gradually once again being released. We may use another illustration. Today we see more about resurrection than those in the past did. As God gives grace to His church, the word increases in richness. He intends to impart more and more to the church.

We can compare the best lectures of the second and third centuries with the ministry of the word today and discover the progress which has been made. The Holy Spirit does not look back; He leads us on. The church in appearance may have many difficulties, yet our God marches forward. He has not ceased upon His having done one thing. He is still working. Hence, what today's ministry of the word touches ought to be deeper than what former ministry had touched. May we see the infinite grace which God pours out upon the church. If the church is to reach matured manhood so as to touch the riches of Christ, today's ministry must increase in its fulness. Do not be content, therefore, with a few careless words. God wishes to give the highest to us.

PART FOUR

THE OBJECTS OF THE WORD

18 The Objects of the Word

We now come to the fourth and final part, which concerns the objects of the word. The word not only has its minister, it also has those for whom it is intended—its hearers. Whether the ministry of the word is effective or not hinges additionally on the audience. No doubt the minister himself is largely accountable, but the objects of the word are nonetheless responsible too. If there is to be the release of the word, both the minister and the audience alike have responsibility. The latter can hinder the coming forth of God's word as well as cause it to flow. There are several places in the Bible where the objects of the word are stressed. We hope to gain some insights from these instances.

(1)

Let us look first at Matthew 13. The Lord is there speaking in parables, since God cannot reveal Himself to "the wise and intelligent" (Matt. 11.25). Such people cannot expect revelation from God, therefore they are not able to receive supply from the word. They are not only incapable of receiving revelation directly from God, they are unable also to receive revelation from the minister of the word. Whenever there are the wise and understanding among the audience the word of God is either weakened or totally obstructed from being released. The more people consider themselves to be wise the harder for them to be enlightened. The stronger they depend on themselves the more tightly is God's word closed to them.

One thing we can observe: in Old Testament prophecies, frequently "the words are shut up and sealed" (Dan. 12.9). This shows that the word may be released, or be shut up after being released. We will not try to explain the meaning of this shutting up nor tell the duration of its being sealed. We merely want to establish a spiritual principle which asserts that man may hear God speaking and yet that word be shut up to him. He may touch God's word, nevertheless it is still sealed towards him. Daniel shows us the fact of sealing, the Lord Jesus gives us its cause—man's own wisdom and understanding. The Lord hides His word from the wise and prudent that they may not perceive. Hence, whoever deems himself wise and understanding, from him the Holy Spirit will hide the word in accordance with God's mind.

One basic principle is revealed in the Bible, which is, that after man has eaten the fruit of the tree of the knowledge of good and evil the tree of life is closed to him. Thereafter, the cherubim and a flaming sword guard the way to the tree of life (Gen. 3.24). As soon as man possesses the knowledge which comes from the tree of the knowledge of good and evil, he is incapacitated from touching life. Such a touch is then not only impossible to man, it is also forbidden by God. This is the meaning of the shutting up. It means more than man's inability; it is also God's forbiddance. How serious this is. Whenever a person focuses on knowledge, life escapes him. Bear in mind that at the time you boast of your own wisdom and understanding, considering yourself superior, the word of God is hidden from you. You perceive not, you see vaguely, even if you strongly desire it. This is God's sealing. Recall what the Lord Jesus prayed: "I praise Thee, O Father, Lord of heaven and earth, that Thou didst hide these things from the wise and intelligent" (Matt. 11.25). God does this purposely. Consequently in the ministry of the word, attention likewise needs to be directed to the condition of the hearers.

Perhaps in speaking to those who are newly saved we need not exercise our spirit too strenuously, nor do we need to draw on much light or words. But how about preaching the gospel to the unsaved? You feel you have to drain much of your spirit and words. And naturally if we touch upon the higher revelation of God—those higher and more practical spiritual things—we obviously need to use more words, more light, and more spirit. But suppose here comes one who considers himself wise and understanding. From him God wishes to hide these things. Not only will God not reveal them directly to him, even the minister of the word is hampered by his presence. If the occasion requires less release of the spirit, his hindrance may not be too great. But if the demand on the spirit is much, he becomes a formidable impediment to the ministry of the word. The strong word of God's revelation fails to come forth because God does not wish him to perceive.

Besides the condition of the minister the hearers of the word constitute another problem. Should one whose condition is adverse to God's blessing be in the audience, he will affect the release of the word. The word will fall to the ground, however strong the minister may be. We are not clear how the hearers affect the word, but we know this is a fact. Therefore, when we learn to be ministers of the word we should remember that sometimes the word is hindered by ourselves while at other times it is due to others.

Suppose after having solved all *your* problems you are still unable to release the revelation and the words. Then you know the difficulty may lie in the objects of the word. To those beginning to minister, the hindrance is largely in themselves, for their revelation is limited and their light is inadequate. But to those who have received a strong and pure revelation and have given sufficient words, their delicate feeling is hampered and their words impeded when they touch those with proud spirits or those debarred from God's blessing.

The spirit is exceedingly sensitive. The one characteristic is that as you deliver the word your spirit and the Holy Spirit, as well as your words, are all released. But here is one in the audience who thinks himself wise. He is an observer. He blocks the word from flowing purely. Sometimes we wish to bring our brethren to the light of God that they might know themselves, or we desire to lead them to the Lord to see the glory within the Holiest. Notice how pure is such revelation. Here is no doctrine nor teaching–just revelation, pure revelation. Now during the process of pure enlightenment and burning away, if there be present three or five brothers who take the attitude of observers (they are merely watching what you can do, with their spirits shut up; they do not need God's word, neither will they gladly submit to God for His word), you will find your words are so frustrated that you can hardly utter them. The more spiritual the nature of your delivery the more easily you will be affected by people; the less spiritual your message the less influenced you are. A minister of the word dreads the "wise and understanding." The Lord will not bless such people. Hence it is most foolish to consider oneself as wise and understanding.

"And didst reveal them to babes," continued the Lord. The tenderer the attitude of the objects of the word, the stronger the word comes forth. The humbler the hearer the more powerful the word. If he is most willing and readily obedient, the word will manifest more light and revelation to him. It is hard to help those who do not want to receive help, but relatively easy is it to help those who are easily helped. This too is a basic spiritual principle.

Many are those who find it difficult to secure help. They resist the word and its meaning; they challenge the Bible; obviously they can hardly be helped, since God's enlightenment must penetrate their many layers of criticism and resistance before it can reach their inward parts. The more childlike a person is the more inclined he is to be helped by the Lord. The softer he is the less prejudiced he becomes. He whose heart is open to God finds that his spirit also opens to God. To him the ministry of the word will be strong and he will receive much revelation.

God resists the hard-hearted but grants grace to the childlike–to those who seek humbly, simply, and tenderly. Why? Because God will destroy the wisdom of the wise, and the cleverness of the clever will He thwart. (See 1 Cor. 1.19) The Lord will bring you to a place where you can say: "Neither my wisdom nor my cleverness is of any avail." If you are in the mercy of God you may look back after three or five years of discipline and confess how much you have suffered under your own wisdom. You should have received more grace but your wisdom stood in the way. How many are yet ignorant of the damage human wisdom has brought to their lives. But on the day they receive the mercy of the Lord they will know.

(2)

"I will destroy the wisdom of the wise, and the cleverness of the clever I will set aside," God says in 1 Corinthians 1.19. His purpose in so doing is "that no man should boast before God" (v.29). In a word, God does not want anyone to be proud. He sets aside the wise and the understanding. We have our own wisdom, but how we need power. We are wise, yet weak. God turns our wisdom into foolishness, but transforms our weakness into strength. This is a most difficult task, yet God has done it. It is marvelous in our eyes. God has destroyed the wisdom of men but given them His power.

How do we explain this? How in destroying man's wisdom is the problem of power to be solved? How does God destroy the wisdom of man in order to bring in His power? By the Lord Jesus Himself becoming our wisdom. "But by His (God's) doing you are in Christ Jesus, who (was made) to us wisdom from God, and righteousness and sanctification, and redemption" (1 Cor. 1.30). In this verse there should be a colon after the word "God", for this wisdom includes righteousness, sanctification, and redemption. How does God make Christ our wisdom? It is after our own wisdom has been destroyed and we become fools for God's sake that we accept Christ as our wisdom.

The power of God is manifested in us in a threefold way: Christ our righteousness, Christ our sanctification, and Christ our redemption. It requires tremendous power to make us righteous and holy and redeemed (the redemption here points especially to the redemption of the body), and all this is embodied in Christ being our wisdom. In other words, God reveals all His grace in Christ. What we are in direct contact with is revelation, but the outcome will be righteousness, holiness, and redemption. This solves the problem of power as well as that of wisdom. When the problem of revelation is solved, all spiritual riches are exposed while all spiritual poverty is deposed. Seeing is basic to spiritual affairs. Once seen, all is solved. We cannot touch righteousness directly, though we can receive revelation that way. When there is revelation, the matter of righteousness is also settled. We are to possess righteousness through revelation, for this is the way God grants us righteousness.

Perhaps this may explain why the Lord rejects our wisdom. Because when we are wise, the wisdom of the Lord has no entrance; therefore, there will be no revelation. As revelation ceases, all spiritual blessings are cut off. Spiritual strength decreases as spiritual insight diminishes, but it is increased when spiritual folly is lessened. The two are closely knit.

No one can receive the works of the Lord directly, since all His works are placed in revelation. He who has revelation has everything. If any should try to accept the Lord's work apart from revelation, he shall find it wholly ineffective. He may know himself as a sinner and consent mentally that Jesus is the Savior, but his prayer is of no avail if there is no spiritual understanding. He may even preach the doctrine of salvation to others; even so, it will fall upon his hearers like cold water. This is attempting to accept the Lord's work apart from revelation. Yet should that person's eyes be opened even slightly to see that the Lord has already died for him, he may immediately and spontaneously accept the Lord's death irrespective of environment, whether he is praying alone in his room or is listening to a message in a meeting. One who touches revelation gains Christ. Similarly, he who has not touched revelation will not be able to possess Christ. The question revolves around whether or not he has received revelation. This constitutes the basic principle. God has placed His work in revelation: hence only in revelation can men be related to His work.

In learning this spiritual principle we can readily understand how much the objects of the word can affect the ministry of the word. Whenever people consider themselves wise and prudent,

God hides Himself from them. But if you come to the Lord as a child—simply, humbly and tenderly— the Lord will just naturally be your wisdom. As He becomes your wisdom your problem of power is equally solved. To you who have Christ as wisdom, then righteousness, sanctification and redemption also become yours. Spiritual reality lies in the revelation of Christ. In touching revelation, you have reality. All the problems concerning past righteousness, present holiness, and future redemption are solved in wisdom. Having Christ as wisdom, you have them all. However, if those to whom the ministry is addressed are proud, self-conceited or spirit-closed, they are unable to receive revelation, nor will God give it to them. For this reason we must learn to be humble, gentle and simple before God. The prouder we are the farther we depart from God's revelation. The minister of the word cannot help us; he may instead be hindered by us. To the wise and understanding God hides all things, but to the childlike He reveals Himself.

(3)

"As it is written, 'God gave them a spirit of stupor, eyes to see not and ears to hear not, down to this very day'" (Rom. 11.8). This refers to the Jewish nation which even to this hour can neither see nor hear. Notice that the condition of Matthew 13 is much more grave than that of Matthew 11. In Matthew 11 the hiding is temporary, whereas in Matthew 13 it is permanent—based on what happened in Matthew 12. The situation in Matthew 12 is this: that after the Lord Jesus cast out demons by the power of the Holy Spirit the Jews insisted He did so by Beelzebub, for the Jews hated the Lord without cause. They inwardly knew He cast out demons by the Holy Spirit, yet they hated Him so intensely that they blasphemed against the Holy Spirit by saying He cast out demons by Beelzebub. They harbored deep prejudice within themselves. They knew they would have to believe in the Lord if they were to acknowledge that He cast out demons by the Holy Spirit. But they had already decided not to believe; and so they would rather reject the Lord.

Consequently they adamantly remonstrated that He cast out demons by Beelzebub. Their hearts were hardened as flint. Towards such as these there can be no forgiveness, not in this age nor in the age to come. The unpardonable sin is committed when people vehemently deny the distinctive work of the Holy Spirit by speaking aloud that it is the work of Beelzebub. Among the many names of Satan this is the foulest, because it means "the king of flies." How stony hard is the human heart. This is the worst sin in the entire Bible. There is none comparable to it. This sin will not be forgiven either in this age or in the age to come.

This explains why the Lord Jesus adopted the use of parables in speaking afterwards in Matthew 13. The disciples came and said to the Lord, "Why do you speak to them in parables?" And His answer: "To you it has been granted to know the mysteries of the kingdom of heaven, but to them it has not been granted." The stony-hearted heard the parable of sowing, but they did not understand what it meant. They heard about stones, birds and thorns, yet they were ignorant as to their applications. They also heard of the good soil, but they did not know what it represented. Here the Lord Jesus gives us a basic principle. Due to the committing of such sin God shuts up His word, that seeing they do not see and hearing they do not hear, nor do they understand. "For the heart of this people has become dull, and with their ears they scarcely hear, and they have closed their eyes; lest they should see with their eyes, and hear with their ears, and understand with their hearts and turn again, and I should heal them" (Matt. 13.15). It appears as if God forbids them to even repent. As long as a person holds to his own inclination and prejudice, refusing to accept the light while attempting to find fault with the truth, the light of God may indeed be closed to him. He who has no revelation, no light, lives in darkness. Therefore we are afraid of sinning, especially do we dread sinning without knowing it. Do realize that a sinner can be saved, even a Pharisee can be saved, for God knows how to deal with a sinner; but He has no way to help that one who refuses to see.

Both Matthew 13 and Romans 11 show us this principle, that

a person may fall into such a position as to be completely shut out of God's light. This we call God's forbiddance or God's sealing. Some are dabbling in the depth of error, not because of their folly but because of their own wisdom. A fault due to folly can easily be forgiven, but an error due to wisdom is hard to be forgiven, because in the latter case the person has not only committed a wrong but something is wrong with his heart as well. As his heart turns against God, God seals up his understanding. This is a most serious matter. To some God is unwilling to reveal himself, therefore He hides from them. Should God treat us this way, how utterly lost we are. What else can be compared with this estate? Let us therefore pray, "Oh Lord, never permit us to fall into such folly as to speak haughty words; never allow us to be so foolish as to resist light, and never let us approach the point beyond repentance."

How can there be repentance if there is no revelation? To seal up revelation is to seal up repentance; and to seal up repentance is to seal up forgiveness. Because they had already sinned against the Holy Spirit, therefore no revelation or repentance was given to them. Hearing they did not hear, seeing they did not see, nor did they understand. In other words, there were only words but no revelation. Some brothers and sisters are unwilling to accept or obey in certain matters. They have their prejudices. Even if a matter is right, they insist on saying it is wrong. How then can they receive revelation on such matters? One who is able to receive revelation from God needs to maintain an attitude that he might be wrong. He does not draw a hasty conclusion for fear that he may be wrong. He who desires light cannot afford to be arrogant. The Lord can easily enlighten him who is gentle and meek. He will give to him both basic and advanced revelations. Hence let us learn to open our hearts before God that we may keep receiving from Him all the time.

(4)

Light never waits for man! We are too often like those who come to the Lord to beg for bread. We are not sure whether we can obtain it. Let us see that God has His work on earth, that the thread of His work has never been broken, and that it continues on. Those with spiritual insight can find out where the thread is. If any falls, he may not be able to catch up. If he is prejudiced, he will not see. Suppose we fail to catch up with what God has done twenty years ago; how then can we keep pace with what God is doing today? Hence never allow yourself to be out of line with God's movings. Be humble and learn. One thing is sure: God has His course and is working step by step towards it. We must follow on year after year. Should our spirit be kept in humility and gentleness, we will be able to touch a little of God's working. But if we should grow proud, arrogant and self-conceited, we shall be laid aside by God.

Ephesians 4 predicts that the church shall attain to mature manhood. God desires to raise His own ministry to a noble level. Some may have touched the higher things of God today, while others may need to spend ten to twenty years before they know how to reach these things. Many spiritual matters have a time element, and we are yet far from having acquired them. So may we ask God for mercy that He may grant us to learn something substantial and real. May God give ministry to His church, and may we learn all that we should learn.